Dr Lee Brosan is a Consultant Clinical Psychologist in the Cambridgeshire and Peterborough Foundation Trust, and Trust Lead for the Development of Psychological Therapies. She is also Clinical Associate at the M.R.C. Cognition and Brain Science Unit in Cambridge and Honorary Lecturer at the University of East Anglia. She has been qualified as a cognitive therapist for over fifteen years.

Dr Gillian Todd is a Senior Lecturer in Cognitive Behavioral Therapy in the School of Medicine Health Policy and Practice at the University of East Anglia. She is also an honorary Visiting Fellow in the Department of Psychiatry at the University of Cambridge. Gillian has been accredited with the BABCP as a cognitive therapist for over fifteen years.

The aim of the **Overcoming** series is to enable people with a range of common problems and disorders to take control of their own recovery program. Each title, with its specially tailored programs, is devised by a practising clinician using the latest techniques of cognitive behavioral therapy – techniques which have been shown to be highly effective in helping people overcome their problems by changing the way they think about themselves and their difficulties. The series was initiated in 1993 by Peter Cooper, Professor of Psychology at Reading University in the UK whose book on overcoming bulimia nervosa and binge-eating continues to help many people in the UK, the USA, Australia and Europe.

Titles in the series include:

OVERCOMING STRESS

A self-help guide using
Cognitive Behavioral Techniques

LEE BROSAN
and
GILLIAN TODD

LONDON

Constable & Robinson Ltd
3 The Lanchesters
162 Fulham Palace Road
London W6 9ER
www.constablerobinson.com

First published in the UK by Robinson,
an imprint of Constable & Robinson Ltd, 2009

Important Note

This book is not intended as a substitute for medical advice or treatment.
Any person with a condition requiring medical attention should consult
a qualified medical practitioner or suitable therapist.

ISBN: 978-1-84529-233-1

Printed and bound in the EU

1 3 5 7 9 10 8 6 4 2

Table of contents

Introduction

Why cognitive behavior therapy?

The approach this book takes in attempting to help you overcome your problems with stress is a 'cognitive behavioral' one. A brief account of the history of this form of intervention might be useful and encouraging. In the 1950s and 1960s a set of therapeutic techniques was developed, collectively termed 'behavior therapy'. These techniques shared two basic features. First, they aimed to remove symptoms (such as anxiety) by dealing with those symptoms themselves, rather than their deep-seated underlying historical causes (traditionally the focus of psychoanalysis, the approach developed by Sigmund Freud and his associates). Second, they were scientifically based, in the sense that they used techniques derived from what laboratory psychologists were finding out about the mechanisms of learning, and these techniques were put to scientific test. The area where behavior therapy initially proved to be of most value was in the treatment of anxiety disorders, especially specific phobias (such as extreme fear of animals or heights) and agoraphobia, both notoriously difficult to treat using conventional psychotherapies.

After an initial flush of enthusiasm, discontent with behavior therapy grew. There were a number of reasons for this, an important one of which was the fact that behavior therapy did not deal with the internal thoughts which were so obviously central to the distress that many patients were experiencing. In particular, behavior therapy proved inadequate when it came to the treatment of depression. In the late 1960s and early 1970s a treatment for depression was developed called 'cognitive therapy'. The pioneer in this enterprise was an American psychiatrist, Professor Aaron T. Beck. He developed a theory of depression which emphasized the importance of people's depressed styles of thinking, and, on the basis of this theory, he specified a new form of therapy. It would not be an exaggeration to say that Beck's work has changed the nature of psychotherapy, not just for depression but for a range of psychological problems.

The techniques introduced by Beck have been merged with the techniques developed earlier by the behavior therapists to produce a therapeutic approach which has come to be known as 'cognitive behavioral therapy' (or CBT). This therapy has been subjected to the strictest scientific testing and has been found to be highly successful for a significant proportion of cases of depression. It has now become clear that specific patterns of disturbed thinking are associated with a wide range of psychological problems, not just depression, and that the treatments which deal with these are highly effective. So, effective cognitive behavioral treatments have been developed for a range of anxiety disorders, such as panic disorder, generalized anxiety disorder, specific phobias, social phobia, obsessive compulsive disorders, and health anxiety, as well as for other conditions such as drug addictions, and eating disorders like bulimia nervosa. Indeed, cognitive behavioral techniques have been found to have an application beyond the narrow categories of psychological disorders. They have been applied effectively, for example, to helping people with weight problems, couples with marital difficulties, as well as those who wish to give up smoking or deal with drinking problems. They have also been effectively applied to dealing with low self-esteem. In relation to the current self-help manual, over several years effective CBT techniques have been developed for helping people overcome their problems with stress.

The starting-point for CBT is the realization that the way we think, feel and behave are all intimately linked, and changing the way we think about ourselves, our experiences, and the world around us changes the way we feel and what we are able to do. So, for example, by helping a depressed person identify and challenge their automatic depressive thoughts, a route out of the cycle of depressive thoughts and feelings can be found. Similarly, habitual behavioral responses are driven by a complex set of thoughts and feelings, and CBT, as you will discover from this book, by providing a means for the behavior, thoughts and feelings to be brought under control, enables these responses to be undermined and a different kind of life to be possible.

Although effective CBT treatments have been developed for a wide range of disorders and problems, these treatments are not currently widely available; and, when people try on their own to help themselves, they often, inadvertently, do things which make matters worse. In recent years, experts in a wider range of areas have taken the principles and techniques of specific cognitive behavioral therapies for particular problems and presented them in manuals (the *Overcoming* series) which people can read and apply themselves. These manuals specify a systematic program of treatment which the person works through to overcome their difficulties. In this way, cognitive behavioral therapeutic techniques of proven value are being made available on the widest possible basis.

The use of self-help manuals is never going to replace the need for therapists. Many people with emotional and behavioral problems will need the help of a qualified therapist. It is also the case that, despite the widespread success of cognitive behavioral therapy, some people will not respond to it and will need one of the other treatments available. Nevertheless, although research on the use of these self-help manuals is at an early stage, the work done to date indicates that for a great many people such a manual is sufficient for them to overcome their problems without professional help. Sadly, many people suffer on their own for years. Sometimes they feel reluctant to seek help without first making a serious effort to manage on their own. Sometimes they feel too awkward or even ashamed to ask for help. Sometimes appropriate help is not forthcoming despite their efforts to find it. For many of these people the cognitive behavioral self-help manual will provide a lifeline to a better future.

Peter J Cooper
The University of Reading, 2009

Preface

When Robinson first asked if I would like to write a book on stress I was extremely pleased. Several weeks later, however, I found myself sitting at the kitchen table with my head in my hands wailing, 'But a book about stress is too big; it has no natural limits – everything in life comes into it.' And I think this is true: stress permeates all aspects of our lives and all aspects of our thinking, feeling and behavior. It can be present in all the situations that are important to us, at work, with the people we love, and at play, if we have time for such a thing. So learning to recognize and understand it, and knowing something about how best to cope with it, could make a huge difference to the quality of our lives. But how to narrow things down to make it possible for myself and others to do this? To my great relief it was at this point that Gillian agreed to join me in writing this book, and managed to bring order into the chaos. Thus, here is our book on stress, which also goes by the alternative, unofficial title 'Stress – or Coping with Life'.

We hope that this book will be useful to almost anyone

who experiences problems related to stress, from its mildest to its most troubling forms. If you are shouting at your children, seething at your boss, unable to face most of the things you have to do, or generally feeling unable to cope, then we hope that this is the book for you.

The book is organized into two parts. The first chapter of Part One provides a theoretical overview of stress, and goes into some detail about the ideas that psychologists have had about it. Central to this discussion is the idea of 'appraisals' – the way in which we weigh up situations – which we come back to repeatedly throughout the book. In Chapter 2 we go on to look at the relationship between stress and the body, looking at the way in which the physical component of stress works, and discussing whether there is a relationship between stress and ill-health. In Chapter 3 we look at links between stress and personality, but emphasize that we believe that not all aspects of personality are fixed, and they can be changed by changing your thinking. These chapters provide a reasonable amount of background information, and the reader who would prefer to skip straight to Part Two should be able to do so without too much trouble, with the exception of a brief glance at Chapter 4, on thinking and cognitive therapy.

The basic idea presented here is that the way that we see things plays an absolutely vital part in our lives, and determines much about the way we feel and much about what we do. But sometimes the way we see things has less to do with the situation, and more to do with our mood and experience of life, than we realize. And sometimes this can lead us to weigh up situations as more negative and problematic than they really are, and thus contributes to how stressed we feel about them. Although it does not naturally occur to us to question the way that we see things, we can learn to do so, and by doing so we can have a very big impact on our lives. These ideas will come up again and again throughout the book.

Part Two starts by helping readers to identify their own symptoms of stress, the situations that underlie it, and the ways in which they cope. We then show how all these fit together into an individual stress profile, or cognitive therapy formulation of stress, and how to begin working on a stress management plan. We go on to present how to identify and tackle ways of thinking that contribute to stress – the detailed techniques that result from the practice of cognitive therapy. We believe that these techniques will be relevant to most people reading this book. We then turn to a number of specific situations that many people find stressful, and to a range of common problems and techniques that might help with them. Finally we try to pull all this together to revisit the overall stress management plan.

The book is, we hope, written so that you can dip into it at almost any point, and don't have to work through things that are neither problematic nor interesting for you. The exception to this is that it will probably all make more sense if you have looked at Chapter 4 and possibly even Chapter 9, which gives more detail about changing your thinking. But if this just seems like more work, we hope that the chapters will make enough sense to be read on their own.

Life is stressful for all sorts of reasons and in all sorts of ways. We hope very much that this book will help to make it a little less so.

Acknowledgements

This book has been an enormous pleasure to write, and has helped us to define our thinking about an important and complex topic; but we would have to admit that it has also helped us understand rather more experientially than we sometimes wanted, just what it means to feel stressed.

We are immensely grateful to many people for their help in enhancing the pleasure and reducing the stress. We would particularly like to thank:

Ian Preston for help with literature searches and general encouragement.

Jacqui Carol for help with earlier drafts.

Fran Brunt, Pip Goodwin, Alison Jenaway, Richard Moore, Hugh Rich, and all members of the Friday Club, for ideas.

Nicola Ridgeway for inspiration about the resourceful self.

Richard Taylor for advice about cancer.

Jo Weston for helpful comments on diet.

Jonathan Todd for interest, ideas and IT rescue.

Angus Mackintosh for thinking it was a gas.

Fritha Saunders for immense patience, tolerance and guidance.

PART ONE

Understanding Stress

Aims of Part One

In this section we introduce the concept of stress, looking broadly at the symptoms and defining exactly what we understand the term to refer to, and what we think it does *not* refer to. We discuss ideas of stress in some detail in Chapter 1, from their first appearance in medical and psychological science to more recent ideas. We emphasize the role of appraisals – the way in which we interpret events – in our approach to stress. In Chapter 2 we look at the physical underpinnings of stress, and the role that these can play in our health. We examine in some detail whether stress really is responsible for physical illnesses, as some people believe it to be. In Chapter 3 we look at the links between stress and personality, discussing whether some types of personality are more or less prone to stress; but we emphasize that our view of personality is that it can change. Finally, in Chapter 4 we introduce the basic ideas of cognitive therapy, since it is the ideas and techniques of cognitive therapy which underpin our approach to appraisals, and to stress in general.

After you've read Part One we hope that you will have:

- Gained a greater understanding of the concept of stress.
- Understood the role of appraisals in the stress process.
- Gained a greater understanding of the role of physical changes in stress.
- Explored the connections between these physical changes and health issues.
- Learned about how stress and personality characteristics may be linked
- Developed an understanding of the way in which the cognitive behavioral approach can be applied to stress.

1

What is stress?

Emma is a forty-two-year-old mother with three young children. Emma is bright and attractive, her children do well at school, she and her husband have a good marriage. Life looks perfect. But is it? Emma never feels that she does anything right and feels desperately inadequate when she compares herself to other people. She is always running around after her family and constantly feels that she can't cope. She gets headaches and finds herself snapping at everyone and then feeling guilty.

Nicola is twenty-nine and living on her own in London. She came to London to work in advertising and was really pleased to get such a good job, but the competition is pretty intense, and she is having to work longer and longer hours to keep up. She is also starting to have doubts about whether she really wants to do this, but is too financially committed to change career now. She is drinking far too much and sleeping and eating very badly.

Gary has his own small building firm, but cannot afford to employ all the workers that some projects need. He is constantly being let down by plumbers and plasterers, and then his clients get furious with him. He has problems with his blood pressure, and has constant pains in his stomach. His family doctor has warned him that he needs to try to relax, but he finds it incredibly difficult to stay calm when other people mess him around and ends up losing his temper and shouting and screaming.

On the surface these people may look very different and have very different lives and different problems, but they have a lot in common, since they are all suffering from stress.

Stress can take many forms and affect people in various ways. The box below shows just some of these.

SYMPTOMS OF STRESS: DO YOU FIND THAT YOU...

- Get headaches
- Have aches and pains in your arms and legs even though you never exercise
- Feel tension in your neck and shoulders
- Feel your stomach churning and have indigestion if you eat anything
- Find that you're getting more coughs and colds than you used to
- Feel tense, anxious, nervy
- Feel low or depressed
- Feel irritable and get angry easily
- Make mistakes doing things that should be straightforward
- Find yourself unable to concentrate properly
- Feel stupid and inadequate most of the time
- Feel you can't cope with everything you've got to do

- Put things off
- Avoid difficult situations
- Snap at people
- Drink too much
- Binge on chocolate and sweets
- Never have time for anything you want to do
- Smoke more than you usually do

If you recognize any of these symptoms, then it is possible that this book is for you, since they are all common symptoms of stress. The book will help you to recognize when you are getting stressed and why, and will offer a general approach to dealing with stress as well as techniques to handle particular stressful situations. In the first part of this book we will talk about some of the theoretical background to stress, and then we will move on in Part Two to the Stress Program. Readers who do not wish for the amount of detail in Part One can skip to Part Two, though a brief look at Chapter 4 before you do so might be helpful.

Before going further though, there are a number of important things we'd like to say.

Firstly, this is a self-help book which we hope contains strategies and techniques which you will find useful. But self-help is not for everyone. Sometimes the problems can just get too much of a hold for you to be able to tackle them on your own. Or some people are just not 'self-help' kind of people. In this case, it could definitely be worth going to your family doctor to see what assistance might be available for you, or contacting one of the organizations listed at the back of this book to see if they could help.

Secondly, not all negative emotions are stress. We talk about this a little more later in this chapter. When we are stressed we certainly do feel tense and anxious, and our mood can be low and depressed. But if you are suffering from more severe forms of anxiety and depression then you may need something that is targeted particularly at helping you cope with those conditions, and again may need help from your family doctor or other people. If you are unsure about what is the right approach for you, then we give more detailed descriptions of anxiety and depression on pp. 84–9 which might make things clearer, or your family doctor should be able to help you to decide. You may also find it helpful to have a look at two other books in this series: *Overcoming Anxiety* by Helen Kennerley and *Overcoming Depression* by Paul Gilbert.

Since we started writing this book there has been a great change in mental health services in the UK, and many places now have workers attached to their family doctor practices who can offer help with a range of emotional and stress-related problems, so the chances of getting treatment which is most appropriate for you is higher than ever before. And happily, the more we recognize just how many of us do have these kinds of problems, the more the stigma about talking about them and experiencing them seems to be getting less, so we hope that it will be much easier to bring up the issue with your family doctor and other people who might be able to help.

And finally – some people talk about 'eustress', or positive stress. While we recognize that there are a lot of situations where it can be good to feel challenged, excited and energized, we don't think that it is sensible to think of these as forms of stress and will not include eustress in our definitions. We will say a bit more about this later in this chapter.

So what is stress?

When we started to write this book we thought we knew quite a bit about stress, but realized that we would have to find out a lot more. So we asked our very helpful local librarian to do a literature search for references to stress in the last five years. He emailed back quite quickly, to say 'I've found 15,000 references to stress – do you think you could narrow it down a bit?'

And what is more, although we could not claim to have checked them all, we bet that most of the 15,000 references will have a slightly different definition of stress. So what we will aim to do in this chapter is to give a very brief overview of the main ideas that seem to be most common, and to define the way in which we think it is helpful to use the term.

Early ideas about stress

One of the first uses of the term stress came not from psychology but from physics, and from a long time ago. In the seventeenth century the engineer Robert Hooke talked about stress when he was considering the design of physical structures. He used the term to refer to the amount of pressure, or the load, which a physical structure such as a bridge might be placed under. Although this might not seem fantastically relevant to studies of human stress, it does contain the crucial notion that stress is to do with being under pressure, which we will come back to repeatedly.

In the 1950s a doctor called Hans Selye talked about stress in terms of human physiology. Selye studied hormones in rats; and in the course of this work he found that when rats were exposed to harsh physical conditions, such as extremes of heat and cold, injection of insulin, or exposure to X-rays (poor rats), they showed a clear physiological response. They experienced enlargement of the adrenal glands, shrinkage of the thymus gland, and the development of stomach ulcers. The meaning of these changes will be discussed in much more detail in Chapter 2; however, it is interesting to note that Selye talked about the bodily or physiological response itself as *stress*, and the source or cause of the response as the *stressor*. The rats in his studies were showing a clear stress response to the harsh environment, or stressor. These distinctions are still used now, and are very useful in helping us to keep in mind the distinction between the stressful situation and the stress response.

Hans Selye also made another important discovery – he realized that not all animals react the same to the same stressor. Now this may be in part because there are differences between individuals in the way that their bodies react. But it also opens the way to a more important individual difference, which psychologists working on stress later picked up on. One reason why two people might not react in the same way to the same situation is because they see it in different ways, and it means different things to them. We use the words perception or *appraisal* to refer to this process.

We can show this distinction like this:

Stressor
The life situation or demand which might cause problems

↓

Perception or Appraisal
How we view the stressor and see it as relating to us

↓

Stress Response
The way that our thinking, our feelings, our bodies and
our behavior change

So stress is your complete response to your perception of
what is going on around you or happening to you.

What makes a stressor stressful? The role of appraisals

To explain this more, imagine that you are lying in bed one
Friday night, alone in the house. Your partner is away at a
business conference and you are thinking about what you
are going to do the next day. Suddenly you hear the back
door rattling. There are a number of things that might go
through your mind. You might think: 'Oh no, someone is
trying to break in; they're going to burgle the house and kill
me.' Or you might think: 'Oh bother, I forgot to unlock the
cat flap and the cat can't get in.' Or you might think: 'Oh
good, he (she) is back early from the conference so we can
have a nice day together tomorrow.' Or of course you might
think: 'Oh drat, he (she) is back early from the conference,

and there goes my day of peace!' So one situation can result in a number of different appraisals – different ways of seeing it, weighing it up. It's also clear that these different appraisals will result in very different emotions. In the first case you might feel very frightened indeed, in the second you might feel slightly irritated, in the third pleased, in the fourth irritated again. The point is that it is not the stressor itself – the rattle at the door – that is causing you to feel how you do, but the way in which you have appraised the situation.

One psychologist who was extremely influential in bringing these ideas of appraisal into work on stress was Richard Lazarus. As in the example above, Lazarus showed how appraisal of a situation can affect how stressful it feels. He and his colleagues created a stressful situation by showing people films – in one example, people watched a bloody accident where a finger was cut off by a circular saw. But before people saw the film they were told different things about it. One group of people was told that the people in the film weren't really injured (so they knew it wasn't real); another group was told that the film was being used to teach people how to avoid accidents (so they could at least distance themselves from the story a bit); but the third group was told that the people in the film really suffered severe pain and infection. Lazarus then took measures of stress, including physiological phenomena such as heart rate and sweating, both thought to be good indications of stress, and people's own accounts of how stressful they found it. Lazarus found that the people who were told that the individuals in the film were badly hurt reported that they found the film much more stressful, and showed more physiological activity, than the other two groups. Lazarus argued that it was these differences in appraisal that were crucial in determining how stressful the film was, rather than the film itself.

Lazarus then went on to talk about different kinds of appraisal. One of these he termed 'primary appraisal'. Primary appraisal means that you weigh up what is going on around you and decide whether there is a problem or not. In other words, is there a stressor present? It is clear that some situations will be seen as a problem by most people – if you are on a boat in the middle of the sea which starts to sink, for instance, you are likely to think there is a problem! Other situations may be seen quite differently by different people. For instance, imagine that a friend asks you to take part in a fun run for charity. You might think: 'Oh no, I can't possibly do that, I'm not fit and I'll just make a fool of myself.' Or you might think: 'Oh good, what a great opportunity to help – even if I have to walk round I'll be able to collect some money.' For the first person the situation would be seen as problematic and as a stressor, and for the second as an opportunity.

One danger of this viewpoint is that some people are likely to think: 'Are they saying that stress is all in the mind then?' And this is definitely not the case. There are some situations that are obviously difficult and stressful for anyone. But even when situations are definitely difficult there may be differences between how people respond.

But there is another kind of appraisal which is also very important. Lazarus termed these 'secondary appraisals'. These have much more to do with whether you think that you can cope with the problem. They involve weighing up your own individual resources, your strengths and the way you have coped in the past, and the helpfulness and availability of other people and other things in the environment that might help. Thus, in the examples above, even the first example might produce different stress responses in different people. One person might think: 'Well, even if the boat sinks, I'm strong and fit and with a life jacket I can keep going for ages; the coastguard will get the distress call so it can't be too long before someone comes.' But another might think: 'Oh no, I will never be able to survive if we end up in the water, and no one will ever find us.' So this appraisal of whether or not you have resources – strengths and abilities – that will help, can make a big difference to just how stressful you find the situation. So too, in the example of the fun run, the first person might know that they are overweight and unfit, and very unlikely to be able even to walk round. This appraisal of their lack of strength in this respect makes the prospect much more problematic. And maybe the second person already walks ten miles a day and knows that the fun run will be fine for them.

So it is not just how you weigh up the situation that is important, but also how you weigh up your chances of coping. Now we can show the diagram as it is opposite. We will come back to these ideas repeatedly throughout the book. But before going on to discuss other ideas about stress, there is one point which we think is absolutely crucial and which we'll look at now.

Not all negative emotions are stress

There are many negative emotions that occur in our lives, sometimes appropriately, and sometimes less so. Depression

Stressor
The life situation or demand which might cause problems

↓

Primary Appraisal
How we view the stressor and see it as relating to us

↓

Secondary Appraisal
How we see our ability to cope and how helpful outside influences might be

↓

Stress Response
The way that our thinking, our feelings, our bodies and our behavior, change

is common, anxiety probably more so. Anger and irritability are problematic in many people's lives. Stress is increasingly being used as a 'catch-all' phrase to include these and any other negative emotion, or indeed any response to a difficult situation. For instance, someone whose favourite dog died recently described how she felt very 'stressed', when it seemed clear to us that she meant that she was very sad. Another friend, writing a thesis for a law degree on absenteeism at work, included under the rubric of stress all time taken off work due to psychological problems. However, a number of these would not normally be considered as stress, but as illnesses or conditions in their own right –

major depression is a particularly good example. These emotions need understanding in their own right. They are not all 'stress', but are particular ways of responding to different situations. Now it is true that some of these emotions overlap with stress. For one thing, if you have been exposed to a stressful situation for a long time, and have found your ability to cope is not sufficient, then it might well happen that you become depressed.

We will talk more about the difference between stress and other emotions in Chapter 5, but since these emotions are not the same as stress itself, it might be helpful to try to think more carefully about what stress is.

Stress as demand

One way of doing this is to go back to the first accounts of stress. It is the idea of being under pressure that we think distinguishes stress from other kinds of emotion. The demands on us all are quite great. Whether or not they really are worse in today's twenty-first-century modern living than they have ever been before we are not sure, but they are certainly high. Many people need to juggle numerous demands, including work, the often very stressful journeys to get there in the first place, homes, children, partners, the desire to pursue hobbies and inter-ests, the needs of other people. And we do this in a modern context where we are aware of competition with our peers, and inevitable comparisons with perfect lifestyles presented in the papers and on TV, so that if we don't manage all these things then we are, it is easy to conclude, failures. Whether or not this is all really more stressful than a more primitive lifestyle where the list of things to do would include 'Find food; keep alive', we don't know. But life does feel pressured.

The idea here is that stress is to do with trying to manage the demands put on you by life – the pressure that you are under. Stress feels different from other emotions. When we first told a group of colleagues that we were planning to write a book on stress they all said: 'Go on then, what is stress?' So we sat in the pub and pictured the following scenarios: you are just about to take an exam, or driving test, or give a talk – it is starting in five minutes. That feeling is probably going to be anxiety rather than stress. But last week when you were thinking about everything that you needed to do to prepare for the exam and realizing that you didn't have time – the feeling that you got then was stress.

One very simple way to think of this is that all emotions are associated with different kinds of situations. Depression tends to be associated with loss and hopelessness; anxiety tends to be associated with threat; anger tends to be associated with times when our personal rules are violated. And, again very simply, stress is associated with ideas of pressure and demand, wherever these come from.

Now it is true that stress and other emotions tend to run into each other. As we have seen, anxiety and stress are quite similar, and stress certainly seems to make people irritable and bad-tempered, and can lead to depression. But it is possible to feel stressed without this leading to other emotional difficulties, and it is certainly possible to feel other emotions, particularly sadness and depression, without these being associated with stress. Because of this overlap, in later chapters of this book we will talk about the different emotions and how best to try to cope with them, and we will talk more about the ideas we've outlined in the paragraph above. But this core idea of stress is that *it is the response that we feel in situations where the demands on us are more than we can cope with.*

INTERNAL AND EXTERNAL DEMANDS

We have seen that one way in which to talk about the idea of being under pressure is to describe it as the demands made on us. There is no doubt that modern living does place many demands on most of us. Like Alice in Wonderland, it can often feel as if you are having to run faster and faster just to stay in the same place. But demand itself can be thought of in two different ways. Firstly, there are the external demands placed on us – things that we really do need to do. We need to go to work, we need to shop for food and cook. But some of these demands come from the inside.

An example might help to illustrate the point. Emma has three children, ranging in age from five to eleven, and currently at two different schools. Her husband works away from home for half the week, so she is on her own for a significant part of the time. They live in the country with no accessible public transport, so Emma needs to spend a great deal of time taking the children to school, and to various clubs and activities. She also needs to shop and cook for them, and to do the thousands of daily tasks that holding a large family together requires. This is quite bad enough as it is, and obviously demanding, and there is never enough time in the day to do everything that needs to be done.

But Emma's friend went round to her house one day and discovered her in the kitchen *ironing the sheets*. 'Emma', she said, 'what are you doing?' Emma looked at her friend as if she was crazy and said: 'Ironing the sheets.' To cut a long story short, the ensuing debate on the necessity of ironing sheets can be encapsulated as follows. Friend: 'Of course you don't need to; you just put them on the bed and tuck them in.' Emma: 'But it's really trampy to put them on the bed without ironing them.' The point is that, whoever is right about sheets, Emma felt that she had to do it – she was responding to an *internal* demand. Her standards told her that it would be completely unacceptable to put sheets unironed on to the bed, and that she would be letting herself down if she did so. So while, some of the demands on her could be considered external – she does need to take the children to school, feed them, etc. – others are much more internal, in this case to do with having very high standards, and finding it important to live up to these.

So demand too is a very individual thing, consisting partly of aspects of the situation which are more or less external, but also partly of aspects that come from internal demands, which have to do with people's individual ideas and values. So there will be huge differences between people in what they consider to be stressful, as a result of these differences in their internal demands on themselves.

THE TIMESCALE OF DEMANDS

Another aspect of demand that can vary greatly is how long the demand goes on for. Interviews for jobs are deeply stressful, but they do not last long (though the preparation may have done). This is very different from the stress of a miserable work environment which goes on and on, often with no great prospect of change. We would refer to the first as an acute stressor, and to the second as a *chronic* one. And demands can also vary in frequency – an interview may be over quickly but you may have to start preparing for the next quickly too. As we will see in the next chapter, a crucial aspect of how we cope with stress physically may be to do with whether our bodies have time to calm down after times of threat and demand. So it is definitely worth bearing the distinction between acute and chronic stressors in mind, since on the whole the impact of *acute* stressors is much less. Of course, the exception to this is when the acute stressor is profoundly traumatic and beyond our normal experience – being caught in the bomb blasts in London in the last few years would be an obvious example – but this requires a completely different understanding, and is for a different book. (You'll find more information on coping with traumatic events in *Overcoming Traumatic Stress* by Claudia Herbert and Ann Wetmore.)

Goals and expectations

Closely related to the idea of internal demands are the ideas of people's goals and expectations. This raises an important distinction. Mostly, when people think of things that make them feel bad, they are thinking about bad things that *happen* – divorce, unemployment, illness, for example. But another way in which people very commonly feel bad is when *good things fail to happen*. We are all familiar with the idea of disappointment. You weren't made unemployed, but you weren't given the promotion that you had hoped for either.

So your goal, or your hope of something nice happening, was not met, and you felt upset and disappointed.

We all have goals, even if these are not very clearly stated to ourselves, and it seems that one reason why different people find different situations stressful is to do with their goals. When personal goals are threatened, situations are likely to be seen as stressors.

For example, Harry is devoted to music technology, and planned to buy a new amplifier. He had found two, but both had different advantages and disadvantages and he couldn't choose between them. Harry started to feel incredibly stressed – indeed lying in bed at night unable to sleep – because he couldn't choose and was afraid that whichever he chose he would feel disappointed. Even though he could see that in the grand scheme of things it was not the end of the world, his goal was to create a wonderful sound system, and it was the prospect of failing in his goal that was creating such stress for him. So stress can result from the fear that your expectations, your hopes and your goals, will not be met and that you will feel disappointment.

STRESS AND CONTROL

In the 1970s some very important research went on in the world of psychology. Martin Seligman carried out some research on dogs, wherein he subjected the dogs to mild electric shocks through the floor of the cage they were placed in. One group of dogs could stop the shock by jumping over a barrier. They couldn't stop the shock happening in the first place, but once it had started they could escape from it. Each of these dogs had a counterpart in a second group – but this second group of dogs had no control over what happened to them. When the dog in the first group escaped from the shock, then the shock was turned off not just for that animal, but for its counterpart in the second group. So the amount of shock that each dog received was the same. But the dog in the second group could not turn the shock off itself, no matter what it did. After a while, the dogs in the second group just stopped trying to do anything to turn the shock off, and became passive and withdrawn. The dogs in the first group continued to be fine, even though they had received no less shock.

So it seemed as if it was not the unpleasantness of the shock itself that was doing the damage to the second group of dogs, but the fact that they *had no control over it.* This famous research is known as the Learned Helplessness experiments – since the dogs in the second group initially tried to help themselves, and then gave up and became helpless. Furthermore, when these dogs were later put in a situation where they *could* escape from the shock, they carried on being passive and did not learn what to do. Later on, Seligman and other psychologists looked at how these ideas operate in humans, and described them more in terms of people's thinking about what was going on. But the basic ideas remain: being out of control of things that are going on around you, and particularly being out of control of unpleasant things, is extremely difficult for people.

PREDICTIVE CONTROL

Sometimes it is true that we cannot do anything about the things that are happening around us; but it seems to be much easier for us to cope with this if we know what is going on and can predict what is likely to happen. Many people will have been stuck in long traffic jams, inching forward with no clue as to what is happening or how long they will be stuck for. Most people in these circumstances will search for information, turn the radio on, and try to establish what caused it and how bad it is going to be. Once you *know* what you have to deal with you seem to be able to cope much better, even if the situation is quite bad.

PERCEPTIONS OF CONTROL

In some situations, the degree of control we actually have is unclear, and depends very much on how we view things; and it is clear that people differ greatly in the extent to which they *feel* in control of what happens, regardless of how much control they actually have. One famous psychologist who wrote about this was Julian Rotter, who described a personality characteristic known as *locus of control*. In this view, people were said to range on a continuum of behavior from External to Internal control:

- People high in *external* locus of control believe that what happens to them is guided by fate, luck or other external circumstances.
- People high in *internal* locus of control believe that what happens to them is guided by their personal decisions and efforts.

On the whole, people who have a high internal locus of control tend to cope better with difficult situations and be more resilient than people who have a high external locus of control. Having an internal locus of control is similar to a number of other similar ideas such as 'self-agency', 'personal control' and 'self-determination'.

What is clear is that feeling powerless and helpless is associated with high levels of stress and with other psychological disorders too. We all need some sense of autonomy and control!

Stress and coping

As we saw earlier, another aspect of stress which is extremely important is not just your perception of the demands placed on you, but also your ideas about how well you can cope with them. This too leads to huge individual differences. We will talk more about different kinds of coping style in Chapter 7.

When a demand is placed on you, whether internal or external, it is clear that there are a number of different ways of reacting. At one extreme, someone could think: 'Okay, that's fine, I can manage that really well.' At the other, someone might think: 'Oh no, that's impossible, I will never be able to deal with it.' There are obviously many shades of grey between these reactions, but in essence, what happens is that you have an idea of your own ability to cope. This might be made up of ideas about the *specific* abilities that are needed – for instance, if you are about to take a driving test you need to have reasonable confidence in your ability to drive. It might also be made up of ideas about your *general* abilities – for instance, you might think that you are generally good at dealing with difficult situations. On the whole, the amount of stress that you feel in a situation is partly to do with how problematic you see that situation as being, but also, crucially, how well you feel that you would be able to cope with it.

Stress and self-efficacy

Another way to talk about this is through ideas of *self-efficacy*. Albert Bandura talked about self-efficacy as a product of two kinds of process. When confronted with a problem, two things need to happen. Firstly, you need to be able to see what the solution to the problem might be – is there something that can be done that would help? And secondly, you need to think about whether you are able to carry out whatever needs to be done. If you are able to think of solutions to problems, and if you believe that you have the skills to carry these solutions out, you are said to be high in self-efficacy. It is not difficult to see that someone high in self-efficacy is likely to feel less stressed when confronted by problems and demands than someone who is not. Interestingly, these two aspects of self-efficacy seem to parallel the primary and secondary appraisals in stress. Where the primary appraisal considers how bad the stressor is, the first process in self-efficacy considers possible solutions. And where the secondary appraisal considers your ability to cope, the second process in self-efficacy assesses whether you have the skills to carry out the solution that you can see. What this should mean is that, as we get better at making our appraisals less stressful and more manageable, our sense of self-efficacy should correspondingly improve.

A definition of stress

It is interesting that ideas from a number of different lines of research all seem to converge. They emphasize that the perception of what is happening is crucial, and they are also interested in our perceptions of control and the ability to cope. So this again comes back to the idea that the stress that we experience is a combination of our perceived views of how difficult and demanding a situation is, and our perception of our ability to exert control over the situation, to cope with and master it.

So, to summarize:

- Stress occurs when there is an imbalance between how you perceive the demands made on you, and on how you perceive your ability to cope with the demands.
- This is true whether the demands are external or whether they are to meet your own internal expectations and goals. Your perception of your ability to cope with demands will also depend on how far you feel in control, and how great your sense of self-efficacy.

This definition leads to one further key idea in the discussion of stress, since it will be seen that people will differ very widely in their perception of these things, and that this will make a substantial difference to how much stress they can tolerate.

Individual differences in stress

One of the authors was stuck in a traffic jam and turned on Radio 4. The radio was playing an interview with the musician Brian Eno. Though people who know Brian Eno's music have rather different views about it, as an interviewee he came across as a fascinating person, seemingly endlessly interested in and captivated by the world and its possibilities. At one point the interviewer said something like: 'I want to go back to a previous interview when you were on *Desert Island Discs*. Apparently on the programme you were asked what your choice of luxury item would be, and you said "a giant man-eating spider". I want to ask you more about it – I think at the time you said that you'd chosen that because it would force you to keep being active, and creative in finding solutions, and stop you just relaxing on the island.' But Brian Eno said: 'Oh – I thought I asked for an endless supply of mind-altering drugs!'

Now whether or not he really did ask for a giant man-eating spider, this does illustrate a point. We all differ in the amount of pressure and demand that we can cope with, or indeed want to cope with, and in how stressful we are likely to find demands that do come along. It seems that we 'like' a certain level of arousal or activity. This level is different for different people, but generally lies somewhere in the middle of the range of possibilities. At one extreme, we are all familiar with people who take part in 'extreme' sports, and seem to love to put themselves in situations where there is a great deal of risk and danger; or who take on challenges at work which many of us would completely draw the line at. At the other extreme are people who find almost anything too stressful to take part in. One of us had a patient who had struggled with Chronic Fatigue Syndrome for many years, and who was invited to attend a conference on an area of medieval history in which he had great expertise. Martin said to me very sadly: 'The problem with chronic fatigue is that things which are opportunities to other people are unacceptably difficult challenges to me – I know if I go to this meeting I will enjoy it, but I will suffer so much afterwards that I just don't know if it will be worth it.' Sadly for Martin, the amount of stress that he could cope with was very small.

Optimal levels of stress

Although there are individual differences in how much stress we can tolerate, we all follow the same basic pattern. This is shown in Figure 1.1 below. If we are bored and understimulated we tend to perform less well; as we become more aroused our performance improves and we become more energized and alert; but if we become over-aroused then our performance is disrupted, and we become stressed and anxious.

Stress and boredom

This may explain why the exception to the rule about stress being associated with excessive pressure and demand is when there are no demands at all, and we become bored. It may be that someone is working at a repetitive job that is well below their abilities, or that they go home in the evening to a lonely house with nothing to do until work starts the next day. When there is simply not enough going on people become bored, frustrated and apathetic, and this too is deeply stressful. It is when we are in the middle of this u-shaped curve that we feel and perform at our best.

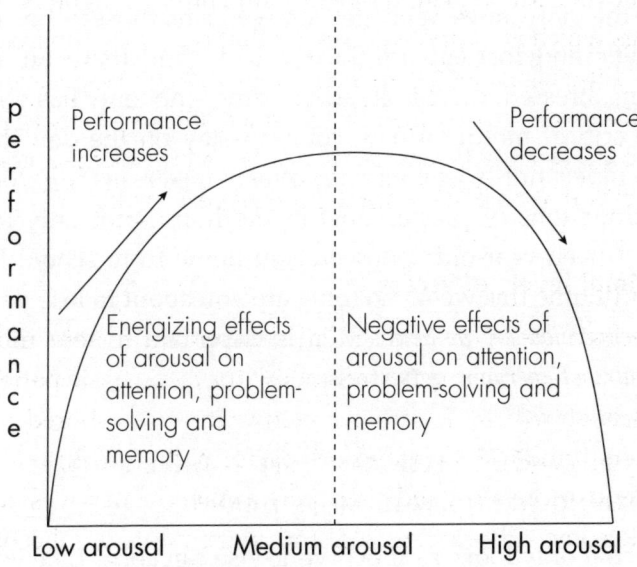

Figure 1.1 The Yerkes-Dodson Law

Myths about stress

Although stress is so prevalent in our lives, and is talked about so widely and openly, there are a number of ideas about it that are still lurking in the background and which make it much more difficult for people when they do feel stressed. Like other myths, these are ideas that seem to carry on in the culture in which they are found even though there is precious little evidence to support them!

MYTH 1: I SHOULDN'T GET STRESSED — IT MEANS I'M WEAK AND PATHETIC

There is a strong tendency among some people to think that the only ones who get stressed are those who are pathetic and inadequate. So if you do find that you are getting stressed, there is an added sting – not only has your very critical mother-in-law come to stay on the day that the builders finish, leaving three cement mixers in the garden and four tons of plaster dust in the house; not only has your fifteen-year-old son been sent home from school for the fifth time this week; not only are you about to lose your job – but *you are pathetic*! So it is important to remember that *almost everyone gets stressed*.

MYTH 2: EVERYONE ELSE CAN COPE — THERE MUST BE SOMETHING WRONG WITH ME IF I CAN'T

In fact, it only looks as if everyone else can cope. Like you, they are struggling to preserve appearances for the outside world, and go to some lengths to hide how they are feeling. As a character in Marian Keyes's novel *Rachel's Holiday* said: 'The trouble about us is that we compare our insides with other people's outsides.' Since we all tend to do this, it is not surprising that we think that other people are doing so much better than we are.

MYTH 3: LIFE IS JUST STRESSFUL, AND THERE'S NOTHING
YOU CAN DO ABOUT IT ANYWAY

Well, yes, it does seem to be true that most people have
quite a lot that is stressful in their lives. But it is not true
that there is nothing you can do. Sometimes this means
doing things that change the situation, but it can also involve
finding ways of managing the way that you feel too – hopefully, as you read on, this book will make some of these
ways of coping clearer.

CHAPTER SUMMARY

- Although some situations are obviously difficult for anyone, the
  degree to which you will find something difficult or stressful
  depends on your appraisal of it (this is called primary appraisal).
- The amount of stress you experience will also depend on how
  you perceive your ability to cope (your secondary appraisal).
- Stress does not refer to any negative emotion, but can more
  usefully be thought of as a response to situations involving
  pressure and demand.
- On the whole we talk about stress when there is too much
  perceived pressure, but a lack of stimulation can also be felt
  as very stressful.
- Sometimes demands can be internal rather than external, and
  may be to do with wanting to meet expectations and goals.
- Stress is also made much worse by feelings of helplessness and
  the inability to control what is going on.
- We define stress as the feelings which occur when you see the
  demands made on you as greater than your perceived ability
  to cope.

2

Stress and your body

So far, we have been thinking about stress in terms of its causes and some of the psychological issues which might be important. But there is, of course, a side of stress which most people are only too aware of. This concerns its impact on the body, and whether or not stress can cause us physical harm.

SOME OF THE PHYSICAL SYMPTOMS OF STRESS

- *Muscular*: tension and pain, particularly headache, neck and shoulder pain, backache.
- *Gastrointestinal*: dyspepsia, indigestion, vomiting, heartburn, constipation, irritable bowel.
- *Cardiovascular*: palpitations, arrhythmia, inflammatory pain, angina.
- *Respiratory*: dyspnoea (shortness of breath), hyperventilation.
- *Central nervous system*: insomnia, anxiety, irritability.
- *Reproductive and sexual*: low libido, impotence, amenorrhoea (absence of menstrual periods), dysmenorrhoea (heavy bleeding).
- *General*: more frequent colds and flu, allergic reactions.

In this chapter we will look at some basic ideas about the way our bodies function in situations of stress, and then look at the issue of stress and illness.

Response to threat: Fight, flight and freeze

As humans were evolving, most of the threats which faced us were physical; we lived in groups in environments which contained a lot of danger, including the presence of predators, the need to find food and shelter in sometimes harsh conditions, and competition for resources and status within the group. Since the threats were largely physical, individuals who were physically most developed were most likely to survive. Consequently we have evolved to be very efficient in reacting to physical threat. Our hearts beat faster, sending blood pumping round our bodies; the extra oxygen derived from the increased blood flow allows our muscles to expand; we start to breathe faster, getting more oxygen into our lungs; we become very attuned to the source of the threat.

All of this makes us stronger and faster, so that we will be better able either to fight or to run. But sometimes this physical activity has a down side. For example, many animals empty their bladders or bowels when frightened. This has a sensible side to it – you will be lighter when you need to run away. But this is obviously not something that you would want to happen when you are talking to your boss! The problem is that many of the dangers that face us now do not require a physical response, so this physical activity is not needed and can feel pretty unpleasant, like when we breathe too fast or our hearts are racing.

The third way in which animals might respond to threat is by 'freezing'. Since predator animals' visual systems are particularly sensitive to movement, many prey animals freeze in the presence of danger in order to reduce the risk of being seen. In order to freeze, muscles need to be tense – this allows them to hold the body still. Again, this tendency, though useful once, may result in problems such as stiffness and pain if muscles are held tense for too long.

Stress and stress hormones

These physical responses are mediated by hormonal systems in the body. Very broadly speaking, there are two main hormonal systems which become activated during stressful situations: that which produces adrenaline and its associated hormones, and that which produces cortisol.

Adrenaline

When we are in a situation that we perceive as threatening, the part of the brain that is responsible for keeping our emotions in balance and appropriate to the situation sends messages to the sympathetic nervous system (or SNS), resulting in the release of *adrenaline* (also referred to as *epinephrine*). The sudden release of adrenaline 'turns on' the fight or flight response. It produces changes in blood flow and blood pressure, such that more oxygen-rich blood can get to the brain and muscles needed to fight or run away. It increases cardiac output and enlarges the air passages. Adrenaline also causes a rapid release of glucose and fatty acids into the bloodstream, so that the body has more energy for what it needs to do. Your senses become keener and you are less sensitive to pain.

As the danger passes, the body attempts to get back to normal. The parasympathetic nervous system (or PNS), releases a hormone called *noradrenaline* which helps to reverse the changes that have taken place. But while the SNS jumps into action very quickly to ready the body for rapid action, it is much slower to turn off and allow the PNS to calm us down. This may in some ways be sensible, keeping us in a state of readiness to respond to threat, but does mean that in some cases it can take quite a while for us to calm down after the danger is over.

Cortisol

The other major stress-related hormone is *cortisol*, which is produced by a part of the brain known as the hypothalamic pituitary adrenal cortex, or HPA. While adrenaline acts very quickly, cortisol is released more slowly. Cortisol levels peak 20–40 minutes after we are exposed to a threat, and continue for longer. So what does cortisol do?

It is essential for the maintenance of some normal functions of the body, including growth and development, as well as for the variations in our metabolism that occur over the course of the day. It plays a key role in the metabolism of proteins and fats, and of glucose. It is associated with the regulation of our blood pressure, and with muscle function, and it is thought to affect our immune system, making some aspects of this work better but inhibiting others. Cortisol also has effects in the brain, particularly in helping to form memories quickly and efficiently. This is thought to be important in helping individuals to remember situations which have proved dangerous in the past.

Cortisol works in the short term to maintain some of the activity which has been begun by changes in adrenaline. For instance, adrenaline quickly elevates blood glucose levels to give us more energy, but cortisol then comes in to keep these levels high. In the long term, if the cortisol response is activated frequently, cortisol levels in the body become generally higher, effectively keeping our bodies in a constant state of stress.

Stages of the stress response

When Hans Selye worked with stress, he built up a picture of what can happen to an animal in terms of three stages, which he described as the General Adaptation Syndrome, or GAS. The first of these stages, which he termed the *alarm stage*, is the fight or flight response, when we respond rapidly to danger. If the fight or flight response is successful, and the danger has been averted – when we have run away from the sabre-toothed tiger, or killed the rattlesnake, then we start to calm down. The intense physiological activity dies down and our bodies revert to a more normal level of functioning.

So long as this doesn't happen too frequently, then everything is fine. But problems occur when the external threat keeps recurring, or never goes away at all. In this case our bodies have to operate at these high levels of arousal over a long period of time, with resulting changes in hormones such as cortisol. In order to stay in an aroused state, our bodies need to 'borrow' physical resources from normal bodily functions like eating and digestion, or the maintenance of the menstrual cycle in women, or from the activity of the immune system. Selye described this as the *resistance stage*, and said that, although it might look as if the body is coping, it is in fact starting to experience problems.

In the third stage, which Selye termed the *exhaustion stage*, the body can no longer cope with the demands put on it, and the problems which might have started in the resistance stage gain ground.

Allostasis

Modern researchers talk about the changes that we make to adapt to stress as *allostasis*. This literally means 'stability through change'; that is, our bodies need to be making constant minor adjustments to keep us in a more or less stable state in which all physical systems function properly. For instance, if we are too hot, then our bodies start to sweat in order to cool us down; if we are too cold, we generate heat by shivering and shaking, or by jumping up and down and stamping our feet. So when we get very aroused and stressed, our bodies are constantly trying to get us back to a more stable state. Stress researchers often talk about the idea of 'allostatic overload', when the demands to restore balance are so great that the body finds it very difficult to cope. The concept of allostatic overload is very similar to Selye's earlier ideas of resistance and exhaustion.

To summarize, our bodies are geared to respond to threat in a very efficient way. But the problem is that in order to do this they have to shut down bodily functions that are not involved in the fight or flight response. Because all the resources of our bodies are going into coping with the immediate threat, there is less energy for non-urgent activities, so that certain other functions, such as digestion, growth, reproduction and the immune system, all go on hold.

Is all stress and arousal bad for you?

Of course, we should absolutely emphasize that all of this *does not mean* that if you experience any sort of physiological arousal then this is bad for you. As we saw from the section on optimal levels of stress in Chapter 1, we all need stimulation, and we function better in some ways when we are aroused. We like feelings of pleasurable excitement – what some people would refer to as eustress – and get bored when we have no stimulation at all. It is only when the arousal gets too much, or goes on for too long, that problems arise.

Stress and health

But the important question for most of us is: does stress make us ill? Is stress really doing harm to our bodies? You may be wondering about the list of symptoms with which we began the chapter: are these symptoms caused by stress?

We can see that many of the physical changes produced by our hormones might have consequences, and that many of the symptoms described above relate very clearly to them.

Muscular aches and pains

The fight or flight response produces a great deal of activity designed to make our muscles more effective. But if the muscles are not being used then something needs to happen to that activity. Usually this means the muscles become tense, then stiff and painful. Since headaches can also be a result of tension in the muscles around our scalp and face, these too could be explained by stress.

Gastrointestinal symptoms

When we are stressed our digestive system is partially shut down, so that if we then eat, we are likely to experience difficulties with digestion, nausea, constipation and diarrhoea. Furthermore, we do not heal as easily, so damage caused to our stomachs by excessive acid in the gut does not repair itself, and can cause further problems with ulcers.

Cardiovascular and respiratory problems

The physical activity of the stress response can put an additional burden on our heart and lungs, leading to palpitations, shortness of breath, or breathing too rapidly and heavily. The stress hormones may also increase the production of cholesterol, which may in turn be a risk factor for coronary heart disease.

Central nervous system problems

We have seen that during periods of danger we become more vigilant to threatening and dangerous stimuli. Over time, this oversensitivity to threat makes us anxious or irritable, prevents us sleeping, and can lead to depression.

Reproductive and sexual problems

Again, some of the problems in our sexual activity may be explained by the idea that during periods of prolonged stress, energy is taken away from functions of the body that are not essential to our immediate survival, so that the menstrual cycle in women is likely to be affected, with periods becoming painful or ceasing altogether. The sex drive or libido diminishes, and in men erectile difficulties may occur.

Colds and flu and other immune problems

One of the factors which may have the highest impact on our health is when stress produces changes in cortisol, which plays a significant role in the immune system. We discuss the effect that this may have on health in more detail below.

As with so much research in this area, the picture is rarely simple. We do not know *how much* stress a person needs to experience in order for his or her body to show any effects, nor exactly why some people are more biologically susceptible to these effects than others. It is also possible that the explanation could be the other way round for some people; that is to say, rather than stress making them ill, being unwell for reasons not associated with stress could then make people feel more stressed. It is also clear that the way in which we respond to stress can have a significant impact on how long it lasts and how badly it affects us. So although prolonged raised cortisol may have detrimental effects, we can learn to control it – and this, of course, is what the second part of this book is all about.

Stressful life events and health

So far we have been looking at the *mechanisms* by which stress might affect health. But another line of enquiry is to explore whether stress and illness seem to go together. In the 1960s, two psychiatrists, Holmes and Rahe, developed a system for looking at life stress. They compiled a long list of events that are likely to be stressful, and asked a large number of people to rate each item according to the intensity and length of time it would take to adjust to it. The list included events that were positive, but would require significant adjustment, such as marriage or promotion at work. The researchers arbitrarily said that getting married would be assigned a stress value of 500, and then rated all other items by comparison. For instance, an event considered to be twice as stressful as marriage would be assigned a value of 1,000, while one considered to be half as stressful would be assigned a value of 250. Some of the items Holmes and Rahe included, with the ratings assigned (but divided by 100), are shown in Table 2.1 below.

TABLE 2.1 LIFE EVENTS AND RATINGS

Death of a spouse	100
Divorce	73
Personal injury or illness	53
Marriage	50
Made redundant	47
Change in financial state	38
Change in responsibilities at work	29
Change in residence	20
Christmas	12

(Adapted from Holmes and Rahe, 1967)

Holmes and Rahe then used this scale to measure the life stress that people were experiencing by adding up the scores for each item that was relevant to them. The total score was known as the Life Change Unit (LCU) score. It is noteworthy that Holmes and Rahe were particularly interested in the idea that it is change, rather than pleasantness or unpleasantness, that makes people stressed, and therefore they included positive items that involve change. This has been a source of some debate ever since.

In a number of studies Holmes and Rahe then used these scores to see whether people with higher LCU scores experienced more physical problems. In a study of 200 doctors, health problems including infectious diseases, allergies and musculoskeletal problems such as back pain, were found to be strongly related to LCU score. Other researchers also found that LCU scores were related to heart attacks, to the onset of leukaemia, and to colds and fevers. It looked, then, as if there was a very strongly emerging relationship between stress and illness.

But other researchers were more cautious about the interpretation of the results. For one thing, the research was mainly carried out by asking people to recall both life events and periods of illness over the last two years. But memory is a fickle thing, and it might be that people who were stressed were more likely to remember illnesses, rather than more likely to have had them. And secondly, sometimes the link could go the other way round. For example, someone who has long-standing problems with back pain may well need to take a lot of time off work and end up losing a job. So in this case, the physical health problems would have caused the stressful life event, rather than the other way round. It is very difficult to reach firm conclusions on the basis of this kind of research.

There are a number of other ways in which the relation between stress and illness has been studied, particularly in relation to the functioning of the immune system.

Stress and the immune system

One of the most important factors in keeping our bodies functioning well is the immune system, the system in the body which protects us against disease. This is a highly complex network of cells which identifies and attacks foreign bodies that might invade us, including bacteria, viruses, fungi and parasites. If our immune system is weakened, it operates much less efficiently and can't fend off the invading foreign bodies, so we are more likely to get ill.

The field of research called *psychoneuroimmunology* shows that there are direct connections between the immune system and the central nervous system (CNS). Changes in the CNS can have a direct effect on the immune system, and chemical changes in the immune system can in turn alter the central nervous system. Since the activity of the CNS includes what goes on in our brains, what this means is that how we think and feel can have a direct effect on the functioning of our immune system. And of course, it is our thinking and appraisal of events that, as we have seen in the previous chapter, play a very large part in determining how stressful we find particular situations.

It's a central belief of psychoneuroimmunology that stress impacts on the immune system to weaken it. Can this have a real effect on our health? Researchers have looked at this in a number of ways, some of which we will explore in more detail below, including the relation between stress and cancer, stress and infectious diseases, and stress and autoimmune disease.

Stress and cancer

One area in which there has been a great deal of interest is the possible link between stress and cancer. Impairment in immune function is thought to be important in at least some forms of cancer, possibly by affecting what are known as natural killer cells. So if stress impacts on the immune system then this might have a knock-on effect on cancer.

One of the best studied areas of cancer research is breast cancer. But when the link between stress and breast cancer has been studied scientifically, the results are very unclear. So many studies have been conducted in this area, and with such conflicting results, that researchers have conducted what are known as 'meta-analyses' of the data. In a meta-analysis, the researchers look at all the relevant studies, and try to combine the results of all of them into a single coherent message. When two meta-analyses were carried out, both initially found that there *was* an association – the probability of developing breast cancer seemed to be higher for women who had experienced more stressful life events than for women who had experienced fewer.

But there is a great difference between research studies in how good their methodology is; that is, how well they have been designed and carried out. Sometimes when the methodology of a study is a bit loose the results can be quite misleading. Bearing this in mind, one of the groups of researchers carrying out the meta-analysis then took a more careful approach. Petticrew and his colleagues gave each of the studies included in their meta-analysis a score for how good their methodology was, and included only those studies that were above the halfway mark. When only the good methodological studies were included, a very different result was found, with *no* association between life events and cancer emerging. On this basis it seems that the link between experiencing stressful life events and developing breast cancer does *not* exist. Now, as Petticrew pointed out, this meta-analysis did not look at the women's appraisals of stress, nor did it look at other forms of cancer, but it did show that there was no obvious and straightforward link between the stressors themselves and the development of breast cancer.

These studies were looking particularly at the question of whether stress affects the *development* of cancer. Another field of research has been concerned with looking at what happens *after* cancer has developed and been diagnosed, and whether stress might affect the way that the disease progresses. Again, the best studies seem to show that the occurrence of stressful life events does not seem to influence the progress of the disease. In one such study for instance, life events such as divorce, death of a close family member, or unemployment, did not increase the chances that women would suffer from a relapse of the cancer.

Yet another field of enquiry looked at ways of *coping* with cancer, and whether this affects health and survival. A fascinating study by Greer and his colleagues in the 1970s looked at a whole host of factors that might influence survival rates. To the authors' surprise, one of the most important factors to emerge was the way in which women responded when they received the diagnosis of cancer: those who responded with a style described as hopeless or helpless ('There's nothing I can do, I will die') or with stoic acceptance ('I'll just have to make the most of things now'), showed less good survival rates than those who responded with a style described as fighting spirit ('This is not going to get to me, I'm going to beat this') or as denial ('The doctors have got it wrong, I haven't got cancer'). The finding about denial was particularly interesting, since there is such a strong bias in psychology towards the belief that facing up to and coming to terms with things is 'good' and denying their existence is 'bad'.

What is clear is that many people do seem to believe that a link between stress and cancer exists. When a group of women who were long-term survivors of breast cancer in Canada were interviewed, nearly half of them said that they thought stress had played an important part in the development of the cancer, and this seems to be a reasonably common view.

So why do many people believe that there *is* a link when the research does not seem to support this? This may be because we see people around us who are stressed and get cancer, so we assume that it is the stress that has caused the cancer. But it may be that the two are related because of what people do when they are stressed. It is, for example, very common for people to resort to smoking or drinking excessively as a way of coping with stress – and we know that smoking, and to some extent heavy drinking, is associated with cancer. So it may be that the *behaviors* that stress leads to have an effect on cancer, rather than the stress itself.

Perhaps another reason is that when people are facing adverse circumstances they have a very strong need to understand what is happening, and to create a sense for themselves that there is something that they can do. In these circumstances people may tend to 'see' links that do not really exist; and for very obvious reasons people may strongly want to believe that dealing with stress and improving their well-being will have a positive effect.

Stress and infectious disease

Infectious diseases are those which are caused by the invasion of the body by bacteria or a virus – known as 'pathogens' since they play a part in the development or 'pathogenesis' of the disease. Not everyone exposed to pathogens develops the diseases; we are probably all familiar with the experience of spending a great deal of time with family or close friends without ever picking up their colds or flu. And some mothers will also be very familiar with the experience of taking their children to see friends with measles, in order to get it over with, all to no avail. In fact, there are always some pathogens in the environment, so that we are exposed to them pretty constantly, but without being (hopefully) constantly ill. Could stress be one of the things that makes a difference to whether we become ill or not?

In a famous study of the links between stress and infectious disease, Cohen and his colleagues took a group of volunteer participants and exposed them to the virus that is responsible for the common cold. Once they had been exposed, the participants were placed in quarantine, and the researchers waited to see whether they would develop a cold or not. The presence of a cold was determined in three ways – firstly by checking for the presence of the virus in nasal secretions, and for antibodies in the blood that are 'virus-specific'; secondly by asking the participants to report symptoms; and thirdly by having their symptoms rated by a medical doctor. (These three measures – physiological, self-report and expert report – are thought to be the best way of deciding definitely whether an illness has occurred, so the researchers were being very methodologically correct.)

Before they were exposed to the virus, all the participants had been interviewed by the researchers about the levels of stress in their lives. The researchers divided the stress into acute stress (in this case defined as stressors that had lasted less than a month) and chronic stress (defined as stressors that had lasted more than a month). Then they looked at whether stress made a difference to whether the participants developed a cold or not. What they found was that the participants who had been experiencing chronic stress were much more likely to develop a cold than those who had not. And the longer the stress had been going on, the higher the probability that the participant would get a cold. On the other hand, acute stress, lasting less than a month, did not seem to make much difference. To demonstrate the complexities of immunology research, though, there was a rather puzzling finding, in that people who were experiencing an acute stressor on top of a chronic stressor were *less* likely to develop a cold than those who just had the chronic stressor.

And what is interesting about this research is that it was the participants' own accounts of the stress that were important. In some cases it was clear that the participants were going through life events that everyone would agree to be stressful; in other cases, however, they were not objectively experiencing more life stress than others, but they reported *feeling* more stressed about their lives. Once again we can see how important one's appraisal process is, because the participants' perception, or appraisal, of the level of stress in their lives was shown to be enough to damage their immune functioning.

Stress and autoimmune disease

Autoimmune disease is the term given to a group of diseases in which the immune system fails to tell the difference between cells that rightly belong in the body and those that do not, and ends up attacking cells that are an important part of our own bodily systems. Rheumatoid arthritis, lupus and multiple sclerosis (MS) are just some examples of these diseases. Could they too be affected by stress?

In multiple sclerosis the cells that line the nerves and conduct messages along them are attacked by the immune system. The progress of multiple sclerosis can fluctuate greatly, with periods of stability interspersed with periods of flare-ups and worsening of functioning. Researchers have therefore looked to see whether these flare-ups are associated with stress, and again the picture is very complicated and seems to depend on the type of stress studied. For example, relatively minor stress, such as problems at work or marital conflict, did seem to be associated with these flare-ups, but more severely stressful events, such as the death of a close relative, did not. It has also been reported that under extremely severe stressful conditions, such as the threat of missile attack during war, the rate of flare-ups in MS patients actually improved!

A similar pattern has been found for rheumatoid arthritis, where again relatively minor stresses seem to be associated with worsening of symptoms, but major stresses do not. It's also been shown that many of the symptoms, including pain and the condition of the joints, improve in people who have taken part in therapy programs aimed at helping them cope with, and reduce, their level of stress.

The role of stress has also been looked at extensively in the development and progression of HIV and AIDS. One study found that there was a dramatic deterioration in immune function in HIV-positive men if their partners died of AIDS. The stress of this is very obvious: there is the grief about the death, but also often the loss of social support which intimate relationships provide; and there is clearly an increased fear that the disease which has robbed you of your partner will affect you too. So it may be that all of this stress may play a part in the deterioration of immune functioning. On the other side of the coin, and more encouragingly, there is also some evidence that social support and stress management can help to improve the immune functioning of HIV-positive people.

Stress and the heart

Finally, there is one kind of illness that has not been covered in this chapter: the effect of stress on heart attacks and cardiovascular disease in general. This is because the impact of stress in this type of illness seems to be very strongly mediated by personality, and so will be looked at in the next chapter on stress and personality.

It seems, then, that there may be a relationship between stress and illness, but this is by no means clear and simple. Some kinds of illness do seem to show a relationship with stress but in others the evidence, when looked at very carefully, is much less convincing. And where there are relationships with stress this can depend on the kind of stress, in quite complicated ways.

CHAPTER SUMMARY

- Our bodies are adapted to respond to threat by reacting physically. Even though many of the things which are 'threatening' for us now don't involve physical danger, we still respond in the same way.
- These physical changes are known as the 'fight or flight' response. A third strategy, freezing, is also common.
- The fight or flight response is a very effective way of gearing us up to cope with threat, but it takes energy away from other functions of our bodies.
- Problems arise when threat goes on for too long and our bodies cannot return to normal.
- The physical changes are mediated by the stress hormones, adrenaline and cortisol. If the stress goes on for too long, then cortisol levels may remain raised.
- Over a long period of time changes in hormones, and other physical aspects of the stress response, may result in physical

problems for the individual. However, these problems do not always occur with long-term stress, and when they do can be moderated by the techniques we describe in Part Two.

- The effect of stress on the immune system may play a part in determining what happens in some cancers, some infectious diseases, and autoimmune disorders, but the picture is unclear, and often no definite pattern emerges.

3

Stress and personality

The issue of what it means to talk about 'personality' has excited debate for many years, indeed thousands of years. In this chapter we will talk briefly about what the concept means, and then go on to look at how aspects of personality may be linked to stress.

What is personality?

Types and traits

We need to start any chapter on personality with some discussion of what 'personality' is. Historically, it has been seen as those characteristics of people which determine what they are like, and which are 'given' from birth and are relatively fixed and immutable. In this view different characteristics were organized into 'types', which were often seen as related to health. For instance in the fifth century BC Hippocrates talked about the four humours – blood, phlegm, yellow bile and black bile – which characterize personality types and which were said to be related to health. People with yellow bile, for instance, tended to be quick to anger, and to get health problems with their spleen. People with phlegm were calm and unemotional, and had problems with their brain and lungs.

In the twentieth century, however, psychologists studying personality took issue with these ideas. On the one hand personality started to be talked about as a set of traits rather than in terms of types. Traits were still said to be stable characteristics, but they could be combined in different ways rather than one set of traits all going together, as in a type. But on the other hand more radical ideas saw personality as no more than a description of people's behavior. This view said that behavior was determined not by personality, but by the demands of the situation in which people found themselves. Far from always behaving in the same way, people would show completely different ways of behaving according to their situation. This became known as the interactionist view.

Interactionism

This view:

- argued that traits are not stable over time and in all situations – people do behave differently in different situations, and they can change over time;
- acknowledged that each of us shows a tendency to behave in certain ways rather than others;
- noted that some people seem to be more consistent across different situations than others.

You can almost certainly think of examples from your own life that fit in with this view. Are you honest? If you found a wallet in the street you would probably hand it in, but given the opportunity to avoid paying tax, would you turn it down?

Fixed personality or learned behavior?

At some level we may have *tendencies* to behave in certain ways or feel certain things. We are, after all, minds set in bodies, and what happens in our bodies must inevitably affect us. In the study of anxiety, for instance, it is clear that some people are much more prone to react physically to threat than others, and this may well be associated with a tendency to feel more anxious and think in a more anxious way. But on top of this basic tendency, much of what we think and feel is determined by what has happened to us in our lives, particularly our early lives. Take two people whose bodily make-up means that they react in a strong physical manner to threat – their bodies are strongly reactive to stress. One of them may have been brought up in a family where people are confident and view the world as an exciting or interesting place. Such a person is likely to feel more confident themselves and to feel less anxious. But someone brought up in a family where other people are anxious, where the parents are overprotective and tell the child that the world is a dangerous place, is much more likely to see things as threatening, and to feel more anxious. So even though both of these people have the same physical response to stress, they have a very different mental one, so that their overall reaction is quite different. It is our learning history, our experience of the world, that plays a very large part in determining how we see things, and how we feel and behave as a result.

Now this, of course, could just be taken to mean that we do have fixed personalities, even though these may be created by a combination of biological or genetic factors and environmental ones, rather than just being caused by genetics alone. But because much of what we are has been learned, it is clear that it can also be unlearned. Although we have tendencies to behave in certain ways, this does not mean that we always have to do that, or that there is no choice for us. So it is important to remember that in any discussion of personality and stress, we are not talking about characteristics that you are stuck with and can never be changed, but about learned ways of feeling and behaving that almost certainly can be altered.

So how do these ideas relate to stress? Later in this chapter we will go on to see how various kinds of personality characteristics have been found to be associated with stress. For now, however, we want to highlight one particular way in which personality and stress have been very closely linked to each other and to health issues. In the previous chapter there was one kind of illness that we delayed discussing, since the links between stress and that illness seem to be so heavily dependent on personality type. This illness is coronary heart disease, and its links to stress are based on the impact of Type A personality.

Personality and illness

Type A personality and heart attacks

In 1959, Friedman and Rosenman identified a particular personality which seemed to be associated with coronary heart disease. The researchers labelled people with this personality 'Type A' and described them as highly competitive and highly achieving, with extremely high desires to meet goals; they were also very impatient with other people, restless, hostile and aggressive. They tended to look tense in the face, to speak in very explosive ways, to sweat easily, and generally to appear to be under pressure. The researchers labelled people who did not show these characteristics as Type B. Essentially, the Type A people could be described as very stressed, whereas Type B people were less likely to get stressed by the demands of the situation they were in. When Friedman and Rosenman looked at people who had heart disease, they found that those with Type A characteristics had approximately *twice* the risk of developing coronary heart disease as the Type Bs. So the personality characteristics were having a very marked impact on their health.

As time went on, however, a familiar complication emerged. As more studies were done, the findings became less and less clear. Some studies just did not find a relationship between Type A characteristics and heart disease. But remember that there were a lot of different aspects to Type A, one of which was to do with being aggressive and hostile. Whenever researchers looked at the relationship between these aspects of Type A behavior and heart disease, they *did* find a relationship. People who were more hostile and aggressive were more likely to have heart attacks. It seems as if it is this, rather than other aspects of Type A, which does the damage. People who showed a cluster of characteristics similar to those of Type A, but without the hostility, did not seem to be at risk.

Another complication concerned the *gender* of the people showing Type A behavior. At the time that the early work was carried out it tended to be mainly men who were in the kinds of positions where Type A behavior was seen rather than women. Later, when women showing Type A behavior pattern were studied, the health risk seemed to be somewhat lower. How could this be? What seemed to be occurring was that the women who showed many of the Type A characteristics did not display nearly so much hostility and aggression as the men, and since it is these aspects which are associated with heart attacks they were not susceptible to the same health risks.

An important issue, given the risks to health, is whether or not Type A personality is a stable characteristic. Some people *have* tended to see it in this way, while others have regarded it as a pattern of behavior. In fact, most researchers now refer to the 'personality' as Type A *Behaviors*, or TAB. Some support for this view comes from the idea that at least some of the Type A behaviors talked about could be seen as learned behavior. Within a pressured work environment, for instance, it is easy to see how people would be encouraged and rewarded for showing very competitive, achievement-oriented behavior.

Another aspect to this is that Type A behaviors seem to be modifiable: in studies looking at people who have suffered heart attacks and who have taken part in programs designed to help reduce these behaviors, the amount of TAB shown seems to decline. So again, it seems as if these behaviors may be learned and unlearned rather than being fixed personality characteristics. In the research studies, the Type A people could certainly learn to be less Type A, and this reduced their risk of another heart attack.

Are there other personality types that are associated with disease?

More recent studies have shown a completely different personality that seems to be associated with heart disease. Described as Type D, or the 'Distressed' personality, this refers to people showing two characteristics: they have strong emotional reactions, and experience high degrees of emotional distress, but they tend to keep these emotions bottled up, particularly in social situations. Their chances of having a heart attack are again higher than for people who are able to be more open with their emotions.

Finally, researchers have also identified another personality that is associated, not with heart disease, but with some types of cancer. When researchers looked at which personality types might be more likely to develop malignant melanoma, or skin cancer, they identified the Type C personality. Type C personalities are described as extremely cooperative, passive, accepting and lacking assertiveness, and they are much more likely than other people to develop not just melanoma, but other cancers too.

The implications of all this may not have escaped you. You cannot be too aggressive, too bottled up, or too passive, and if heart attacks don't get you, cancer will. This seems to leave depressingly little room for a healthy personality that is *not* prone to disease of some sort.

But in fact the picture may indicate that *extremes* of emotion could be the problem. The personality types describe the way in which people deal with difficult situations and negative emotions. One type responds with anger and hostility, a kind of externally explosive way of dealing with emotion. Others respond by bottling things up, not speaking, not trying to make changes to the situation that is causing the difficulties. Between these extremes, however, there is room for a very extensive middle ground, of reasonably appropriate expressions of feeling, and reasonably appropriate behavior, that is not associated with disease.

Personality and stress

So far we have looked at the influence of different personality traits or behavior on the development of a particular disease. But there is also the issue of whether there are particular personality traits which are more associated with stress in general.

The hardy personality

The idea of the 'hardy' personality, or 'hardiness', was introduced by Susanne Kobasa in 1979. She was interested in personality characteristics that might distinguish between people who seemed to be susceptible to stress and its impact on their health, and those who seemed to be resistant to it. Kobasa looked at many personality measures, and found three characteristics that make up the hardy individual, which she termed commitment, control and challenge.

- *Commitment*: This refers to the degree to which people are committed to and involved in all aspects of their lives. Hardy people believe strongly in the importance and interest of what they are doing, and have much higher belief in themselves than others who would not be described as committed.
- *Control*: We have seen in Chapter 1 that the issue of control seems to be very important. Not surprisingly, this emerged as one of the characteristics associated with the hardy personality. Essentially it refers to the degree to which people feel that they have control over what happens in their lives, with hardy people showing a high belief that they do have control.
- *Challenge*: The third element is that of challenge, which refers to the idea that change is seen as an opportunity and a challenge rather than as negative and threatening. So hardy people exposed to a situation where they need to change would be able to embrace this as a positive move, rather than necessarily a bad one.

People who display these hardy characteristics seem much more able to cope with stressful situations, and to show less impact on their health when they are exposed to stress, than others who do not. Like everything in stress research, the true extent of the relationship between hardiness and resilience in stressful situations is uncertain, but there does seem to be enough of a core of agreement to make it worth bearing in mind. And what is also encouraging is that it seems that these characteristics can be learned, and that by doing so stress can be made more manageable.

Optimism and pessimism

Other personality characteristics which seem to be associated with stress are optimism and pessimism. These are concerned both with your anticipation of what will happen – how likely it is that things will turn out positively for you – and with your sense of having some positive control over the outcome. A range of studies have found that optimism and pessimism are related to a number of issues surrounding both psychological and physical wellbeing. Optimists have been shown to have more of a sense of control over stress, and to be more likely to use positive coping measures when confronted by stress. In studies of depression following childbirth, optimists have been shown to be less likely to become depressed than pessimists. In older men with coronary heart disease, optimism has been associated with better health.

It seems that there are a number of personality characteristics that may help us deal with stress which have been described in different terms by different people, but which all have something in common. The ideas of self-efficacy and locus of control described in Chapter 1 have a lot in common with those of hardiness and optimism/pessimism described here. The common factors seem to be that people who respond well to difficult situations tend to have confidence in themselves and their abilities, a sense that they can exert some control over what happens, and a belief that things will turn out well rather than badly.

This of course sounds all very well if you are one of those people. But what if you are not? The key is to think about the discussion at the beginning of this chapter. One view of personality is that these characteristics are 'fixed' and there is not that much you can do about them. But we believe strongly that many characteristics described as 'personality' are in fact ways of behaving which have been learned, and which depend very heavily on people's thinking about themselves and the situation that they are in. And this thinking can, therefore, be changed. It is at this point that we need to go on to a more detailed discussion of the role of thinking in stress.

CHAPTER SUMMARY

- Many theories of personality recognize that people's behavior can change over time and over different situations.
- Much of what we think of as personality may be learned behavior that can be changed.
- Certain types of personality characteristics, particularly those described as 'Type A', seem to be associated with heart attacks, but research indicates that these characteristics too can be modified.
- Coping well with stress seems to be associated with personality characteristics that relate to a sense of control, confidence and optimism, which again can be learned.

4

The role of thinking in stress: An introduction to cognitive therapy

HAMLET: Denmark's a prison.
ROSENCRANTZ: Then is the world one.
HAMLET: A goodly one; in which there are many confines,
wards and dungeons, Denmark being one o' the worst.
ROSENCRANTZ: We think not so, my lord.
HAMLET: Why, then, 'tis none to you; for there is nothing
either good or bad, but thinking makes it so: to me it
is a prison.

William Shakespeare, *Hamlet*,
Act 2, Scene 2 (our emphasis)

The role of thinking in stress

We saw in Chapter 1 that the role of appraisal was absolutely crucial in determining how stressful an event can be, whether it is appraisal of the situation itself, or of our own ability to cope. So too, many of the so-called personality characteristics described in Chapter 3 depend on our beliefs, or our thoughts, about ourselves and the situations in which we find ourselves. So one of the things that we have learned about stress is that it is the way in which we see situations that makes them more or less stressful. *The way in which we see things plays an absolutely crucial part in determining how we feel about them and how we react to them.* This idea is important not just in stress, but in all emotional disorders, and it is this idea that was the foundation of cognitive therapy. This chapter will therefore explain more about the basic ideas of cognitive therapy. Detailed descriptions of how to use it to help manage your stress are given in Part Two.

Before moving on, however, consider the following two people, both of whom have been told that they need a pretty serious medical check-up:

Susie went to see her family doctor for a routine cervical smear. When the results came back her doctor said that he would like her to see a specialist for a follow-up appointment, since it was possible that some of the cells might be showing abnormalities that could indicate a risk of developing cervical cancer. On the day of the appointment Susie felt extremely wound up. She was terrified of what the specialist might find, and also deeply embarrassed about having to expose her body to a stranger for the examination. She felt sure that the new tests would show that she was really ill, and might die. Even if it turned out to be okay she was worried about needing to take time off work, because she was afraid that her colleagues would be really fed

*up with her. As the day wore on she felt more and
more tense, and at the appointment was so shaky and
tearful that she could barely concentrate on what the
doctor said.*

*The same thing also happened to Martina. Similarly,
her family doctor suggested that she should see a
specialist to investigate the results of her smear. On
the day of the appointment Martina was a little nervous,
but also felt almost relieved. She was thankful that, if
there was anything wrong, the test had picked it up,
and that someone was going to check it out and take
it seriously. Even if the worst came to the worst she
knew that the prognosis for cervical cancer was good
if it was caught early, and she was convinced that she
would be able to overcome it.*

So what we can see is that, in very similar situations,
these two people felt very different – one desperately
worried, the other almost relieved – because the way in
which they were thinking about the situations was so
different.

The psychologist Albert Ellis was interested in the relationship between thinking and emotional problems and
developed a psychological treatment called Rational
Emotive Therapy (an early form of cognitive therapy). Like
others, he argued that it is not what happens to you (the
situation) that distresses you, but the meaning which you
attach to it. He emphasized the importance of being rational
rather than negative in responding to problematic situations. In stressing the importance of this point Ellis said:

'Even if you are being tortured to death, you could be tortured to death *slower*.' The implication was that even if you think you are in the worst possible situation, there might be a worse one, and thus your appraisal of it as 'the worst' is in fact a matter of opinion – a way of seeing things. Behind this somewhat extreme example is the serious point that appraisals make all the difference to how you feel about things. Shakespeare, speaking though Hamlet, clearly knew this too!

These ideas became formalized by Aaron T. Beck, who is often referred to as the founding father of cognitive therapy. The word 'cognitive' comes from the Latin *cogito* – I think – and the therapy is thus all about our thinking.

Cognitive therapy is based on three important ideas:

1 *We all actively construct the meaning of what goes on around us.*

   There are a lot of ways to describe this – cognitive therapy initially referred to thoughts, but we have also talked about appraising a situation, weighing it up, attaching meaning to it, 'seeing it'. All of these are really referring to the same process. And sometimes we weigh things up deliberately or consciously, but as often as not, this 'weighing up' process goes on without our being much aware of it. What we are aware of is the end product – the ideas or thoughts that we have about a situation.

2 *The way that we see things, or our thoughts about them, plays a crucial role in determining our emotional response to them.*

If we see things in their best light we will feel optimistic and cheerful; if we tend to see the worst in situations we are likely to feel gloomy, sad or frightened. Martina felt relieved and hopeful in a situation where Susie felt stressed and anxious.

3 *Thoughts and feelings form cycles that keep things going.*
Once we have thought something, our emotions are affected – but then this emotional state takes over. When we are in any emotional state our brains process everything in terms of that emotion, and screen out anything that doesn't 'fit'. It is as if that way of seeing things becomes the only way our brains can imagine, and we tend to get deeper and deeper into that emotion. So Susie started out feeling stressed, but as the day of her appointment grew nearer she thought of more and more things that could go wrong, and felt worse and worse.

This relationship between thinking and feeling is shown in Figure 4.1.

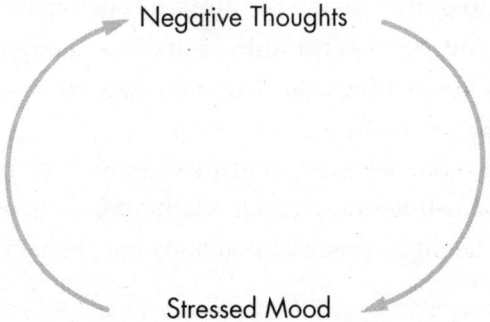

Negative Thoughts

Stressed Mood

Figure 4.1 The vicious cycle of negative thoughts and stressed mood

The influence of our bodies and behavior

Another very important feature is that it is not just the way that we think and feel that are involved in these cycles. The way that our bodies react, and the way that we behave, become influential too. When she started to get stressed, Susie experienced a lot of physical symptoms. We saw in Chapter 2 that when we're anxious and stressed, our physiology changes, adrenaline is released into the system, and a number of physical alterations occur. Often these changes can add to people's discomfort. Susie was already very tense, but when she became aware of feeling shaky and tearful she was even more embarrassed about being examined by the doctor because of what he might think of her.

Once we get trapped in these negative cycles of how we think and feel, and how our bodies react, this can have a big impact on what we do. For instance, it is very common for people to want to avoid situations that make them feel stressed and afraid. The trouble with this and other behavioral responses to stress is that, although they may make the situation better in the short term, in the long term they reinforce people's ideas that they are inadequate, cannot cope, or are 'bad' in some way.

As you can see, the cognitive model displayed in Figure 4.2 illustrates the circular relationship between Susie's thoughts, feelings, physical reactions and behavior.

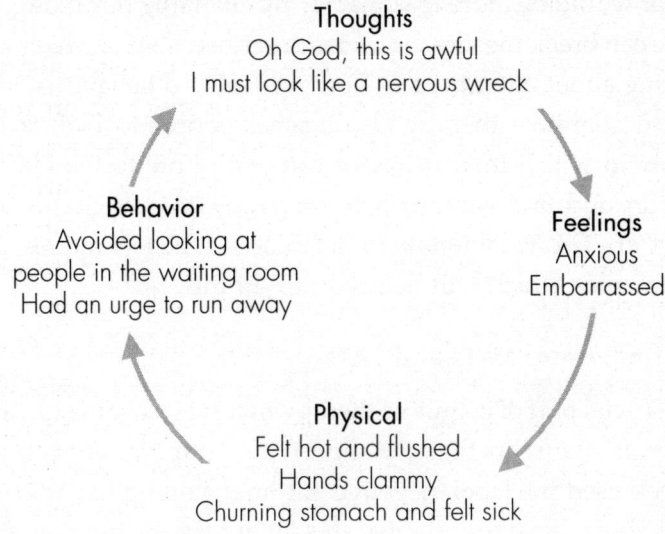

Thoughts
Oh God, this is awful
I must look like a nervous wreck

Feelings
Anxious
Embarrassed

Physical
Felt hot and flushed
Hands clammy
Churning stomach and felt sick

Behavior
Avoided looking at
people in the waiting room
Had an urge to run away

Figure 4.2 The basic cognitive model

What can cognitive therapy do to help?

What we have shown is that the kinds of thoughts that people have contribute greatly to their experience of stress. And we have discussed how this 'stressful thinking' becomes part of a bigger picture that involves feelings, symptoms in the body, and how we behave. So what can cognitive therapy do about all of this? Well, firstly it can teach people to recognize when they are having thoughts which are contributing to the stress that they feel; and secondly it can teach how to challenge these thoughts. Is the stressful thought really the most rational and realistic way of seeing things, or is there another way of thinking that would be more reasonable? By changing our thoughts, we can break the vicious cycles described above, which will bring about alterations in how we feel and behave as well. And cognitive therapy also teaches people to look at the way in which their behavior can contribute to the vicious cycle, and find ways of helping people to change this too. In Part Two we will talk in detail about the techniques and strategies which will help you to do this.

A final note: NATs and SATs

A crucial part of cognitive therapy involves learning to identify the thoughts that are underlying your emotional state. Beck used the label 'negative automatic thoughts' or NATs for short. We have adapted this label to make the thoughts specific to stress, and will refer in Part Two to 'stressful automatic thoughts', or SATs. These are the thoughts, or appraisals, that underlie your experience of stress, and which can be identified and changed to help reduce the amount of stress you feel.

CHAPTER SUMMARY

- People can interpret similar situations in very different ways.
- The way in which we interpret – or think about – a situation plays a crucial part in determining our emotional response to it.
- Our thinking also has a big impact on how our bodies react, and what we decide to do. These elements then feed into 'vicious cycles' that keep the problems going.
- Learning to change the way in which you think about a situation can greatly reduce the amount of stress you experience.
- We will refer to the thoughts that underlie stress as stressful automatic thoughts, or SATs.

PART TWO

The Stress Program

Aims of Part Two

In Part Two we start by helping you to recognize three aspects of stress – your signs and symptoms, the situations that make you stressed, and the way in which you cope. In each case we include tables and worksheets for you to use to identify and keep track of the problems. We then show you how these different aspects fit together in what we refer to as the 'cognitive formulation of stress'. We introduce the overall strategy for your stress management plan, and show how cognitive therapy can help you to identify and change the thoughts or appraisals that underlie stress.

We then go on to discuss a wider range of problems and techniques. We look at how some ways of behaving can make stress worse, and show how you can combat these. We examine stress at work, and in relationships, and look at difficulties you might have in organizing and managing your time. We then identify some common styles of thinking and behaving, such as procrastination and perfectionism, that can easily make stress worse, and we discuss techniques to enhance your ability to cope with these and other stress-related difficulties. We talk about how to look after yourself, and how by concentrating on positive aspects of yourself you can increase your confidence and your ability to cope with stress. Finally, we provide a brief summary of how to manage your stress plan.

After you've read Part Two we hope that you will have:

- Learned to recognize your signs and symptoms of stress.
- Learned what makes you stressed and how you cope with stress.
- Developed an individualized stress profile and stress management plan.
- Understood the techniques and strategies that will help you change your stressful thinking and behavior.
- Identified particular techniques and strategies relevant to your individual stress management plan.
- Learned how to take care of yourself and to enhance positive aspects of your thinking in order to further reduce your stress.
- Thought about how to carry all this forward!

5

Is stress a problem for you? Recognizing signs and symptoms of stress

We know that stress covers a wide range of symptoms, and can affect people in all sorts of ways. In this chapter we will look at the main symptoms of stress, and suggest ways in which you can keep track of your own stressful feelings. We will also discuss the difference between stress and other negative emotions so you can be sure that this is the right way of thinking about how you are feeling.

It can be helpful to classify the symptoms of stress into four different groups:

1 *Cognitive* symptoms concern ways that you think – such as 'I can't cope' – and problems with concentration and memory.
2 *Emotional* symptoms concern ways that you feel – such as 'tense' or 'wound up'.
3 *Physical* symptoms concern the way that your body reacts to stress – such as with headaches, stomach aches or tense and aching muscles.
4 *Behavioral* symptoms concern ways that you respond to stress – such as by avoiding difficult situations, drinking too much or losing your temper.

TABLE 5.1 SYMPTOMS OF STRESS

Cognitive symptoms

- Difficulty making decisions and feeling that you have too many things to do
- Finding it difficult to concentrate and feeling easily distracted
- Forgetting what you are supposed to be doing
- Difficulty remembering things
- Noticing that you are having more anxious thoughts
- Racing thoughts, flitting from one thing to another
- Trouble thinking clearly and feeling a bit muddled
- Constant worrying and not being able to put your mind at rest
- Predicting the worst happening and blowing the situation out of proportion
- Ruminating or brooding on what's happening to you and not being able to let go
- Only seeing the negative in a situation and discounting the positive. Lots of 'yes, buts'
- Making poor judgements
- Finding it difficult to be objective and rational and letting your emotions rule
- Being critical and beating yourself up
- Demanding high standards of yourself and others
- Experiencing thoughts of not coping

Emotional symptoms

- Moodiness
- Feeling irritable
- Feeling agitated
- Feeling overwhelmed
- Feeling tense and edgy
- Generally feeling unhappy and miserable
- Feeling on the edge of tears or bursting into tears easily
- Feeling emotionally numb
- Feeling hopeless about being able to change your situation

Physiological symptoms

- Loss of appetite or increased appetite
- Breathing difficulties
- Skin problems
- Increased heart rate
- Increased frequency of colds/viruses
- High blood pressure
- Physical aches and pains, muscle tension
- Frequent headaches or migraines
- Increased nausea/tummy upsets
- Loss of interest or pleasure in sex
- Sleeping more or less than usual
- Tiredness/exhaustion

Behavioral symptoms

- Being accident-prone and generally clumsy
- Overreacting to situations
- Weight loss or weight gain
- Change in smoking/drinking habits
- Rushing to places and being regularly late for work or appointments
- Increase in compulsive behaviors such as checking
- Teeth grinding (bruxism)
- Having angry outbursts and entering into arguments
- Putting off or avoiding seeing friends, colleagues and family
- Procrastinating – 'I'll do it tomorrow'
- Nervous habits, e.g. nail biting, hair pulling, skin picking

People vary widely in the way that they experience stress. For some, the primary problem will be physical symptoms like tension headaches, aches and pains, or feeling sick. Others may be much more aware of the emotional aspects of stress; they may feel overwhelmed and experience extreme moodiness, being irritable one moment then bursting into tears the next. And for some people the cognitive aspects of stress might be most prominent; they might worry and brood over things every waking hour and feel as if they are unable to control their thoughts. Some people might not be aware they are stressed, but will have an impact on others around them. Sometimes this can take the form of blowing up at other people without even acknowledging to themselves they are stressed, or finding that they are avoiding doing things, or overeating or drinking too much. On the whole people are likely to experience a combination of the different types of symptom, but often one kind is likely to be more prominent.

Table 5.1 provides a long list of common symptoms of stress. Looking through, you will probably find that some of these are not relevant to you, while others will sound only too familiar. You can use this list to identify your own symptoms: put a tick by every symptom that you experience, and two ticks by those that are particularly frequent or troublesome for you.

Exercise: Monitor your stress symptoms

You can track and keep a record of these symptoms of stress using the Stress Symptom Rating Scale displayed in Table 5.2.

TABLE 5.2 STRESS SYMPTOM RATING SCALE

Under each of the headings make a list of the symptoms of stress that have been most troubling for you over the course of the past week. Then rate the symptoms on a scale of 0–10. The first rating is how often you experienced this symptom (0 = not at all, 10 = all the time). The second rating refers to the severity of each symptom (0 = not at all severe, 10 = the worst it could be).

Stress symptoms	Frequency 0–10	Severity 0–10
1. My cognitive symptoms of stress are:		
2. My emotional symptoms of stress are:		
3. My physiological symptoms of stress are:		
4. My behavioral symptoms of stress are:		

You may find it helpful to use this rating scale as a way to monitor your progress over the next few weeks. Note the scores that you have made today, before you have started to make any changes. If you think that your scores are likely to change day by day anyway, then it might be good to make ratings every day for a week. These scores will now act as the comparison point. As you start to use the techniques described in Part Two, you can use the scale to see if they are working for you. If they are, you should find that your scores on the symptoms rating scale start to drop.

Stress or something else?

Before going on to the following chapters, however, it may be helpful for you to be sure that stress is the right way of thinking about your problems. Remember that at the beginning of the book we said that not all negative emotions are stress? The symptoms of stress overlap with those of other common psychological conditions, particularly anxiety and depression, and some of the treatment approaches use the same kinds of strategies. But if your main problem is anxiety or depression, then it would probably be more sensible to use an approach targeted specifically at that problem. If you have any doubt, read through the descriptions of anxiety and depression below, and see if these seem to fit your problems better. If you are still not sure, then your family doctor will be able to help you to think about it. Have a look at *Overcoming Anxiety* by Helen Kennerley or *Overcoming Depression* by Paul Gilbert, or the other self-help books for anxiety and depression listed at the end of this book. Your family doctor will be able to talk to you about other kinds of help available.

Anxiety disorders

Anxiety is a normal reaction to stress and most people who suffer with stress have symptoms of anxiety. In small amounts it can help you to deal with difficult situations –

for example, studying harder for an exam, or managing a tense situation at the office. Typically, once the triggering ✓ event is resolved anxiety subsides. But when anxiety becomes an excessive, irrational dread of day-to-day situations, an anxiety disorder might have developed. Anxiety disorders are disabling conditions where the experience of fear and worry is out of proportion with the situation. The feeling of anxiety is frequent and so intense that it interferes with a person's quality of life. The six major types of anxiety disorder are: Generalized Anxiety Disorder (GAD), Obsessive-Compulsive Disorder (OCD), Panic Disorder, Social Anxiety Disorder (or Social Phobia), Health Anxiety and Post-Traumatic Stress Disorder (PTSD). The characteristics of the different types are displayed in Table 5.3. These descriptions are adapted from the latest edition of the *Diagnostic and Statistical Manual of Mental Disorders.*

TABLE 5.3 ANXIETY DISORDERS

Generalized Anxiety Disorder

Generalized Anxiety Disorder (GAD) is characterized by excessive anxiety and worry about a number of everyday events. Individuals with GAD tend to see things in the worst possible light, and constantly anticipate disaster. Worry usually occurs every day for a prolonged period of more than six months. Often people feel unable to control their worrying thoughts. People with GAD experience a variety of physical and cognitive symptoms including irritability, muscle tension, feeling fatigued, difficulty concentrating or the mind going blank, sleep disturbances and feeling restless. These symptoms cause distress and impact on occupational and social functioning.

Obsessive-Compulsive Disorder

Obsessive-Compulsive Disorder or OCD is characterized by obsessional thoughts, images or impulses, and for some people (though not all) by related compulsions in the form of rituals which attempt to neutralize the obsessions. Obsessions are experienced as intrusive and cause marked anxiety and distress. Compulsions are often repetitive behaviors such as checking, or mental acts that are performed rigidly in response to an obsession. The aim of compulsions is to reduce distress or to prevent a negative event occurring. The person with OCD is able to recognize that their obsessions and/or compulsions are unreasonable or excessive. They are time-consuming, often taking up more than an hour a day. The affected person experiences considerable distress and normal life, such as work and social activities, can be significantly affected.

Panic Disorder

Panic Disorder is characterized by intense episodes of extreme anxiety or panic that are unexpected and recurrent. People experience a sudden onset of physical symptoms such as palpitations, sweating, nausea, shaking and breathlessness. They worry about the consequences of having a panic attack such as losing control, going crazy, fainting or having a heart attack.

Agoraphobia is often precipitated by the fear of having a panic attack in a setting from which escape might be difficult or embarrassing. As a consequence, people with agoraphobia might avoid public or unfamiliar places (e.g. being in a crowd, travelling by public transport, queuing in a shop) unless they are with a companion. When severe, the agoraphobic might become confined to their own home because it is perceived as a 'safe' place.

Social Anxiety Disorder

Social Anxiety Disorder, sometimes referred to as Social Phobia, is characterized by an intense fear of being judged negatively by others and feeling embarrassed or humiliated by one's own actions. Physical symptoms often include blushing, sweating, stammering, trembling, nausea and palpitations. Panic attacks might occur when the fear is intense. Social situations are often avoided or endured with considerable difficulty and distress.

Health Anxiety

Health Anxiety, also known as *hypochondria,* is characterized by excessive worry that minor bodily symptoms might indicate a serious illness. The person is preoccupied with their body and might engage in constant self-examination. Often a person's anxiety persists after they have been assured by a medical doctor that their symptoms are not a sign of illness. If the person *is* suffering from an illness, their concerns are excessive and inappropriate. Often doubt and disbelief in the doctor's diagnosis is expressed, or if reassured this tends not to last. A further feature of Health Anxiety is requiring constant reassurance from doctors, friends and family. Some people will actively avoid discussing their concerns or events that trigger their anxiety, e.g. reading medical books.

Post-Traumatic Stress Disorder

Post-Traumatic Stress Disorder, or PTSD, can develop after a person is exposed to a traumatic event or psychological trauma in which physical harm occurred or was threatened. The stressor might involve someone's actual death, threat to life or serious injury. It is characterized by a severe and ongoing emotional reaction to the trauma that persists one month after exposure to the event. The person might persistently re-experience the event in the form of flashbacks or nightmares, and will avoid situations that are associated with the trauma, often in fear of losing control or harming another person. The person experiences symptoms of increased agitation such as difficulty falling asleep, anger and excessive sensitivity to the possibility of danger around them. Their work and social life are usually adversely affected.

If you recognize yourself in any of these descriptions and feel that these problems are taking over your life, then it would be worth discussing things with your doctor. Because of the overlap between anxiety and stress it is possible that you will experience some of these symptoms, but if they are not overwhelming and continuous it is more likely that you are stressed.

Depression

As with anxiety, people may experience low mood or mild depression in the context of stress. Indeed depression is such a common condition that it is often referred to as the 'common cold of psychiatry'. It can be relatively mild, and can get better spontaneously. But for some people the depression becomes much stronger and overwhelming, and may need to be treated independently. We talk about 'clinical depression' when the symptoms have become very severe and unrelenting, and are having a major impact on people's lives. So what is depression? The symptoms listed below are adapted from the latest edition of the *Diagnostic and Statistical Manual of Mental Disorders.*

SYMPTOMS OF DEPRESSION

You might have developed depression if you have experienced five or more of the following symptoms during the past two weeks or longer and these symptoms represent a change from how you felt previously, and if at least one of the symptoms is either (1) depressed mood or (2) loss of interest or pleasure.

In addition, to meet the criteria for depression your symptoms must:

- Cause you significant distress or have impaired your social, occupational or other important areas of functioning in your life.
- Not be due to the physical effects of a substance such as a drug of abuse, a medication, or a general medical condition such as an underactive thyroid.
- Not be better accounted for by the loss of a loved one.

1 Your mood has been depressed most of the day, nearly every day, for example feeling sad or empty.

2 You have noticed a marked decline in interest or pleasure in all, or almost all, activities most of the day, nearly every day.

3 You have lost a significant amount of weight (when not dieting), or you have gained a significant amount of weight, for example more

than 5 per cent of body weight in a month. Alternatively you have noticed an increase or decrease in your appetite nearly every day.

4 You have had difficulty sleeping or have been sleeping a great deal more than usual nearly every day.

5 Other people have observed that you have been agitated or sluggish nearly every day.

6 You have been fatigued or have experienced a loss of energy nearly every day.

7 You have extreme feelings of worthlessness or excessive or inappropriate guilt nearly every day.

8 You have noticed a decline in your ability to think or concentrate, or be decisive, nearly every day.

9 You have recurrent thoughts of death (not just fear of dying), recurrent suicidal thoughts without a specific plan, or have been considering a suicide attempt or a specific plan for committing suicide.

As with anxiety, if you recognize yourself in this description then it would definitely be worth discussing things with your family doctor. Because of the overlap of depression with stress, you may recognize some features we have described, but if these are not overwhelming then it is more likely that you are stressed.

CHAPTER SUMMARY

- There are four key types of stress symptoms: cognitive, emotional, physical and behavioral.
- The Stress Symptom Rating Scale can be used to monitor your progress through the stress program.
- Stress overlaps with anxiety and depression, but when these become a problem in their own right then a different treatment approach is needed.

6

What makes you stressed? Identifying stressors

Jessica had recently separated from her husband and was going through a divorce. She had financial problems and needed to sell the family home and find a job. She hadn't worked for seven years since having children and had lost confidence in her ability to resume her career in retail. Her husband would drop by to see the children without any prearrangement and she felt unable to relax in her own home. She was deeply upset about the end of her marriage, and was often tearful and overwhelmed with feeling that she could not cope with all the things that she had to do. She started to experience a lot of physical ailments, and worried that these meant there was something seriously wrong with her.

Alex was feeling extremely unhappy at work, but felt trapped because he could not find alternative employment. He had been transferred to a new engineering project, without any consultation, in a new location that meant he had an additional ninety minutes' travelling

time through heavy traffic to get to work. His super-
visor constantly quarrelled with him over minor things
and Alex didn't think that his skills and ideas were
being used. He missed socializing in the pub with his
previous work colleagues and was too tired to go to
football practice. He believed that he was a failure and
that whatever he did it was never good enough.

Allie felt that her life was chaotic with one minor
thing after another going wrong. In the latest crisis she
had struggled to operate her new computer and
somehow lost the data that she needed to do a
PowerPoint presentation. She had no filing system and
couldn't find the papers she needed, so had to make
an extra trip to the library to retrieve documents not
available on the Internet. After being stuck in a traffic
jam for twenty-five minutes she accidentally parked in
a parking bay reserved for doctors and got a parking
fine that she could not afford. By the evening she had
a throbbing headache and felt physically exhausted.

As we discussed in Part One, people experience stress when
they perceive the demands that are made on them to be
greater than their sense of their ability to cope. These
demands are known as stressors – things that make you
stressed. In this chapter we will discuss common ways of
describing stressors. These tend to fall into two categories.
Life events are comparatively major occurrences, such as
divorce or changing job, which are likely to have a big
impact on people's lives. The other category is *'hassles'* –
aspects of life which are part of our daily existence and
which we probably don't pay much attention to, but which
can nevertheless build up to cause significant stress.

Life events

As we saw in Chapter 2, in the 1960s two psychiatrists, Holmes and Rahe, developed a system for looking at life stress. They used a long list of events that are likely to be stressful, and asked a large number of people to rate each item according to its intensity and the length of time it would take to adjust to it. (see Table 2.1 on p. 42).

In Chapter 2 we looked at whether this measure of life event stress could be related to physical health, and saw that the picture is pretty complicated. One of the complications is that the ratings were arrived at by taking the average scores given to the events by a large number of people. But this begs the question of how stressful an event may be to the particular individual involved. For instance, divorce is rated as extremely stressful, and most people would concur that it is; but for someone who has been in a deeply abusive relationship divorce may represent freedom and relief. Similarly, a major house move and renovation project may be seen as exciting and fun to one person, and an overwhelming burden to another.

We cannot get away from the idea that individual appraisals of events are key to how stressful they are! We can, however, use the kinds of items included by Holmes and Rahe as a starting point for considering our own stress.

The Life Events Questionnaire

This Life Events Questionnaire is adapted from Holmes and Rahe's list and will help you to identify whether you have been affected by events in your life over the past year, since it allows you to make your own rating of how stressful you have found the event.

TABLE 6.1 QUESTIONNAIRE: LIFE EVENTS

Below is a list of commonly experienced life events. Read though each one carefully and indicate by ticking the 'Yes' box if the event has taken place in the past year. Next rate how stressful you found the event using the scale below with 0 = not at all stressful and 10 = extremely stressful, could not have been worse.

Life event	Yes	Stress rating
1. Financial difficulties		0 1 2 3 4 5 6 7 8 9 10
2. Pregnancy		0 1 2 3 4 5 6 7 8 9 10
3. Divorce		0 1 2 3 4 5 6 7 8 9 10
4. Separation from husband/ wife/partner		0 1 2 3 4 5 6 7 8 9 10
5. Marital/partner problems		0 1 2 3 4 5 6 7 8 9 10
6. Marriage		0 1 2 3 4 5 6 7 8 9 10
7. Retirement		0 1 2 3 4 5 6 7 8 9 10
8. Unemployment		0 1 2 3 4 5 6 7 8 9 10
9. Fired from work		0 1 2 3 4 5 6 7 8 9 10
10. Made redundant		0 1 2 3 4 5 6 7 8 9 10
11. Sexual problems		0 1 2 3 4 5 6 7 8 9 10
12. Suffering from a serious physical health problem or injury		0 1 2 3 4 5 6 7 8 9 10
13. Caring for a loved one with a health problem		0 1 2 3 4 5 6 7 8 9 10
14. Illness in a family member		0 1 2 3 4 5 6 7 8 9 10
15. Imprisonment or probation		0 1 2 3 4 5 6 7 8 9 10
16. Ending of a relationship		0 1 2 3 4 5 6 7 8 9 10
17. Puberty		0 1 2 3 4 5 6 7 8 9 10
18. Engagement		0 1 2 3 4 5 6 7 8 9 10
19. Broken engagement		0 1 2 3 4 5 6 7 8 9 10
20. Getting back together with a partner		0 1 2 3 4 5 6 7 8 9 10
21. Working more than 37.5 hours a week		0 1 2 3 4 5 6 7 8 9 10

Life event	Yes	Stress rating
22. Moved house		0 1 2 3 4 5 6 7 8 9 10
23. Major changes in financial status		0 1 2 3 4 5 6 7 8 9 10
24. Problems with friends		0 1 2 3 4 5 6 7 8 9 10
25. Death of someone close to you		0 1 2 3 4 5 6 7 8 9 10
26. Problems with relatives		0 1 2 3 4 5 6 7 8 9 10
27. Work-related problems		0 1 2 3 4 5 6 7 8 9 10
28. Birth of a baby		0 1 2 3 4 5 6 7 8 9 10
29. An important personal achievement		0 1 2 3 4 5 6 7 8 9 10
30. Child started nursery, school, left home		0 1 2 3 4 5 6 7 8 9 10
31. Increased mortgage		0 1 2 3 4 5 6 7 8 9 10
32. Change of job		0 1 2 3 4 5 6 7 8 9 10
33. Difficult relationship with a significant other		0 1 2 3 4 5 6 7 8 9 10
34. Change in responsibilities at work		0 1 2 3 4 5 6 7 8 9 10
35. Going into debt		0 1 2 3 4 5 6 7 8 9 10
36. Legal problem		0 1 2 3 4 5 6 7 8 9 10
37. Going on holiday		0 1 2 3 4 5 6 7 8 9 10
38. Christmas		0 1 2 3 4 5 6 7 8 9 10
39. Other life events? List any other significant life events that are not included above		0 1 2 3 4 5 6 7 8 9 10
–		0 1 2 3 4 5 6 7 8 9 10
–		0 1 2 3 4 5 6 7 8 9 10
–		0 1 2 3 4 5 6 7 8 9 10
–		0 1 2 3 4 5 6 7 8 9 10
Now add up your total score		Total score =

The questionnaire will have given you some idea of the extent to which life events may be a problem for you, either highlighting single events which have taken over your life, or by showing the number of things you are trying to cope with. On the whole, the higher the score the more stressed you are likely to be, but even a single score of nine or ten means you could be under a considerable degree of stress.

Hassles and uplifts

On the whole, life event researchers have concentrated on the more major events in people's lives, and on *changes* in people's lives that they need to adjust to. But there are also sources of stress that do not relate to single or major events, but to aspects of daily experience that may be a constant in people's lives and are demanding and difficult to deal with.

Hassles are events that annoy or bother you in your routine day-to-day life and can make you feel anxious, irritable and upset. Having to cope with heavy traffic jams on a daily basis in order to get to work would not be a major life event, but it is certainly stressful. Ordinary events such as buying a new TV and trying to make sense of the instruction manual, or being asked to work late the day you are due to go on holiday, would also be examples.

The case studies at the beginning of the chapter should demonstrate the difference: Jessica was clearly experiencing a major life event; Allie was experiencing ongoing hassles; Alex was probably undergoing a mixture of the two, since his job had changed and he needed to adjust to this but the change had also increased the amount of hassles in his life. And in fact Jessica had also experienced an increase in daily hassles as well as the emotional impact of the divorce, since the absence of her husband increased the amount that she had to do, and the general difficulty of daily life.

In contrast to hassles, *uplifts* are positive events that can give you a lift and make you feel good, or give you a sense of achievement and satisfaction. Like hassles, they can be relatively minor events, but their impact is still felt. Going to a party and socializing with friends, being given positive feedback about your performance at work, or spending time doing a pleasurable activity, would be good examples of uplifts.

Some hassles and uplifts can occur on a daily basis whereas others are quite rare, but both are thought to have a cumulative effect. If hassles regularly outweigh uplifts in people's lives then the effect will be negative. Like life events, they may have an effect on health. For instance, a psychologist called Stone examined the relationship between hassles, uplifts and symptoms of a cold, and noticed that people reported an increase in the amount of hassles and a decrease in uplifts prior to the onset of the cold!

Table 6.2 shows examples of hassles and uplifts from Allie's week.

TABLE 6.2 ALLIE'S HASSLES AND UPLIFTS WORKSHEET

Hassles	Rate the hassle on a scale of 0–10 0 = no hassle, 10 = extreme hassle	Uplifts	Rate the uplift on a scale of 0–10 0 = no uplift, 10 = extreme uplift
1. Losing data required for a presentation at work	9	1. Going shopping for summer clothes	5
2. Getting stuck in a traffic jam	3	2. Planning a holiday	6
3. Getting a parking fine	10	3. Sharing a bottle of wine with a close friend	2
4. Taking on too many responsibilities at work	8	4. My boss told me that I was doing a good job	4
5. No time for myself	9	5. Being complimented on my new hairstyle	6
6. Not getting enough sleep	8		
7. Wasting time surfing the net	4		
Hassles total score	= 43	Uplifts total score	= 23

So the next step is to consider how far hassles are contributing to your stress, and whether you have uplifts that help to reduce the stress. Take a moment and think about hassles and uplifts that you have experienced in the past week and make a note of them in the worksheet below. Then rate each hassle and uplift on a scale of 0–10. You may find that you are only too aware of what your hassles are, but if not Table 6.4 on p. 100 may help.

TABLE 6.3 HASSLES AND UPLIFTS WORKSHEET			
Hassles	Rate the hassle on a scale of 0–10 0 = no hassle, 10 = extreme hassle	Uplifts	Rate the uplift on a scale of 0–10 0 = no uplift, 10 = extreme uplift
Hassles total score		Uplifts total score	

Looking at your completed worksheet, are there more hassles than uplifts? Are there things which clearly stand out as major sources of stress for you? Are there things which you would really like to change? Taken together, the hassles and life events worksheets should give a reasonable picture of the sources of stress in your life. In Chapter 8 we will come back to this issue in order to help you decide where to try to start making some changes.

TABLE 6.4 EXAMPLES OF HASSLES AND UPLIFTS

Areas of hassle and uplift	Examples of hassles	Examples of uplifts
Relationship	– Conflict with a friend/partner (including criticism, disagreement, arguments) – Being let down or rejected by a friend/partner	– Support from a friend/partner – Giving support to a friend/partner – Receiving positive feedback – Positive communication – Pleasurable activities with friends (party, out for drinks) – Intimacy
Family	– Problems with children – Home maintenance (inside and outside)	– Having fun with your children/siblings/parents – Support received from your family
Work	– Overloaded with family responsibilities – Dissatisfaction with your job/duties – Meeting deadlines/goals – Underuse of your skills – Organizational changes – Hassles with your manager/supervisor – Problems getting on with a colleague – Dislike of a colleague – Clients/customers giving you a hard time – Dislike of current work duties – Considering changing jobs – Problems with employees – Sharing an office and being distracted – Noisy environment	– Type of work – Use of your skills and ideas – Having job security – Support from your manager/supervisor – Receiving positive communication and feedback – Being organized – Working in the home (cooking, special dinners, gardening, DIY)

Areas of hassle and uplift	Examples of hassles	Examples of uplifts
Finances	– Not enough money for basic necessities (food, housing, clothing, transport) – Not enough money for recreational/social activities – Concerns about not enough money for emergencies – Too many responsibilities (home/work)	– Having enough money to be comfortable – Receiving a pay rise/increment – Winning a prize (bingo, raffle) – Money to buy non-essentials
Time pressure	– Have too many things to do and not enough time – Too many social obligations – Not enough time for social engagements – Not getting enough rest/sleep – Attending too many meetings – Too many interruptions/ demands placed on time	– Having a good night's sleep – Having a lie-in at the weekend – Time to enjoy social events – Chilling out/down time – Time to rest/relax
Organization	– Not being able to find important documents – Office space/desk is cluttered – The pile of ironing is so great that you have nothing to wear – Forgetting to make credit card/bill payments	– Having a good filing system – Domestic chores completed – Clean and tidy environment – Drawers and cupboards organized and being able to find things without effort
Health	– Side-effects of medication – Suffering with a minor physical illness (e.g. cold, tummy bug) – General concerns about health – Concerns about your medical treatment – Concerns about bodily functions – Concern about your physical abilities	– Feeling physically well – Having energy – Exercising
Environment	– Crime – Recycling/pollution – Traffic congestion – News events	– Good weather – Green space and pleasant surroundings

Areas of hassle and uplift	Examples of hassles	Examples of uplifts
Inner concern	— Having regret about past decisions — Concerns about an inner conflict — Loneliness — Concerns about progressing — Difficulty making decisions — Fear of being rejected — Fear of confrontation/conflict — Worry about the future — Questioning the meaning of life	— Feeling a sense of well-being — Confident about decision-making — Feeling accepted and experiencing a sense of belonging — Being able to communicate concerns and be understood — Letting worries go

CHAPTER SUMMARY

- Major life events are clear sources of stress in people's lives.
- Assessing the seriousness of these events for an individual involves taking account of their appraisal of the event.
- A significant amount of stress comes not from these major events, but from ongoing hassles in people's lives, particularly when these are not redressed by uplifts.
- Filling in the worksheets for life events and hassles should help to clarify the sources of stress in your life.

7

How do you cope? Identifying harmful and healthy ways of coping

For every problem under the sun
There is a remedy, or there is none
If there be one, try and find it
If there be none, never mind it.

Anon.

'Coping' is a word that is used a great deal and covers a wide range of feelings and ways of doing things. In order to make sense of this in relation to stress, in this chapter we will talk about various kinds of coping, how you can identify your own coping style, and its impact on how stressed you feel.

To begin, imagine a situation where you are at work and are snowed under. Just as you are trying to sort things out, your boss comes in and asks you to prepare an important report for the next day – but you can't cope with the work already piled up on your desk.

Now look at the descriptions below – these people have all just been in a similar situation.

Samantha did what she could, and then went home from work, poured herself a glass of wine, and sat moodily in front of the TV. Her husband and teenage children came in to chat but she couldn't face talking, and tried not to take any notice. Eventually when they kept going on she slammed her fist down on the table, yelling at them to shut up. Her younger son started crying, and her older one stormed out of the room yelling that she didn't care about any of them.

Ellie, on the other hand, talked to her boss at work and explained that she had so much to do that she didn't know how she would be able to fit the report in. She asked the boss if anyone else could help, and when it seemed there wouldn't be anyone, she and her boss agreed which of the other pieces of work piling up could be left a bit longer.

Mike didn't talk to his boss, and went home in the evening feeling dreadful. But over a glass of wine he started chatting to his wife about how difficult he was finding work. She was really sympathetic and said how awful it must be for him. He felt a bit better and then started to think about whether he could talk to his boss.

Exercise: Identifying your coping style

In order to identify your coping style, think of the last time that you were feeling very stressed. It's best if you use a specific example rather than general types of situation. For example, 'Taking Mum to the supermarket last Wednesday when she forgot her shopping list' would be better than 'Trying to help other people'.

Give yourself a minute to think about this example, and get a clear picture of where you were, what was happening, etc. Write this down in the box opposite, and then rate how

stressed you felt using the ten-point scale (0 = not at all
stressed, 10 = most stressed you could imagine feeling).

> **STRESSFUL SITUATION:**
>
>
> How stressed I felt: 0 1 2 3 4 5 6 7 8 9 10

Now think carefully about what you did. How did you
respond to the situation, and to the stress that you were experiencing? What did you do? What did you try not to do? It
is important to think about what you really did, not what
you think you ought to have done. Again, if you find it helpful,
write down everything that you did in the box below.

> **HOW DID I RESPOND?**
>
>

Now think about how you felt after you had carried these
things out. Did doing them reduce the amount of stress
that you felt? Try re-rating this on the ten-point scale.

> **HOW I FELT AFTER RESPONDING TO THE SITUATION:**
>
>
> How stressed I felt: 0 1 2 3 4 5 6 7 8 9 10

Make a note of whether the things that you did reduced
your rating or not. Are the ratings lower? The same? Possibly
higher?

In this exercise we asked you to think about 'what you did', not 'how you coped'. But in a sense everything that you do in response to a stressful situation could be thought of as your intrinsic coping style. Sometimes you will think: 'But the problem is that I can't cope'. But even if all you do is tear your hair out and wail, this is your way of coping. Some of what you do already will probably be very helpful, but some of it may be less so. By identifying these patterns of coping style it should be easier to spot how you can improve the amount of helpful coping you do.

Types of coping

We can classify types of coping very roughly as follows:

Emotion-based coping

This refers to people who cope with stressful situations by trying to manage the emotions which the stress produces. They might do this by talking about how they feel, getting sympathy and support from other people, or letting their emotions out. They might use meditation, or physical exercise, to make themselves feel better. Mike was showing this kind of emotion-based coping when he went home and talked to his wife about how difficult he was finding work.

Stress carrying

'Stress carrying' can be thought of as a kind of *failure* of emotional coping. People find it difficult to manage their emotions, or to contain the stress that they feel. Instead of being able to work on this themselves in a helpful way, they respond by taking their emotions out on other people. This is known as stress carrying because of the stressful knock-on effect of this behavior on other people. Samantha was being a stress carrier when she went home from work and first tried to ignore and then shouted at her family. We have described stress carrying specifically because we think it is important to identify it clearly if this is something that you do. We are indebted to Stephen Palmer and Cary Cooper, in whose book *How to Deal with Stress*, we first came across the label.

Avoidance-based coping

This refers to people who like to pretend that everything is okay and deny that there is a problem. They might do this by retreating into fantasies and dreams about the future – for example, thinking that winning the lottery will solve all their problems – or by generally sticking their head in the sand. People are likely to avoid talking to other people about anything that causes stress, and to resent it when people try to talk to them. They may also avoid the emotional pain stress can cause by doing very unhelpful things like drinking much too much, taking other drugs, legal or illegal, or bingeing on chocolate and crisps.

Problem-based coping

This refers to people who like to cope with stress by concentrating on the situation that seems to be causing it, and by seeing what they can do to make a real difference to it. Sometimes people prefer to do this on their own, but problem-based coping can also include seeking practical help from other people, so it includes elements of social support. In the examples at the beginning of the chapter, Ellie was clearly showing this kind of problem-based coping when she spoke to her boss, explained the problem and asked for help.

What kind of coper are you? Go back to your description of how you coped, and see if it clearly falls into one of the categories described above. If you're not sure, have a go at the questionnaire below. It may be that your coping included elements of more than one style. Furthermore, some people will respond in the same way to all kind of stress, while others will respond differently according to what is happening.

TABLE 7.1 QUESTIONNAIRE: WHAT KIND OF COPER ARE YOU?

For each response circle the number which best corresponds to how frequently you use them:

0 = Never use

1 = Use a bit, in some situations

2 = Use quite frequently

3 = Use in most situations

When I get stressed I tend to:

A

1. Talk to friends or family about how I feel		0 1 2 3
2. Let my feelings out – cry, get upset		0 1 2 3
3. Worry about it all the time		0 1 2 3
4. Try to see it in a different light, make something positive of it		0 1 2 3
5. Talk to someone I know will be supportive		0 1 2 3
6. Accept that it has happened and can't be changed		0 1 2 3

B

7. Get irritable or aggressive	0 1 2 3
8. Shout at my family	0 1 2 3
9. Want to be on my own — cold shoulder everyone	0 1 2 3
10. Be nasty/sarcastic/unkind	0 1 2 3
11. Bully other people	0 1 2 3
12. Throw/bang things	0 1 2 3

C

13. Try and put it out of my mind	0 1 2 3
14. Hide how I feel from other people	0 1 2 3
15. Hope for a miracle	0 1 2 3
16. Go to a film or watch TV to think about it less	0 1 2 3
17. Act as though it hasn't happened	0 1 2 3
18. Take to drinking, smoking or bingeing to take my mind off it	0 1 2 3

D

19. Talk to someone who might be able to give advice or help	0 1 2 3
20. Analyse the problem and make a plan	0 1 2 3
21. Make changes in how I do things	0 1 2 3
22. Ask someone for help with the practical side of things	0 1 2 3
23. Think hard about what steps to take	0 1 2 3
24. Take direct action to get around the problem	0 1 2 3

SCORING THE QUESTIONNAIRE

You will see that the responses are arranged in four groups. For each group of questions, add up your total score and enter it below:

A Emotion-based coping: _____

B Stress carrying: _____

C Avoidance-based coping: _____

D Problem-based coping: _____

The higher the score, the more likely you are to use that kind of coping. You may find that you are mainly using one type of coping, or that your responses are fairly evenly distributed between one or more types.

Are some kinds of coping better than others?

It can be seen from the above descriptions that there are a couple of types of coping which probably are not helpful in any circumstances. Stress carriers, who react by taking it out on people around them, almost certainly worsen things by making the people around them more stressed. This just adds to an atmosphere of fearfulness or resentment, and makes it hard for anything very constructive to take place. Although the behavior may relieve the person's stress in the very short term, it is likely to make them feel guilty and ashamed when they have calmed down. In the examples above it is hard to imagine that anyone in Samantha's family felt very good when they went to bed that night, including Samantha. Of course, there may be people who are stress carriers who do not feel guilty or ashamed, and may be oblivious to their impact on other people.

The other kind of coping which is fairly clearly unhelpful is that of drinking too much, taking too many illegal or even prescription drugs, bingeing or doing other things that are harmful to the self. These things are likely to result in a hangover of some sort which makes your mood even worse, and quite possibly bring feelings of guilt or shame as well.

But as far as the other kinds of coping are concerned, there seem to be good and bad aspects of both.

Advantages and disadvantages of different ways of coping

Emotion-based coping: This can be very useful in a lot of situations. Being able to calm yourself down and soothe your emotional state can be extremely helpful. As we know, some sorts of stress go on and on, and practical problem-solving may make things a bit better, but will very often not take the source of stress away completely. In this case, finding a way of coping with your feelings, by talking to your family and friends, taking exercise or doing meditation, can be extremely constructive as a way of calming yourself and increasing your ability to tolerate what is going on. But people who rely too much on this way of coping may be making it difficult for themselves to concentrate on more practical problems. Moreover, people who rely too much on this way of coping can sometimes make things worse for themselves. At times, concentrating on how you think and feel can become counterproductive, as it takes over and you find it difficult to *stop* thinking about your problems. At its worst, this worry or rumination tends to make people's mood worse rather than better.

Avoidance-based coping: It is often thought that avoidance-based coping is unhelpful, and it is true that if it goes on for too long, and if this is the only kind of coping that people do, then it probably isn't great. It means that people don't think of solutions to problems, and instead of finding a way of managing their emotions, they bottle them up. This in turn can mean that the stress may come out in people's bodies, with muscle tension or headaches, or it may mean that eventually people's emotions will explode in an unhelpful way. But on the other hand, we all need fantasies, and we all need to escape reality from time to time. So the odd daydream about how winning the lottery will solve your problems, or deciding that just for this evening you will let yourself concentrate on something nice, could well provide you with just the kind of break that you need.

Problem-based coping: This is, obviously, often a very good strategy. If you can do something about the source of stress, and tackle the real-life situation in a constructive way, then things are likely to get better. Tackling problems in a practical way also has the very strong advantage of helping people to feel in control. In the examples above, Ellie tackled the problem by discussing things with her boss; happily for her, the fact that she had a reasonable boss meant that she was able to come up with a constructive solution which vastly reduced the stress that she felt.

The problem with this kind of coping comes when you are in a stressful situation which you realistically don't have much control over. There can be very few people reading this book who have not been stuck in major traffic jams, often when they are desperate to get to work, catch a plane, or enjoy a holiday. But generally there is *nothing* that you can do in these situations.

The problem, therefore, for people who rely too heavily on problem-based coping is that when it is not really relevant they may not be very good at mobilizing other types of coping, and may end up with the dreaded stress carrier response of irritability and anger at people around them, thereby making everything worse.

Social support in emotion- and problem-based coping

People vary enormously in the amount of social support which they need and want, but the right levels of support can be extremely helpful. Having people around whom you can talk to, who are sympathetic, and who can help with practical steps is almost always a bonus. But as with everything, there are dangers. Relying too heavily on people can sometimes put a burden on them; this can end up alienating them and making them feel resentful and angry. On the other hand, sometimes people might decide that they love helping you and pop round at all times of day or night to 'offer you support', resulting in more stress as you politely make a cup of tea and wish they'd go away! Relying too heavily on other people can also make you feel that you are too dependent on others, and undermine your confidence in being able to deal with something yourself.

'Goodness of fit'

There is a theory that different types of coping are appropriate for different types of stress, and this does seem to make obvious sense. There is not much point meditating on your emotional state when the washing machine has just broken down and water is pouring on to your new floor. Some kinds of stress require problem-solving and action; others require that you can manage your emotions. Many require both at different times. In the earlier examples Mike came home from work in a bad state, but through talking to his wife managed to calm down and feel happier. In this frame of mind he was able to think about how to talk to his boss the following day. So emotional coping enabled him to get to the point where he could use problem-based coping.

What does this mean for how I cope?

The upshot of all this is that we need to learn to recognize when our coping is helpful, and when it is unhelpful. Do we have a style that we tend to cling to regardless of the demands of the situation? Are we able to be flexible? Do we have strong beliefs about ways of coping? For example, some people might believe that they *must* let their feelings out and if they don't they will damage themselves somehow. These people would be much more likely to use emotional coping, even when it might not be the most sensible choice at the time. And some people might believe that it's wrong to talk about their feelings at any time, and concentrate on looking for practical solutions in situations where there really isn't anything to be done.

Go back to your example and ask yourself two questions:

1 Are there elements in what I did that are clearly unhelpful? If so, can I think of different ways of doing things?
2 Do I tend to use the same kinds of strategies in every stressful situation? Do I need to try different ways of doing things?

It can sometimes be very difficult to think that you need to change strategy! We are very familiar with clients who respond to problems by working harder at their old strategies. But sometimes it can be helpful to be able to say to yourself: 'Okay, that isn't working!' Subsequent chapters of this book will help you to identify different ways of coping, including both general strategies of dealing with stress by managing your thinking, as well as specific techniques aimed at particular problems.

CHAPTER SUMMARY

- There are many different kinds of coping, the main categories being:
  - Emotion-based coping (including stress carrying)
  - Avoidance-based coping
  - Problem-based coping
- These different kinds of coping all have advantages and disadvantages, but being a stress carrier or overusing substances are almost certainly not helpful strategies.
- Different kinds of stress probably require different kinds of coping.
- People vary in the kinds of coping style that they prefer, and in their flexibility to use different kinds of strategies.
- You have identified your own common coping strategies and thought about whether you tend to use the same strategy in all situations, or different ones according to the source of stress.

8

Your stress profile and stress management plan

So far we have discussed a number of different aspects of stress and coping, with a number of questionnaires and worksheets to help you to identify your own symptoms and patterns of thinking and behavior. In this chapter we are going to put all these together to make sense of your stress profile and start your stress management plan. The different aspects of stress are summarized in the box overleaf.

We can now put all of these things into what cognitive therapists would call the 'formulation' – this is your map of how the stressful situations, your symptoms and coping all fit together. Your thinking, or your appraisals, play a central role in the formulation.

In essence, what happens is that when confronted with a difficult situation, you have two kinds of thoughts about it: your primary appraisal, or just how difficult this is for you; and your secondary appraisal, or just how able you feel to cope with it. These appraisals could also be described as the cognitive components of the stress response. They in turn trigger the other components of the stress response,

THE VARIOUS ASPECTS OF STRESS

Stress symptoms

- Cognitive
- Behavioral
- Physiological
- Emotional

Stressors

- Life events
- Hassles
- Uplifts

Coping style

- Avoidant
- Emotional
  - Including the use of alcohol
  - Stress carrying
- Problem-solving

your emotional and physical symptoms. Finally, you then respond to the stress by doing something to cope, sometimes helpful and sometimes not. If your coping behavior is successful, then the stress subsides, and you will feel better. But if your coping behavior is not successful, then your stress response is likely to get stronger, and the thoughts that you have about the situation and yourself are likely to get more and more negative. These vicious cycles are often what keeps the stress going. Furthermore, sometimes the emotional and physical response can also have a direct effect on your

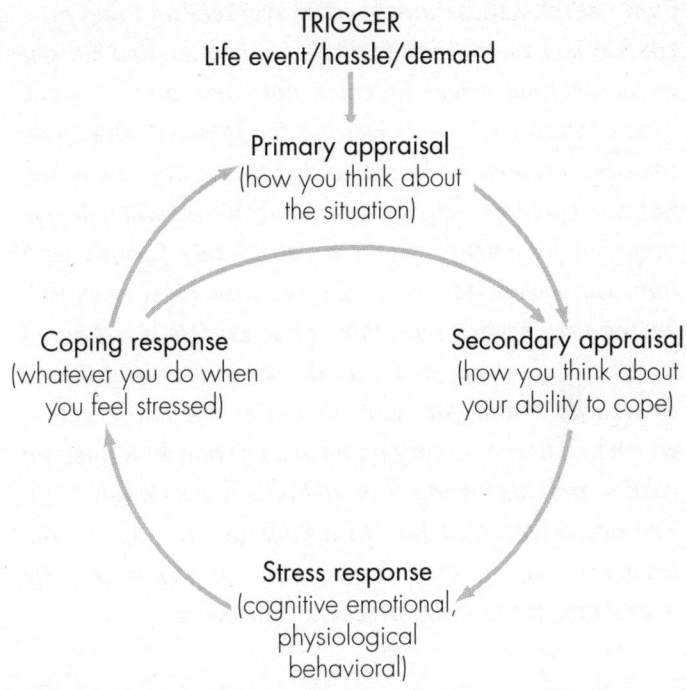

Figure 8.1 Cognitive formulation of stress

appraisals, for instance by making you feel inadequate, or frightened by the way in which you are responding.

The way in which these fit together can be illustrated by the following example:

Gary was a builder who employed a small number of permanent workers, but also relied on a much larger number of other independent workers such as plumbers, electricians or plasterers, whom he would call on at various stages of the building process. But because he didn't employ these independent workers and had little control over their timetabling he would often find himself in the position where he could not carry on with work himself because he was waiting for someone else to do their bit. Because he was afraid of losing work he would not warn potential customers about this, so when delays occurred his clients would be absolutely furious with him. Gary went to his doctor because he was experiencing very severe symptoms of stress. He was finding it difficult to sleep, and was drinking heavily at home as well as in the pub with his mates. He had eczema, which had flared up very badly and left him with weeping rashes, and his blood pressure had got worryingly high. The doctor referred him to a cognitive therapist, who used the map to show Gary what was happening. He asked him to describe a recent bad event.

The plasterer ends up saying he won't do it at all. Gary goes home and doesn't answer the phone when the client rings to find out why nothing has happened. Later the client phones again, and again Gary doesn't answer. The next day the customer writes to say he will send Gary a cheque (not a big one) for the work he's done but will get someone else to finish it. Gary's stress levels increase. He is also very worried that his blood pressure has risen again, and this makes him feel more worried and angry.

In this example, therefore, it is easy to see how Gary's coping behavior kept things going. Instead of trying to talk calmly to the plasterer to get a realistic idea of when he could come, and then explaining this to the customer, Gary got angry and alienated both the plasterer and the client. This

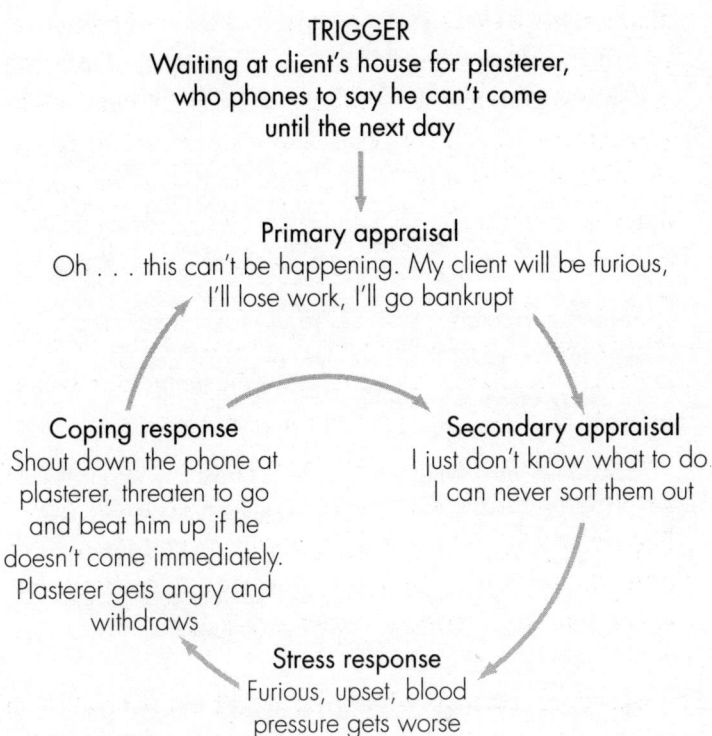

TRIGGER
Waiting at client's house for plasterer,
who phones to say he can't come
until the next day

Primary appraisal
Oh . . . this can't be happening. My client will be furious,
I'll lose work, I'll go bankrupt

Coping response
Shout down the phone at
plasterer, threaten to go
and beat him up if he
doesn't come immediately.
Plasterer gets angry and
withdraws

Secondary appraisal
I just don't know what to do.
I can never sort them out

Stress response
Furious, upset, blood
pressure gets worse

Figure 8.2 Gary's formulation of stress

brought about the very consequence he was afraid of – a very common feature of the way these vicious cycles operate!

It might be helpful to think of a recent example of when you were feeling particularly stressed, and see if it fits this way of mapping stress out. The questions in the following table might help you. When you have read these, try completing the stress formulation worksheet in Figure 8.3.

Trigger: Think of a recent situation where you got stressed. Where were you doing? What was going on around you?

Primary appraisal: What went through your mind about the situation? How bad did it seem to you, and what did you think the impact or consequences for you were going to be?

Secondary appraisal: How did you think you were going to manage the situation? Could you think of what to do? Did it seem unmanageable? Did you feel helpless?

Stress response: What did you notice about how you felt? Did you feel panicky? Hopeless? Depressed? How bad was this feeling? What did you feel in your body? What did you notice about any physical changes, like your heart racing, breathlessness, pains in your body?

Your coping response: What did you do? What did you do when you were in that situation? Did you find that you just wanted to get away? Did you become tearful or angry? Did you try to tackle the situation?

What happened? Did your coping response help you to get through the situation and feel better or calmer? Did things escalate and get worse? Did you find that the only thing to do was to get out of the situation? If the situation did not improve, try to think about the consequences of your coping response, and how this might have kept the situation going.

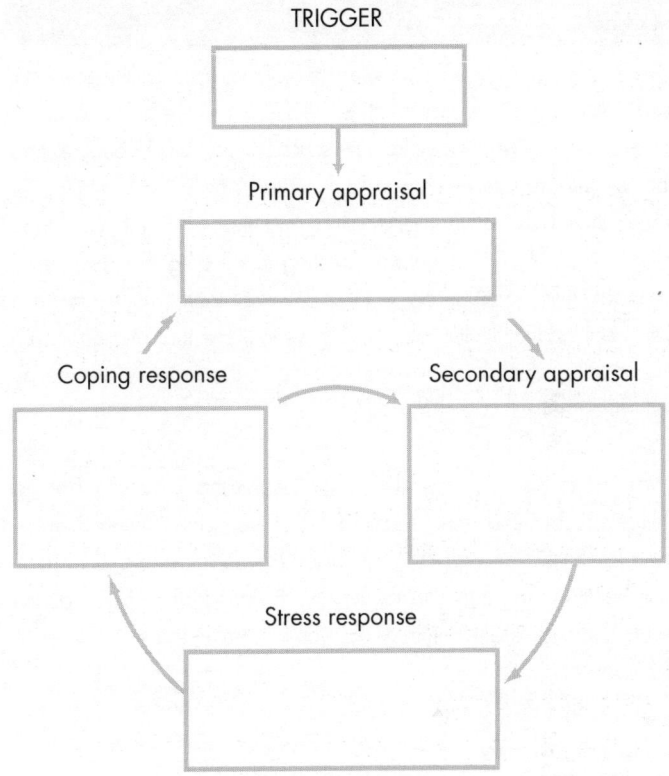

Fig. 8.3 Your cognitive therapy formulation of stress

Having formulated this one situation, you may find it helpful to repeat the exercise for other stressful times (use the blank worksheet at the back of this book), so that you can see if there are patterns that are repeating themselves, and investigate the impact of your coping responses. Hopefully this will help you to see the way in which your appraisals and responses play a part in the stress process, and should highlight areas it would be helpful to change.

TWO IMPORTANT PROVISOS

We should emphasize that we are not saying that the fact that you are experiencing stress is just because you are thinking in the wrong way. We know that the situations in which people find themselves are often extremely difficult to cope with. Similarly, we know that stress is very distressing and that you will have tried many ways of coping before resorting to reading this book, and probably with some success. We know that there is likely to be a very real and difficult problem, but we believe that understanding the way in which appraisals contribute to the process can be an extremely helpful way forward.

We should also say that if you try to use this way of mapping things out but it doesn't seem to fit, or you don't find it helpful, then don't give up and think this approach is not going to be relevant for you. You can still go on with the program outlined below even if the different components don't seem to hang together in this way.

Your stress management plan

Now that you have identified the different components of stress, and the way in which these hang together, you can start to think about what changes might be helpful and possible to make, and to set goals for change. But we will start by giving an overview of the stress management program so that you can map out your general approach.

The general approach to stress management

We have seen in the formulation above that there are a number of vicious cycles that occur when you are feeling stressed. When things are stressful you start to think in a negative way about the situation (your primary appraisal) and about your ability to cope (your secondary appraisal). These are the cognitive aspects of your stress response. Your feelings and your physical responses kick in (the emotional and physiological aspects of the stress response) and then you start to do something which we have termed your coping response, even if by 'coping' all you are doing is running away or reaching for the bottle.

Because so much of our stress depends on cycles between these different components, anything that we do at one point of the cycle should have an impact on the others too. So we can tackle stress by concentrating on one part of the cycle, or by looking at strategies and techniques aimed at each part.

STRESS MANAGEMENT FOR EVERYONE: TACKLING APPRAISALS

As we have said (once or twice!), the role of appraisals is central in the stress response. Therefore, being able to identify and change the appraisals that are contributing to stress is absolutely vital. So the first component of your stress management plan involves learning to identify and to challenge the thoughts and appraisals that underlie your stress. Chapter 9 will show you in detail how to do this.

TACKLING OTHER ASPECTS

Because stress covers such a wide variety of feelings and responses, other aspects of your stress management plan will be much more individual and tailored to you. Chapter 10 refers specifically to general aspects of behavior and how you can modify these. Subsequent chapters cover different situations that are often associated with stress (relationships, work and time management), and then a variety of specific problems (such as procrastination or rumination) that contribute. Chapter 15 talks about general aspects of taking care of yourself, and techniques of relaxation and other strategies that should help you directly with physical and emotional aspects of stress. Finally, Chapter 16 talks about ways of enhancing your positive qualities and your sense of self-efficacy.

Making your plan

There are four stages in this process:

1 The first is to think about which areas of your life are causing you the most difficulty.
2 The second is to think about what changes you could make in these areas, and to set specific goals for change.
3 The third is to work out the strategies and techniques that you need to take to achieve the specific goals.
4 And the fourth is to review how you are doing and revise your plan.

In order to do this it may be helpful for you to start a stress management notebook or folder so that after a while you can look back on what you decided at the beginning and see how far you have progressed. It may seem too obvious to need saying, but our experience in clinics is that people often don't think of keeping notebooks for personal changes, and often find it helpful when they do.

The worksheet below is something that you can use to keep track of your progress week by week. It may be helpful to print a number from the blank copy at the end of the book, or make your own version.

USING THE WORKSHEET

At this point of the book you should have enough information to fill out the first two columns of the worksheet, concerning the problems and the goals that you would like to achieve. What goes into the third column should emerge as you read on through the next chapters of the book. In particular, Chapter 9 explains stressful automatic thoughts in more detail. Keep the worksheet to hand, and as you read on come back to it when you come across a technique that you think might be useful. The last column gives space for you to review your progress.

TABLE 8.2 STRESS MANAGEMENT PLAN

Stressor 1	This week's goal	Techniques 1. Identify and challenge stressful automatic thoughts (SATs) 2.	Review progress
Stressor 2	This week's goal	Techniques 1. Identify and challenge SATs 2.	Review progress
Stressor 3	This week's goal	Techniques 1. Identify and challenge SATs 2.	Review progress

Drawing up your stress management plan

1. WHICH PROBLEMS ARE CAUSING THE MOST DIFFICULTY?

What areas of your life do you want to change? How would you like to see your life six months from now? If you could wave a magic wand, what would you do with it? (This needs to be realistic – no lottery wins!)

As you will see, we have chosen to label the problem areas on the worksheet as *stressors* rather than problems. This is because it is much better to pick a stressor to put in here, rather than a feeling or other aspect of the stress response. It usually makes it easier to set specific and measurable goals that will direct you to a clear action plan. And it makes it clear that the reason that you are feeling stressed is because of what is going on in your life, and your reaction to it, rather than it just being a problem in you.

The areas that you pick may be large and all-embracing such as 'my relationships' or 'my career', or they may be much smaller – 'my relationship with my mother-in-law', 'my journey to work'.

Try to pick three areas that you know would make a big difference to you if you could do something about them. Write these in the first column of the worksheet.

2. DEFINE YOUR GOALS

Now that you have identified these stressors, the next step is to work out a reasonable goal in relation to them. Think about where you would ultimately like to get to with the stressor.

The Chinese philosopher Lao-tzu said: 'The journey of

a thousand miles begins with a single step'. So if your ultimate goal seems a thousand miles away do not despair. Sometimes we need to approach our ultimate goal step by step rather than all at once. This doesn't mean that you won't be able to reach the large goal in the end, only that you need to get there by stages.

So in the next column on the worksheet, write down what the goal for the first step could be.

Remember that goals should be SMART, that is:

- **S**pecific
- **M**easurable
- **A**chievable
- **R**easonable
- **T**imed

Jane had been very unfit for a long time and had never been very good at organized sports – although she had been quite a decent runner when at school. Jane's teenage children used to tease her mercilessly about being unfit and a bit overweight, and she was finding both their teasing and her poor general health increasingly stressful. One day she finally snapped. 'Okay', she stormed, 'I have had enough of this. I am jolly well going to apply to run the London Marathon, and I will jolly well finish it, and I will jolly well finish it in reasonable time, and then you will all have to jolly well shut up!' After much spluttering with mirth from the children and sense of impending doom from Jane, she decided that she would go ahead. So her overall goal was: Complete the marathon in a reasonable time.

But obviously, in order to get to this point Jane needed to break things down into a number of much smaller specific goals. She thought about what she would need in order to achieve the goal, and how she was going to go about it. So the next steps involved:

1 *Find a trainer at the local gym who could help and advise me – within the next two weeks.*
2 *Find out what a suitable diet for someone on an intense training regime should be – within the next month.*
3 *Work out what my training regime should be over the next eight months – ditto.*
4 *Start the first step – walking and jogging two miles four times a week.*
5 *Review progress and increase jogging the following week.*

Jane also realized that the way in which the children were teasing her was something that she would need to tackle, and decided to take steps in relation to this too.

Using this example we can see how the SMART rules work. Jane's goals were:

- Specific – she said exactly what each step would be.
- Measurable – it would be clear when she had carried them out.
- Achievable – each step was within her abilities.
- Realistic – she was not planning something that was completely out of touch with reality.

- Timed – she gave herself two weeks to find a trainer, and then gave herself a week to carry out her exercise and review at the end of the week.

3. CHOOSE YOUR TECHNIQUE

The third column is called Techniques. This is where you enter the technique that you think would be most appropriate to help you meet your goal. As we have explained, we have included 'Identify and challenge SATs' for each goal because of the importance of tackling appraisals. After this, however, the techniques you choose will depend on your stressor and on the kind of approach that you think might be helpful.

When choosing techniques think of your current ways of coping. Do you need to try something completely different? Or make your current style a bit more efficient? Think about what you've tried that has worked a bit, or that hasn't.

You may already know how you are going to go about making changes, but if not, then leave this column and read on. Once you have identified something suitable then come back to the worksheet and write it in. Now it is time to start making changes. Put the technique into action, and give it your best shot for the next week.

4. REVIEW YOUR PROGRESS

This of course is why it is important to have measurable and achievable goals. At the end of the week, sit down and review what you have done. Were you able to achieve your goal? Did it work? Would it be good to carry on, or modify it according to what you have learned? Are you ready to specify the next goal related to the stressor? Think about all of this, and make a plan for the following week.

Over the next few weeks while you are working on your stress package, there will be a four-stage sequence:

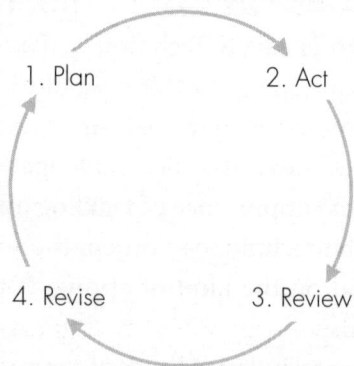

1. Plan   2. Act

4. Revise   3. Review

So at the end of every week you need to review and revise, change goals, plan techniques, and act! We will come back to this in Chapter 16.

CHAPTER SUMMARY

- You have identified your stress responses, stressors and coping responses.
- We have looked at a way in which these fit together, and you have been able to see if this is a helpful way of understanding your own stress profile.
- You have started your stress management plan. This involves:
  - Identifying stressors;
  - Pinpointing goals;
  - Starting to look for techniques;
  - Using the worksheet to monitor and review progress.

9

Changing your stressful thinking

We have seen that appraisals – the way in which we think about things – play a very large part in determining how stressful we find things, and how we cope with them. Chapter 4 introduces the ideas of cognitive therapy, that show how thinking is related to how we feel and behave. So a very important part of learning to cope with stress involves learning to tackle the negative thinking associated with stress – what we call *stressful automatic thoughts or SATs*. This is why we have included working with SATs in the techniques for the stressors in the stress management plan (see pp. 124–5). In this chapter we will describe how you can tackle these thoughts – which, in a nutshell, involves learning to identify, and then to question and challenge, the thoughts that are making you feel stressed.

Characteristics of negative thinking

But first it may help to understand something about the nature of the stressful automatic thoughts. Mostly, people do not think very much about thinking. Ideas form in our minds without us really questioning where they came from or why we have them, and mostly we do not question whether they are right or not – we just have them. So the thoughts that we have in our emotional states have the following characteristics:

Firstly, the thoughts are *automatic*. They are not the result of a rational process in which we think about all options, weigh up possibilities, etc. The thoughts just appear in our mind fully formed. It is helpful to have the idea of a 'back-room' in your brain – we know that a lot of our processing of information goes on in this 'backroom', out of our aware-ness, and only the end result comes into our more conscious minds. This idea was described delightfully by the eminent physician Richard Asher in the early twentieth century, who said that he likened his brain to an oven, but knew that a lot of what came out of it was half baked. This is a very helpful way to think about a lot of our stressful thinking!

Secondly, the thoughts are *plausible*. They are presented to our conscious minds as a fait accompli. We just accept them as reality, and very rarely question them. Of course this is not true of all our thinking – there are probably many times when we question whether we are right about some-thing or not. But it does seem to be true of the thinking associated with negative emotions.

Thirdly, the thoughts are *unfair*. The automatic processing makes sure that we ignore anything that does not fit. So we ignore positive events and interpretations, and we overemphasize negative ones.

And fourthly, the thoughts are *unrealistic*. Negative thinking is based on very biased ways of processing events, so our negative thoughts are often based on guesswork and exaggeration, and even small problems are blown up out of all proportion.

It is important to point out the qualities of these thoughts because the fact that they are automatic and plausible can make it quite difficult to catch yourself having them – but this is the next step.

How to identify your stressful thoughts

Aaron T. Beck called the thoughts that are associated with depression negative automatic thoughts (NATs for short!). Since we are going to be talking about the thoughts that occur in stress, we call them stressful automatic thoughts (SATs). Sometimes people are all too aware of the stressful thoughts that they have in their mind – the thoughts are there all the time, as worries or fears or memories. Sometimes, however, they are not so aware of their thoughts – just of how they feel. It can take quite a bit of training to become aware of them. One of the things that undoubtedly helps some people is to write the thoughts down, and the worksheet below is a good way to start to do this.

TABLE 9.1 A DIARY OF YOUR STRESSFUL AUTOMATIC THOUGHTS

Date and time	Situation (where you are, what you're doing)	Mood (e.g. sad, anxious, stressed)	Stressful automatic thoughts (exactly what is going through your mind when you feel bad)

Using this worksheet, you could think about the last time that you felt stressed. The more recent the occasion, the easier it will be to think about it. Try to get a clear picture of what happened in your mind.

Now jot down the date and time. Then look at the Situation column: where were you, what were you doing, what was going on around you? This is usually what is going on outside you, but perhaps you were just starting to think about something.

Jot down how you felt – this could just be one or two words to describe the emotion. Next, try to recapture exactly what went on in your mind when you were feeling bad, and jot that down too.

Imagine Anna, who is in the middle of a very important course for her work – one that she really wants to do, but is afraid that she isn't actually quite up to. Anna needs to finish a report for the course, but keeps putting it off.

TABLE 9.2 ANNA'S DIARY OF STRESSFUL AUTOMATIC THOUGHTS

Date and time	Situation (where you are, what you're doing)	Mood (e.g. sad, anxious, stressed)	Stressful automatic thoughts (exactly what is going through your mind when you feel bad)
Mon. 2 p.m.	Sitting at home – meant to be writing a report for my course, but I keep putting it off and can't concentrate.	Anxious (terrified actually) Stressed	There's no point me doing this, I'm never going to be able to get it done. Everyone will know that I shouldn't have been signed up for this.

See myself having to go into the tea room and no one will look at me because they know I've messed it up. |

Tips on identifying stressful automatic thoughts

THE DIFFERENCE BETWEEN THOUGHTS AND FEELINGS

It is very easy to get muddled about the difference between thoughts and feelings, particularly when you are in the thick of quite strong emotions. Imagine the following situation: you are at home and feeling very lonely, and you ring up a friend to see if she can meet you that week. She says she can't because she is too busy. Many people would say they 'felt rejected'. But in fact 'rejected' is not what we would describe as a feeling, or an emotion. The *feeling* here would be sad, humiliated or something like that. This feeling would be there because you had the *thought* that you had been rejected. On the whole, in describing emotions we tend to use single words; when describing thoughts we tend to need a bit more to explain things (although 'rejected' is an obvious exception to this). It is good to try to sort the difference out at this stage, because it will make it easier when we look at questioning thoughts.

PICTURES IN YOUR MIND

Anna's diary brings out an important feature of negative thoughts. Sometimes these are not in the form of words, or sentences, but are in pictures. Some people tend to think more in images than in words, and these images can be very powerful. In Anna's image she saw herself going into the tea room and everyone turning their backs on her and avoiding her.

If this is the case with you, then you could either write down the visual image, as Anna has done above, or you could try to think about what it means.

I'M NOT HAVING ANY THOUGHTS

It can be very difficult to identify your thoughts. This might be because you are swamped by the feeling that is associated with them. Sometimes the thoughts can go through your mind very quickly, leaving only the feeling behind. And sometimes it's quite scary to start to identify your thoughts. If this happens to you, then the best thing to do is to give yourself time, and try to tune into the thoughts you are having.

A GOOD TIME TO WRITE THINGS DOWN

Whenever you feel particularly stressed about anything, this is your opportunity! Stop what you are doing, if at all possible, and ask yourself: 'What is going through my mind right now?' Again, if at all possible write the thoughts down straight away – it is much easier to get a clear picture if you do it at the time, rather than trying to remember later. If you can't write it down, make a mental note of what is going on in your mind so that you can write it down later.

How to question and challenge stressful automatic thoughts

Once you have been able to identify the thoughts that are associated with your feelings of stress there are a number of things that you can learn to do to question and challenge them.

Identifying cognitive errors or 'distortions'

The first of these involves thinking about the reasoning processes that have helped produce a thought. We know that the automatic thinking processes that lead to stressful thoughts are very biased, and we can identify a number of different types of bias, or cognitive distortion (see overleaf). The point of identifying these errors is this:

if a thought is based on a faulty line of logic or reasoning, it is very unlikely to be true.

TYPES OF COGNITIVE ERRORS

All or nothing, or black-and-white thinking is the tendency to perceive your qualities in an extreme way. Sam was an undergraduate studying history at Oxford; at school he had been very bright and came top in every subject, but when he came to university other people were just as bright as him. Sam found himself thinking: 'But if I'm not the best then I'm complete rubbish.' So whenever he was set an essay he would get very stressed, thinking that if he couldn't do it better then everyone else then he would be an absolute failure.

Overgeneralization is the tendency to take one negative thing and make it true of everything. For instance, Sarah cooked a really nice meal for her family, but the potatoes were a bit overdone. Sarah thought that the meal was ruined and that she was a useless cook, despite the fact that everything else was really nice.

Catastrophization is another process by which a negative event can get blown out of proportion and in your mind lead to disastrous consequences. Geoff was a car salesman whose sales figures were down by 10 per cent compared to the previous month. Geoff thought: 'This is a total disaster, my reputation is ruined; this is the start of a slippery slope and it's just a matter of time before I'm fired – I won't be able to pay the mortgage, I'll lose my home.' Again, he became extremely stressed about going to work, assuming that the worst would happen.

Discounting the positive occurs when you ignore any positive experiences, or even turn a positive experience into a negative one. For example, Gina was complimented on how skilfully she conducted a sales meeting at work and thought: 'They're just saying that. I can't do with all this flattery: it's so superficial and insincere.' When she clinched a deal that was going to be extremely profitable for the company, she thought: 'That's just a fluke.'

Mind-reading occurs when you assume you know what another person is thinking. Ross was talking to a girl he was interested in and when she sighed, he thought: 'Oh god, she's really bored, she must be desperate to get away.' He had assumed that he could tell what she was thinking!

Fortune-telling is similar, but this time means that you assume that you know what will happen in the future – and specifically that bad things are going to happen to you. Tom found it very difficult to study for his A levels, assuming that they would go badly however hard he worked. Every time he sat down to study, he started thinking that no university would have him anyway.

Emotional reasoning occurs when you assume your feelings are facts. Because you *feel* stressed, it must mean that things are difficult or impossible. You don't take the time to see whether your feelings really fit the situation, but assume that they must be a true reflection of it.

Personalization occurs when you take everything to be related to you, even though there is little basis for doing so. For instance, you might conclude that something bad that happened is entirely your fault and assume that you are responsible, and believe the mistake reflects your personal inadequacy. Marcia visited her sister in hospital who later developed a virus and on hearing this she believed she was responsible for infecting her and felt crippled with guilt.

Labelling is an extreme form of overgeneralization that involves defining yourself and others by negative labels – for example, when you make one mistake you might think 'I'm an idiot', or 'I'm a loser'. The trouble is that you then respond emotionally as if this label were true. The same is also true for judgements on others – Ian labelled his secretary a 'shirker' when she took an extra fifteen minutes for her lunch break and got very angry, but didn't notice that she was the first person to arrive in the morning and the last person to leave at the end of the working day.

Shoulds, musts, oughts are statements that start with a 'should', 'must' or 'ought to'. They can cause you to feel pressured and resentful – they are like issuing a command to yourself and leaving no room for error. Anne set herself unrelenting high standards and would come up with rules for herself such as 'I should go to church every Sunday' and 'I should always have a clean and tidy house'. David had an appointment with his family doctor and on arrival at the surgery discovered that his doctor was running late. He found himself feeling resentful and thinking that he ought to be seen on time and the doctor should be more considerate towards his patients. Both Anne and David felt stressed when their own behavior or that of others fell short of their standards.

A QUICK GUIDE TO COGNITIVE DISTORTIONS

All or nothing thinking
Seeing things as black or white with no middle ground or shades of grey. Either you do things perfectly or you've failed.

Overgeneralization
Believing that a single or small event is evidence of a much bigger problem.

Catastrophization
Exaggerating an event and imagining the worst possible outcome.

Discounting the positive
Ignoring any positive experiences or turning a positive experience into a negative one.

Mind-reading
Assuming you know what another person is thinking, and that it's bad.

Fortune-telling
Assuming you know what will happen in the future, and that it will be bad.

Emotional reasoning
Assuming that because you feel something is bad then it must be.

Personalization
Assuming that bad things are related to you when there is little basis for doing so.

Labelling
Defining yourself and others by negative labels that make you feel bad.

Shoulds, musts, oughts
Setting unreasonable standards and feeling guilty when you can't live up to them.

When you have written a stressful thought down, look at the list of distortions and see if you can identify these biases in your thinking. Write the distortion down next to the thought. Remind yourself: how can a thought based on such faulty logic be true?

Looking at the evidence

The next step is to start thinking about the *evidence* for our thoughts. Some people find it helpful to imagine a court of law. Your thought has to convince you beyond reasonable doubt that it is correct. So there are a number of questions that you can ask yourself:

- Is there any evidence *for* this thought? Is there anything at all that would back it up?
- Is there any evidence *against* the thought?
- Is there an alternative way of seeing things that would fit the facts of the situation?
- Is there a less extreme way of seeing things?
- How would someone who wasn't so upset view the situation?
- What would you say to someone else if they were in this situation?

Essentially, you are trying to come up with a more fair and realistic way of viewing the situation that you are in. Once you have asked yourself these questions, go back to the original worksheet on p. 136, but this time use the empty column to write down the results of your questioning.

Table 9.3 shows Anna's attempts to come up with alternatives to her stress-inducing thoughts.

TABLE 9.3 ANNA'S UPDATED DIARY OF STRESSFUL AUTOMATIC THOUGHTS

Date and time	Situation (where you are, what you're doing)	Mood (e.g. sad, anxious, stressed)	Stressful automatic thoughts (exactly what is going through your mind when you feel bad)	Alternative way of seeing things
Mon. 2 p.m.	Sitting at home – meant to be writing a report for my course, but I keep putting it off and can't concentrate.	Anxious (terrified actually) Stressed	There's no point me doing this, I'm never going to be able to get it done. Everyone will know that I shouldn't have been signed up for this.	I know really that my boss wouldn't have put my name down if she didn't think I could do it.
			See myself having to go into the tea room and no one will look at me because they know I've messed it up.	My colleagues were pretty nice to Sam last week when he messed his first assignment up! They didn't ignore him.
				I've been mind-reading and fortune-telling!

Tips on questioning thoughts

When you have filled in the 'Alternative way of seeing things' column, ask yourself how that makes you feel. Do things seem less stressful and difficult? Can you detect a difference between how you felt when you filled in the 'Mood' column and now? If you can detect even a small improvement then you have done well.

Sometimes, however, you will feel that the so-called fair and realistic new thought is pretty rubbishy and you don't really believe it. In this case it is unlikely to make you feel any better. But don't dismiss the thought – write it down anyway. Seeing things on paper can sometimes make them seem a bit more real.

Keep practising – at first it will be difficult to come up with alternatives, or you will come up with them and not believe them. But questioning thoughts is like learning any new skill – the more you do it, the easier it gets and the more faith you have in your skills as a result. Remember that you have probably been thinking in the stressful way for quite a long time, and that it will take time to make changes. Don't give up! (In case you need them, we've included blank copies of the worksheets at the back of the book.)

Why do we think like this? Identifying patterns in thoughts and behavior

As we have seen, it is clear that for any given situation, there are a number of different ways of seeing what is going on. Yet another very important feature of this is that people seem to tend naturally to think in one particular way more than another. Some people generally see the more positive and optimistic side of things; others notice the gloomiest or most threatening aspects of a situation.

Most people know about Eeyore in the Christopher Robin stories, who was unremittingly gloomy about everything. And it does seem to be true that, for whatever reason, we acquire habits of mind. We were once shown a wonderful poem, written in 1895 by Sam Walter Foss, about a calf walking home (rather erratically) through the woods. The next day a dog took up the trail, and the day after a sheep. So a path was made, and men started to follow it. The path becomes a road, and the road a village street, and then the central street of a 'renowned metropolis'. The calf by now is long dead. And here are two excerpts from the poem:

> But still they followed – do not laugh –
> The first migration of that calf,
> And through this winding woody-way stalked
> Because he wobbled when he walked
>
> . . .
>
> A hundred thousand men were led
> By one calf near three centuries dead.
> They followed still his crooked way,
> And lost one hundred years a day;
> For thus such reverence is lent
> To well-established precedent.

This seems to us to be a very good analogy for how habits of mind might occur. We follow a path that is already there, and the more we do it, the bigger and stronger the path gets, and the more difficult it is to get off it. So if we start to think in a particular way, then we are likely to carry on doing it – going along with 'well-established precedent'.

But why should we start to think in a particular way? When Beck began to talk about cognitive therapy the emphasis was very much on the 'here and now'; on what people think in the present, and not what happened to them in the past. But it soon became clear that different people did tend to think in different ways. Beck went back to looking at what had happened to people in their childhood, and saw that early experiences play a large part in determining the paths that their thoughts would travel on.

Imagine a child of a single mother. Mother has to go out to work and comes home very tired. The child wants to play, but Mother is too tired, and says: 'Leave me alone; let me sit down.' She gets tea, but wants to read the paper, not talk about the child's day. Then a friend comes round – suddenly Mother is not too tired to talk, but does want the child to go away so that she can gossip. After a while the message becomes loud and clear to the child: 'I am not wanted'; 'I am not lovable'; 'There is something wrong with me.' These ideas become fixed in the child's mind – they are not necessarily things that she says to herself, but they are fundamental, core beliefs about herself that will colour her experiences through her life. Later in life, if she were to ring someone up and they were too busy to see her, her core beliefs would be activated – it would be proof that she was unlovable and unwanted.

So these core beliefs sit at the back of your mind, and become the framework through which other experiences are seen. They are easily activated, and when they are activated they tend to result in very strong emotions.

Beck talked about how there are two very common types of core belief. One set of beliefs concern how lovable you are, whether you are wanted by other people, as in the above example. Beck labelled people for whom these beliefs are central as 'sociotrophic'. The other set of beliefs is much more to do with achievement. This is where people are very concerned with what they have accomplished – they tend to be very concerned with issues of success and failure rather than with issues of being close to other people. Beck labelled people for whom these beliefs are central as 'autonomous'. It will not come as a surprise to learn that these two sets of beliefs tend to be unevenly split between the sexes! The form which core beliefs take does not have to follow one of these patterns, but they are common ones.

The idea of core beliefs also explains why people find it easier to cope with some events than others. If you tend to be sociotrophic, then what happens in your relationships will be very important to you. If your marriage breaks up it will be devastating for you. If you lost your job, on the other hand, or didn't get promoted, you would be upset or cross, but you would not be devastated. By contrast, someone who tends to be autonomous would be devastated by losing their job but might cope a lot better with the break-up of a relationship. Once, a patient one of us encountered while working in a psychiatric hospital explained why she and other people there had become patients and, to our amazement, described this scenario exactly. 'It's not that worse things happen to us,' she said, 'it's just that the things that have happened to us are the things we can't cope with.'

These beliefs can be very powerful in our lives – but does that mean that we are stuck with them? Sometimes when these beliefs are very strong it *is* difficult to overcome them – after all, we have had them a long time and thought them many times. But any change we make to our thinking will start to bring about small dents in these beliefs. Every time we identify and tackle a thought that belongs to the old pattern we are effectively helping to shrink and weaken it. The more we can do this, the better it will be.

Using these techniques to combat stress

Now that you have learned to identify and challenge your thinking, it is time to start putting this into practice when you are stressed. Try to make it a rule that every time you notice that you are starting to feel stressed you will stop and reflect on what is going on. On the whole it is better to try to do this as soon as you notice the stress starting, but sometimes circumstances just don't allow this. Some people find it extremely helpful to carry a little notebook with them to jot down things as they occur, so that they will be sure of remembering them later. Other people can just make a mental note about it and come back to it later.

It's also important to remember that tackling your thoughts is a skill like any other and gets better with practice. At first you may not feel that it's doing any good, but as your skill increases you will start to feel more and more effect. It will also help at the beginning if you make yourself write things down rather than just trying to do everything in your head. As time goes on you may find you don't need to do this, but it is probably better to start off doing so.

These techniques should be used to tackle the particular stressors that you have identified in your stress management plan, but they will also be useful to you in any situation which is making you stressed. In subsequent chapters we will go on to talk about techniques for dealing with particular stressful situations, but being able to tackle your thoughts is a general skill that should be helpful in all situations, and will certainly enhance any other techniques that you use.

CHAPTER SUMMARY

- Stressful thoughts are often automatic and plausible, so we often accept them as real and do not think to question them.
- We have shown how to recognize and identify the stressful automatic thoughts (SATs) that underlie your feelings of stress.
- We have also shown how to question and challenge these SATs and to come up with fairer and more realistic alternatives.
- We have discussed the way in which the tendency to think like this develops, and how you can use the techniques outlined in this chapter to tackle the 'core beliefs' that make you vulnerable to SATs.

10

Changing stress-related behavior

So far we have been talking about how to work with your thoughts in cognitive behavior therapy (CBT). But the other aspect that CBT is concerned with is your behavior – hence its name. In this chapter we will look at the role of behavior in stress. Later chapters will talk about specific techniques that will include making changes to your behavior, but there are also two general ways in which behavior is important in stress. Firstly, the way that you behave gives powerful messages to yourself and others about how you feel; and secondly, one very common way in which stress can affect us is by prompting us to avoid difficult situations, which can sometimes make the stress worse in the long run. Let's look at these two points in more detail.

Behavioral messages

The way that people behave sends powerful messages about how they feel. We believe what people do – including ourselves – much more than we believe what they say.

Imagine that you have a 'friend' who tells you that she likes you, but never invites you to her parties, and crosses the road to avoid you if she sees you in the street. And imagine that you have another friend who never particularly says what she feels about you, but rings you a couple of times a week to see what you're up to, and suggests getting together at quite frequent intervals. Which of these friends do you believe likes you better?

Hoping that you picked the second, then this illustrates the first way in which behavior is important – it is what we *do*, rather than what we say, that sends powerful messages about how we feel. This is true of what we do in relation to other people, but it is just as true in relation to ourselves. We believe what we do, not what we say. If you *tell* yourself that you're confident, but in social situations hide in the background and never put yourself forward, you are not really going to feel very confident! But if you tell yourself that you're confident, and then make sure that you *act* confidently, then you are much more likely to feel it too. This means that when we have dealt with our thoughts, as described in Chapter 9, it becomes very important to *base our behavior on the new thoughts, not on the old ones.* Although it may feel uncomfortable and alien at first, the more we behave in the new ways, the more solidly we will believe in them. There are a couple of things that you can do to help with this.

The non-stressed twin: Imagine that you have a twin who is exactly the same as you in every respect except that they don't feel stress. Imagine them going into a situation, and see what they would do. Would they cope differently from you? Would they be able to come up with different kinds of solutions? If you can imagine this, then try to see if you can put your non-stressed plan into action. The idea of the non-stressed twin came from a patient who had read about the 'non-obsessional' twin. We have been unable to track the source but are grateful to the unidentified author for the idea.

Plan A and Plan B: Think about how you behave when you are stressed, and write down what you do. This is Plan A, and you know how well it works, and how it makes you feel. Now think about what you would like to do if you felt brave or clever or confident enough. This is Plan B. Imagine yourself carrying out Plan B, even thinking about what you would be wearing, how you would hold your-self, what your voice would be like, what you would be able to see and hear around you.

Sam was a twenty-four-year-old scientist at the begin-ning of his career, doing work that he believed was going to be genuinely useful. But his research involved working with chemicals, and even though he knew rationally that these were not harmful to himself or other people, he could not get rid of the sneaking feeling that they might be. Sam told himself that he did not have a problem with this, and that he knew that the chemicals were safe. But at the end of the working day Sam found it extremely difficult to leave work. He would check that every surface that he had worked on was scrupulously clean, and after a while he started to keep separate clothes at work so that he could wash and change out of his work clothes before he went home at the end of the day. Sam kept telling himself that he didn't think there was a problem with the chemicals – but in the end it was taking him two hours a day to go through a series of rituals to make sure everything was safe. He would justify this by saying that it was sensible to take precautions. But one day he knocked over a small container, and splashes from the chemicals got on to his skin. He found that his heart was racing appallingly, his breath coming in pants and gasps, he was sweating in the cool room – and he knew inside that he was absolutely terrified, despite anything that he tried to say to the contrary.

After this Sam knew that he really did have a problem, and that it was no use telling himself that he didn't. His fear was governed by what he did, not what he said. So using the techniques above he asked himself: 'How would my non-stressed twin behave with these chemicals?' He realized that his non-stressed twin would do exactly what the other people in the lab did – clean up after themselves in a reasonable way that took no more than five or ten minutes, and go home without washing. He thought up a detailed Plan B which entailed working out exactly what he would do, and then he forced himself to go through with this. After a while, he started to think he had been a bit silly, and began to realize that there really wasn't anything to be afraid of. His fears had been allayed by behaving as if there was nothing to be afraid of!

Avoiding stressful situations

The second way in which behavior is important is that when people are stressed and anxious, they naturally tend to avoid the situations that are making them feel bad. We know that avoidance almost always contributes to problems rather than solving them. For instance, a lot of people find it very difficult to open official-looking mail, particularly if they are in the middle of stressful transactions – house-buying, for example, or dealing with the tax man! But this means that crucial deadlines can be missed, or demands intensified, and the situation can get very much more complicated and difficult to sort out. Furthermore, when we are anxious we naturally tend to avoid the things that make us feel that way, and in the short term that does help, at least in the sense that we stop feeling anxious. But in the long term avoidance can only add to the problem.

There is therefore another vicious cycle that increases our stress:

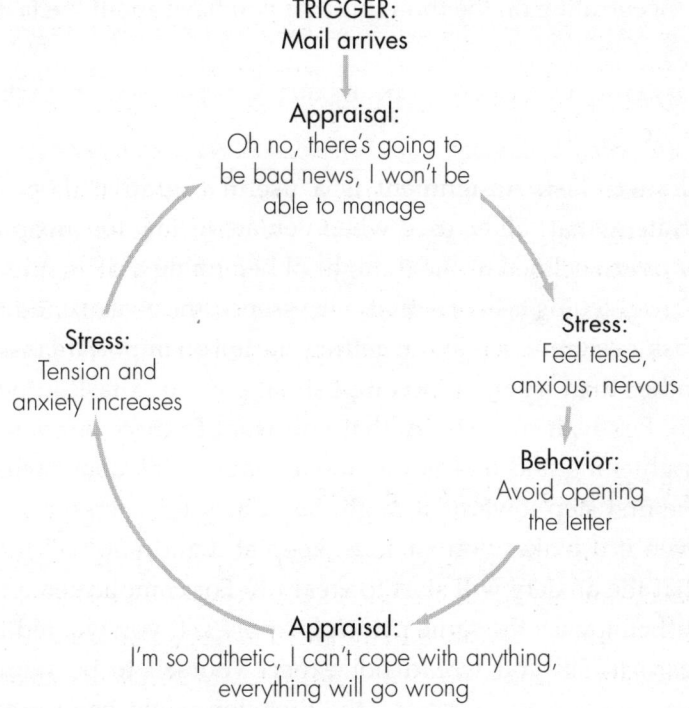

TRIGGER:
Mail arrives

Appraisal:
Oh no, there's going to be bad news, I won't be able to manage

Stress:
Feel tense, anxious, nervous

Behavior:
Avoid opening the letter

Appraisal:
I'm so pathetic, I can't cope with anything, everything will go wrong

Stress:
Tension and anxiety increases

Figure 10.1 The vicious cycle of avoidance

In the long term, therefore, we know that avoiding things we are afraid of makes us more frightened, and undermines our confidence. So dealing with avoidance is crucial in cognitive therapy. We will talk more about some types of avoidance, particularly procrastination, in later chapters.

Two ways of working with avoidance

For now, however, there are two main ways in which you can try to deal with avoidance in general. The first of these involves thinking about the task itself, and breaking it down into manageable steps, and the second involves concentrating on the thoughts that you have about the task.

BREAKING TASKS INTO MANAGEABLE STEPS – GRADED TASK ASSIGNMENT

Graded Task Assignment is a useful cognitive therapy strategy that can be used when you are feeling too anxious or overwhelmed at the thought of beginning a demanding or frightening task or activity. In essence, the goal of Graded Task Assignment is about getting started on important tasks rather than trying to accomplish all parts of a task in one go. Firstly, if the activity that you want to carry out is too frightening and makes you too anxious, think about what the first step towards it might be. Carry this step out and even if it makes you anxious, keep at it and you will find that the anxiety will start to wear off. For complicated and difficult tasks the same principle applies. If you wanted to learn to ski you would not expect yourself to be skiing black runs after one day – the first step might be to practise standing up with your skis on! When you are feeling stressed and expecting yourself to accomplish a big and important task this principle is no different. The process of Graded Task Assignment involves breaking the task down into specific and achievable steps so that you can succeed at each step before moving on to the next. It is important that you are able to manage each step so that you feel more confident and more motivated to continue.

When you have a problem like this, write it out in steps. It might help to use a worksheet like the one below.

TABLE 10.1 GRADED TASK ASSIGNMENT WORKSHEET

1. Describe the task that you are finding difficult to do.

2. What is the first step that you can take? (Remember that small achievable steps must come first.)

3. Having accomplished the first step, how do you feel? How motivated do you feel?

4. What is the second step you can take?

5. What is the third step you can take? And so on until the task is completed.

6. What have you found helpful about using this strategy?

Mark was a forty-two-year-old head teacher who had to produce an end-of-year report for the board of governors in his first year. It was particularly important for him to present a good case since the funding for crucial projects for the next year depended on the governors approving his report. At the same time he was juggling many other tasks and felt overwhelmed with stress. He was aware of his tendency to procrastinate and recognized he was avoiding this task because he was convinced that he had blown all chances of obtaining extra funding. Using Graded Task Assignment, Mark considered what steps he needed to take to get started with writing the report. Step one involved opening a new Word document on the computer and typing the title of the report. He felt particularly pleased having taken the plunge to start. Step two involved writing the main headings of the report and step three the subheadings. By step three Mark's confidence had increased and he felt motivated to continue on to the more complex steps. By breaking the task down into small steps he had been able to make a start.

It is of course possible, however, that there will be times that you have done this and have written out all the small steps that you need to take, but still cannot get started. In this case the problem may be to do with the thoughts you are having about the tasks, and these need to be tackled in their own right

DEALING WITH NEGATIVE PREDICTIONS

One of the things that lies behind problems with avoidance, or with making other changes to behavior, is that without realizing it people are implicitly making negative predictions of what will happen. 'If I talk in that meeting I will make a complete idiot of myself and everyone will howl with laughter'; 'If I open that letter I'll find that the buyers have dropped out.' These negative predictions then create additional anxiety and make it very difficult for people to do what they need to do.

Millie was feeling incredibly stressed because her colleague had gone on maternity leave and not been replaced, and Millie was doing the work of two people. She was working extra hours to meet her targets, but felt constantly that she wasn't managing to do things properly and that her work was not good enough. She thought – that is, predicted – that if she discussed her concerns with her manager he would become angry and see her as weak and pathetic. As a result she avoided talking to him about the difficulties, and carried on desperately trying to keep up, but ended up feeling resentful and taken for granted. Rationally Millie recognized that the real problem was her own belief about not being good enough, and that it was unlikely that her boss would be so unreasonable; but because even the slightest risk of her prediction coming true was too scary to contemplate she was unable to change her behavior, and carried on feeling stressed.

To see if this applies to you, take a moment to think about a time when you have avoided doing something that you needed to do. What negative predictions did you make? Were you assuming that things would go badly for you, or that someone else would respond badly? Cognitive therapists view these predictions as similar to a theory or hypothesis in a scientific experiment – and like all theories, they should be put to the test. So every time you make a negative prediction, you need to design an experiment to test it out!

HOW TO DO A BEHAVIORAL EXPERIMENT

In essence behavioral experiments are similar to testing a scientific theory, except that the theory is about you and your behavior. Doing the experiment involves the following:

- Identify what your negative prediction is – what do you think will happen?
- Devise an experiment to test it – how can you work out whether your prediction is going to come true?
- Carry the experiment out.
- Review the prediction in the light of what happened.

In the example above, Millie was predicting that if she spoke to her boss about her workload he would get angry and think she was pathetic. So she avoided talking to him, carried on working incredibly hard, but felt stressed and resentful. Millie's experiment had three parts:

1 Identifying the prediction.
2 Designing an experiment and carrying it out.
3 Reviewing the prediction.

Table 10.2 shows Millie's completed behavioral experiment worksheet:

TABLE 10.2 MILLIE'S BEHAVIORAL EXPERIMENT WORKSHEET

Prediction	Experiment	Review
What am I predicting will happen?	What is my plan for designing an experiment?	Did my prediction come true? What have I learnt?
If I tell my boss that I am having difficulty keeping up with the volume at work he will get angry and shout at me. He will tell me that I'm weak and pathetic and should consider looking for another job.	1. Email Richard and ask if we can organize a meeting. 2. Gather information — time sheet that includes tasks and hours worked. 3. Be open and honest with Richard, stay with the facts and figures.	Richard was really understanding and told me how much he valued my contribution to the team. He agreed that my current workload was unsustainable and helped me to prioritize my work. We agreed to meet in two weeks for a review. I felt so relieved. I learnt that you cannot second-guess how someone will react and that it's better to face the problem than avoid it.

You can use this worksheet to help you tackle situations where you know that you are avoiding doing something, particularly when you realize that this avoidance is making you feel more stressed. There are additional blank worksheets in the back of this book for you to use should you need them.

TABLE 10.3 BLANK BEHAVIORAL EXPERIMENT WORKSHEET		
Prediction What am I predicting will happen?	**Experiment** What is my plan for designing an experiment?	**Review** Did my prediction come true? What have I learnt?

Of course, not all predictions are proved quite so wrong as Millie's were! Sometimes the predictions might come partially true, or even completely true. But cognitive therapists have described this as a win-win situation! That is, if your negative predictions are proved to be false, then that's a win. But it's also a win if they do, because at least you now have accurate information, and can deal with a problem on a factual and realistic basis.

CHAPTER SUMMARY

- Behavior is important in two ways.
- Firstly, it gives us very strong messages about ourselves.
- It is therefore very important to make sure our behavior fits with our new way of thinking.
- Secondly, in stressful situations we often avoid things and end up feeling worse.
- One way to deal with this is by breaking tasks down into manageable steps.
- Often we avoid situations because we are making negative predictions about what will happen.
- We can deal with these negative predictions by the techniques of behavioral experiments.

11

Stress and relationships

There is no doubt that one of the main sources of stress for people is what happens in their relationships with others. In this chapter we will focus on close relationships and friendships, rather than the relationships that you might have at work, which will be discussed in the following chapter. In later parts of this chapter we will talk about how you can tackle some of the problems in relationships. We will refer to skills and ideas described in Chapter 9 on stress and thinking, so it may be a good idea to have a look back at that chapter to refresh your memory.

Relationships are crucially important for most people. Perhaps there will be some people whom you know who are happy with very little contact or closeness with others, but this is unusual, for like most other primates and many mammals, humans are social animals. A famous study in the 1970s, by George Brown and Til Harries, looked at depression in women in a disadvantaged part of London. This study identified a number of factors that made women more vulnerable to developing depression. These included the death of the woman's mother before she was twelve; having three or more children under fourteen, and having no occupation outside the home. And one of the most important factors that protected women from depression – that is, made it less likely that they would become depressed – was having someone whom they felt close to and could talk to. The presence of this close, confiding relationship reduced the likelihood that women would get depressed by a very significant amount, even when all the risk factors were present. So it was clear that the nature of relationships played a big part in determining whether the women got depressed or not.

How does this relate to stress? The diagram below may help to make this clear

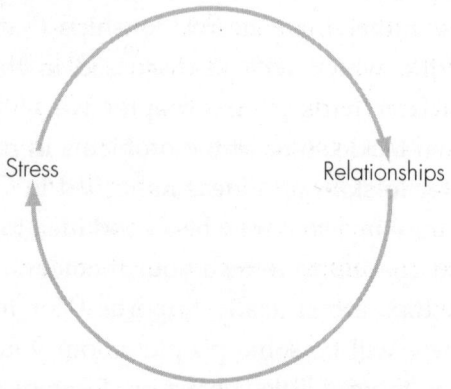

Stress   Relationships

Figure 11.1 The vicious cycle of stress and relationships

What this demonstrates is that there is a very close relationship between feelings of stress and what happens in your relationships. Sometimes this vicious cycle might start with something going wrong with relationships that are important to you. Perhaps you and your partner have started to have terrible rows, and you are feeling constantly criticized and undermined. Or perhaps your teenage daughter wants to spend all her time hanging out with her friends instead of studying, and you are having endless fights about it. As these difficulties continue, you may well find that you are feeling increasingly stressed and unhappy. But sometimes the vicious cycle can start with stress that arises from other kinds of difficulty. Perhaps you are having a terrible crisis at work, and just can't decide whether you should try to change career or not, or you have moved to a new job with a long and horrible commute. When you get home in the evening and your partner says 'Did you have a good day?' you snap, and then you both start to argue. As time goes on this pattern starts to build up resentment and anger, so that the problems in the relationship become a new source of stress, and the vicious cycle continues. Of course, the good thing about a cycle like this is that it can also go the other way, so that if you get home and you and your partner can be supportive and warm to each other, then this can play a great part in reducing your stress, and making it easier for you to face the things in the world that might be causing you problems.

Locating the stress in your relationships

It may be that you know only too well which people in your life are problematic for you, in which case you should skip to the following section. But sometimes the feeling of stress can permeate your life so widely that you lose sight of exactly that others are contributing too, or that your problems with one person are spilling over into other areas. In this case, it may be worth taking stock of all the relationships around

TABLE 11.1 RELATIONSHIP STRESS WORKSHEET

	Who is in my life in this area	How stressed I feel around them (0–10)	Frequency of contact 1 = too much 2 = about right 3 = too little
Home			
Other family			
Friends			
Neighbourhood			
Work			
Hobbies			
Other			

where it is coming from. Or maybe you have become so focused on a problem with one person that you don't realize you. One way to do this is to use the worksheet opposite. For each of the types of relationship, think about who is around, and how you feel when you are with them.

For each relationship, rate how stressful you find it to be around that person. A rating of 0 would mean that you didn't find it at all stressful and 10 would be absolutely as stressed as you can ever be. Don't forget that a relationship can cause you a great deal of stress even when it involves someone you care greatly about. Then think about how often you see the person, whether you want to see them more or less than you actually do, or whether this is about right.

Now you can use the box below to clarify where the stressful relationships lie.

Which are the least stressful relationships in my life?

Which are the most stressful relationships in my life?

Changing the frequency of contact

Once you have identified these relationships, the first thing to do is to think about how frequently you see the people involved. We are going to go on to talk about the *quality* of your relationships, but sometimes just simple changes in how often you see people might be possible. Are there people in your life whom you feel good around, but don't see much of? Remember that the presence of a close relationship had a very protective effect on whether women got depressed or not. And we know that social support in general makes people feel better. Could you do things that mean you see more of someone that you have a supportive relationship with?

On the other hand, looking at the relationships that cause you stress, are there people in this category that you can reduce the amount of contact with? Obviously if these are your partner or children that could be a bit tricky! But it may be that there are people who cause you stress that you don't need to see so much of.

Harry had a regular arrangement to play squash with a friend, and thought this was a good way to unwind at the end of the week. But when he completed his relationship stress worksheet he realized that he had rated this friend as very stressful. In fact, it turned out that when they went to the bar after the game his friend always wound him up about how much he was earning, and told Harry he should change his job. So he would go home feeling more stressed about his life, rather than less. Harry knew that the friend would not be likely to change this, and decided that he would reduce the frequency of the games to once a month to see if that would help.

It may also be that looking at the worksheet has made you realize that you are more isolated than you thought, and this too could lead to stress. One of us was once teaching a group of clinical psychology trainees who were due to submit an important piece of work very soon. We asked them to complete this worksheet, and at least half the class said that they hadn't realized that they were spending all their time working, had stopped doing any of their hobbies, and never saw anyone if it wasn't related to work. No wonder they were feeling stressed! Despite the time pressure, they all agreed that they would cope a lot better if they reintroduced some of the positive people in their lives.

Sometimes people become isolated when they are going through periods of change in their lives. Perhaps you have moved house and have not been able to make friends in your new neighbourhood. Perhaps you have changed job and no longer see your old colleagues. Or perhaps you have lost an important relationship and found it difficult to pick up friendships on your own. In each of these cases, it may be helpful to concentrate your efforts on re-establishing networks with people.

Mary and her family had moved to a new town and she and her husband had agreed that her priority would be to get their new house sorted out. But she realized after a while that she never saw anyone except her husband and children. Although she kept in good email contact with her friends, it was just not the same as meeting for coffee or drinks, and whenever anything went a bit wrong she would find herself fretting about it endlessly. She decided that she would make a definite effort to start finding out about local societies that she might join, even if it meant that the family would be in chaos a lot longer!

Of course, not all relationship problems can be helped by changing how often you see people! Often the most stressful relationships are with people whom you are closest to, and whom you want things to be better with.

Changing stressful relationships

So how can you make these relationships better? Much of what we will go on to talk about is most relevant to your closest relationship with your partner, but the ideas can also be applied to other relationships, with children or parents, or with important friends.

We believe that there are six areas to think about in any kind of relationship:

- Firstly, relationships are systems.
- Secondly, relationships in the present are influenced by relationships in the past.
- Thirdly, problems in relationships are often affected by hidden expectations that each partner has about how the other should behave.
- Fourthly, problems in relationships are affected by just the same kinds of irrational appraisals that affect other areas of our lives, and by the same kinds of cognitive errors.

- Fifthly, communicating well does not seem to come naturally to many of us, and we need to learn how to do it better.
- Sixthly, we need to increase constructive behavior – to relearn how to be nice.

1. Relationships are systems

Janie was really unhappy with her relationship with her partner Mike. He seemed increasingly cold and hostile towards her, and never wanted to spend any time with her. Janie was desperate to get things back on to a good footing, but could not tell Mike how sad she was feeling, and ended up shouting at him and accusing him of neglecting her instead. It is, of course, easy to see what effect this would have on Mike. It certainly did not make him feel warm and romantic and keen to spend time with her! But after a long heart-to-heart with a good friend Janie went home and put her arms round Mike and said she really loved him and was sad they were drifting apart. And Mike put his arms round her too and said he was sorry he'd been so detached but was very worried about the credit crunch and afraid he would lose his job and let the family down.

It is in this sense that the relationship is a 'system' – that is, the different components of the system (in this case, the people) do not operate in isolation from the other parts but continually react and respond according to what else is going on in the system. When Mike was cold and with-drawn Janie got upset and angry, and pushed Mike further away. When she was able to show warmth to him his behavior changed towards her.

USING THIS IDEA TO BRING ABOUT CHANGE

The implication of thinking about relationships in this way is that in order to make a change in the system you need to think about the part *you* play in it. It is very difficult to get other people to change while remaining the same your-self, because the system just doesn't work like that. So in order to bring about change, you need to think about what *you* can do differently, not what the other person *should* do differently to make things right for you. If you try to force change on another person they are more likely to resist it than anything else, causing escalating stress for themselves and for you as you both become frustrated and resentful. So remember: if you want change in a relationship system, you can only change yourself!

2. Relationships are affected by experiences from the past

In the chapter on thinking and stress we spoke about how your early experience can have a profound effect on how you feel and think about yourself. Your early experience also has a very profound effect on how you think about other people, and how you expect them to behave towards you. We know that patterns of behavior in relationships are

TABLE 11.2 EXERCISE: CHANGING YOUR RELATIONSHIP SYSTEM

Ask yourself:

- What do I want to change in our relationship?
- Am I expecting the other person to change rather than me?
- Is there anything that I can do to change the system?

Use the space on the next page to jot down your thoughts:

set up very early in people's lives, and that they often repeat these patterns in other relationships as they get older.

Marie was the only child of a single mother who had always feared that she would never have children. Marie was the apple of her mother's eye, and her mother almost

*always put Marie's feelings and needs before her own.
When she was older Marie started dating a man who was
fun and attractive, but she could not understand why he
would not always put her first. In the end she left him
for someone who wasn't nearly so much fun, but was
older and doted on her, just as her mother had done.*

*Tilly, on the other hand, had been badly treated by
her father and brothers, and made to feel like a second-
class citizen. When she finally left home and started
seeing people she kept falling for men who were similar
to her family – men who seemed caring at first, but
quickly began to put her down.*

These examples show ways in which the entire relationship recapitulates earlier relationships, but sometimes the
patterns can be much more subtle and hidden. It may be
that, without realizing it, you assume that someone you
are close to will automatically know how you feel without
you needing to tell them, much as a mother will often be
good at discerning the moods of her child. So you may get
very cross if your partner does not pick up on how you
feel. It may make you feel that they don't really love you
or aren't really interested in you.

These voices from the past can be very powerful indeed
and, without us realizing it, can often affect our relationships very detrimentally. And we can seem to get stuck in
these repeating cycles – partly because we feel safer with
what we know, even if it is horrible, and partly too because
we may have a kind of fantasy that it will be better this
time and we'll be able to put it right.

USING THESE IDEAS TO BRING ABOUT CHANGE

When you come up against a problem, ask yourself:

- Have I done this before, or been in the same kind of situation before?
- What is my earliest example or memory of being in this situation?
- Am I carrying something from my past over into my present?

If the answer to the first and last of these is yes, and particularly if your earliest example is of something that happened when you were very young, then it is likely that your current relationships are being affected by what happened to you in the past, and that you may be in the grip of a repetition of earlier problems.

If this is the case, then try to catch yourself when you start to get into this pattern, and take a deep breath. Ask yourself whether this is really the sensible way to react in the present. Try to use the techniques for identifying your thoughts (see pp. 135–9) to get to the bottom of how you are reacting, and then to use the challenging techniques (see pp. 139–46) to see if there is an alternative way of behaving that would fit the current situation better.

3. Expectations play a big part in relationships

Hugo and Allie had been married for two years. Hugo was a very keen and talented writer, and Allie a keen and talented painter. They got married on a tide of hope and optimism, that they would live as two young artists, devoted to their work and rejecting the conservative values of their families. But after two years things were wearing a bit thin. Neither of them had had much success in their artistic endeavours, and the reality of life in the garret was a lot less fun than the idea of it. At this point Hugo made a decision. He would give up the idea of becoming a writer and train to become a teacher instead – something that he would be very happy with. But Allie was furious, and berated him for this decision. Hugo could not understand her rage, and was in turn furious that she was trying to undermine his efforts to be realistic and helpful. Eventually things got so bad that they went to see a therapist, who quickly identified the expectations that they had brought to the marriage.

For Allie, the problem was not, as one might have thought, that Hugo was giving up the dream, but that he was giving it up for an occupation that would not provide them with a very substantial income for some considerable time. And behind this was the expectation that a husband should provide for his wife, and protect her from adversity. For Hugo, the problem was that Allie would not support his decision, and undervalued the sacrifice that he was making. For him, the expectation had been that a wife should always support her husband.

So much for rejecting conservative values. Both Allie and Hugo were shocked to learn that they were still carrying these values from their childhood fami-

lies. But once these expectations had been made clear to them, and they had been able to admit that they were still affected by them, then they were able to come to terms with the realities of their life in a much more positive way.

This example also shows the way in which Hugo and Allie's experience of past relationships continued to affect them in the present, even though they were unaware of them, and also that it was possible for them to examine and change them.

These examples of expectations concern quite general and all-encompassing ideas, but sometimes expectations can concern more specific areas of life. Problems with expectations affect not only close relationships but friendships too – for example, expectations such as 'a real friend would always put himself out for me if I needed him' or 'a real friend would always make time to listen' are fairly common examples. Other examples of expectations might be:

- You don't need to work at a good relationship.
- I shouldn't have to ask for what I need – my partner should know.
- My partner should know how I feel without me having to explain.
- My partner should think about me as well as him/herself.

When expectations are unrealistic, or demanding of the other partner, relationships can easily run into difficulties.

So it is important for both partners to be able to identify and questions their expectations, and to try to modify them if they are causing problems in the relationship.

IDENTIFYING EXPECTATIONS

Very often, the sign that an important expectation has been activated is that you will find yourself feeling very stressed and emotional. Sometimes you may feel that this strong emotion is justified, but at other times you may be surprised at just how bad you feel about what the other person is up to. When this happens, go somewhere quiet and ask yourself:

- What did the other person do that upset me?
- What did I think they ought to have done in this situation?
- What is the general expectation that underlies this?

For example, one day Allie came home with expensive new acrylic paints that they could not really afford, and Hugo got very cross. Allie was outraged that he should have objected. Her answers to these questions would be:

- 'Hugo objected to me buying something I need.'
- 'I think he should have been more supportive and agreed that this is a priority.'
- 'Ah – I am expecting him to provide for me again!'

QUESTIONING EXPECTATIONS

Once you have been able to identify the expectation that is causing the problem, then you can subject it to the same kind of questioning process that we have discussed before:

- Is this expectation reasonable?
- Is it fair?
- Is there an alternative way of thinking about what the other person should do?

For Allie, she needed to remind herself time and again that Hugo and she had entered into their marriage as equal partners, and that he was in fact doing his best to look after her. So she tried to get herself to think that maybe he was wrong to have got so angry with her but that actually he did have a right to object that she had spent their scarce cash on herself without asking him!

PUTTING THE ALTERNATIVE INTO PRACTICE

Once Allie had come to this thought, she and Hugo were able to agree that the next time she felt that she really needed something in order to get on with her art work, then she would ask him first, and would not expect him to carry on providing for her when they really couldn't afford it.

PROBLEMS WITH EXPECTATIONS

As with other kinds of stress-inducing thoughts, it can sometimes be difficult to identify exactly what the expectation behind your emotional state really is. In this case it may be helpful to keep a diary of the times when you are angry or upset in your relationship. It may be that looking back on this diary will help you to see themes emerging that you can identify as expectations.

Sometimes expectations are rigid and unreasonable, and are held with such conviction that one person truly believes that they have the right to impose this on the other partner. In this case it can be very difficult to move forward, and sometimes people might need to go for professional help.

Sometimes expectations are merely incompatible. We live in a multicultural society that embraces a wide variety of values and ideas about marriage and friendship. A belief that may be entirely reasonable in one culture can cause major problems in another.

Sometimes expectations trigger very drastic appraisals of what the other person is doing – you may believe that the fact that the person has such unreasonable expectations means that they are truly horrible, or that they want to hurt you on purpose. And of course it is not impossible that this is true. But sometimes people are unaware of how strongly held, or how unreasonable, their expectations are. In the world in which they grew up, these expectations may well have been normal and they have never questioned them. It may be that by bringing these expectations into the light it is possible for the other person to reflect on them, and for you to reach some kind of compromise that is manageable for you both.

4. Problems in relationships are often affected by 'faulty' appraisals of what the partner is doing

Mike and Janie had been living together for a couple of years when they started to have problems in their relationship. Mike was getting very stressed by his job, and finding it increasingly difficult to stop working when he got home. One evening he got home very late, pecked Janie on the cheek and went straight into his study to work. Janie thought, as many of us might: 'He really has gone off me; he just doesn't want to spend any time with me at all. Oh god, I bet he's started an affair.' She became very angry with Mike, and yelled accusations at him. Mike started to think: 'She is being completely unreasonable. I can't stand this on top of everything else.'

So just as our appraisals influence how stressful we find other things in our lives, so they also influence our relationships. Janie was showing very clearly negative appraisals of Mike's behavior, and cognitive errors too. She was generalizing from his behavior that evening, thinking that it meant he did not want to spend any time with her, and then catastrophizing about the reason for this, fearing that he might be having an affair. As with unrealistic appraisals in other areas, she did not bother to check it out with Mike in a calm way, but was carried by her emotion into behaving in ways that made things worse – until she started to realize what she was doing, as we have described earlier (see p. 182).

Another example shows how these appraisals can operate:

On another evening Mike walked into the kitchen, hoping that he and Janie could get on a bit better. As he walked in, Janie – who was cooking – thought: 'I bet he's going to ignore me and go straight into the study, I'm not going to risk him rejecting me again.' So she turned away from him and carried on with what she was doing. Mike thought: 'God, she can't even be bothered to say hello to me. She must still be furious. I'm not staying in here.' And he walked through into his study.

So both Janie and Mike had behaved in ways that were brought about by their appraisals of what the other was doing, and both made the situation worse.

In order to try to prevent these appraisals making relationships worse, it is extremely important for people to try to notice what they are doing, and to identify and question the appraisals. It may be helpful to use the worksheet below to start to tackle these appraisals, especially at the beginning.

One way of tackling the appraisal may be to try to check things out in a calm and reasonable way with your partner. Of course, doing things in a calm and reasonable way can be a lot more difficult than it may seem – which is why we need to think about communication skills.

TABLE 11.3 WORKSHEET: IDENTIFYING AND QUESTIONING YOUR APPRAISALS

Behavior
What my partner did that upset or annoyed me:

Identify appraisal
Why did he or she do that? What does it say about what they feel about me, or about what kind of person they are?

Question appraisal
Is this really a fair way of understanding what was going on? Am I bringing my past, or my own expectations into this? Can I think of another way of viewing things that would be more fair and reasonable?

5. Problems in relationships are often affected by faulty communication

In the 1980s Aaron T. Beck wrote a book about relationships which he called *Love is Never Enough*, and sadly it seems that this is true. No matter how much you love someone, it is still possible to get things completely wrong! We don't listen, we shout when we want to be heard, we almost wilfully misinterpret what is said to us because we're cross anyway... the list goes on. So we need to learn to communicate better to stop things going so wrong that we really cause harm to our relationships.

The essence of good communication is listening and talking clearly. Below are descriptions of some of the unhelpful and helpful ways of communication.

LISTENING TO PEOPLE – WHAT NOT TO DO

Firstly, do not switch off. This might easily happen if the other person is talking about something you don't really want to hear about, or think you have heard quite enough of. So you switch off and just let it wash over you. If the other person is talking about something that is important to them this is guaranteed to drive them mad and throw them into shouting or nagging.

Do not half-listen. This tends to happen if you are in the middle of something else – you may be cooking supper or watching the TV or reading. You hear what the other person is saying and could probably repeat it back if forced, but your attention isn't on it, and they know! So this gives a powerful message that you are not really interested in them and their concerns.

Do not interrupt. Even interrupting a casual conversation can send a message to the other person that they are boring and not worth listening to. When arguing, people are usually so concerned to get their view across that they start to interrupt and shout over each other, and are completely unwilling to listen to the other, or to give way on anything. This guarantees that the argument will end badly.

Do not mind-read. Mind-reading is a way of saying that we assume we know what the other person is thinking. It is very difficult to really listen to what someone is saying when you think that you know what they mean already.

Do not watch out for things just in order to prove your point. Often, particularly in arguments, people hear only what they want in what the other person is saying. They will latch on to things that confirm their view of what the other person means in order to be able to continue to blame them and show that they are right!

So, if you manage to stop yourself doing all of this, what should you do?

LISTENING TO PEOPLE — WHAT TO DO

Do decide that you are going to listen. There may be times when it just isn't possible because you need to get other things done or you need time to yourself. But if that is the case, don't let the other person rabbit on when you know you're not listening. Tell them that you need time for something else but that you'd love to sit down and chat or talk later.

Do stop thinking about yourself! In order to really listen to what someone else is saying you have to be able to put your own thoughts and feelings aside, so that you can try to understand how they are feeling. And if possible don't illustrate that you do understand by giving an anecdote from your own experience – let this be about the other person.

Do check that you have understood. If you are not sure what the other person means, then ask them to put it a different way, or to give a specific example. Don't let this degenerate into courtroom-style inquisition, as in 'Perhaps the witness could attempt to clarify this rather muddled point…', but sound as if you are genuinely interested in finding out. And if you are feeling really brave, then try reflecting back what you think they mean, as in 'So, is what you mean that you feel frightened when I'm late and don't let you know?'

Do wait to give an opinion until you're asked. The temptation is to step in and start to give your opinion on facts, feelings, general reasonableness of the case etc. Wait! The other person will be much more receptive to your views once they've got their own off their chest.

TALKING TO PEOPLE – WHAT NOT TO DO

Don't assume that the other person can read your mind and will know how you feel. Sometimes the other person is not thinking about you, and has no idea that you are fizzing with rage or on the brink of tears, or have been dying to get something off your chest for the last six weeks. If you want them to know something, you will have to tell them.

Similarly, don't assume that if they really loved you they would know that you are knackered and would love a cup of tea. You can ask!

Don't retreat by not talking at all. For example, if the other person says 'You seem upset, what's wrong?', don't answer 'Nothing'. The other person will correctly interpret this as 'there is a great deal wrong, but I'm furious and I'm not going to tell you' and will almost certainly respond by feeling enraged or cold shouldering you back. Not talking is also a very good way of ensuring that you can't address difficult issues, or of sticking your head in the sand and hoping the problem will blow over or solve itself. Mostly this doesn't happen, and the problems and issues fester until they explode.

On the other hand, don't talk too much. Sometimes one partner will talk about everything on their mind, feeling like they're getting everything off their chest, and not allow the other person to take part in the conversation or notice the effect that this might be having on them.

Don't make an issue out of the wrong thing. Sometimes we can blow up about something small – say your partner or friend forgets to buy the milk – when really the whole issue for you is that they never pay bills or contribute to any household expenses. The issues need to be addressed properly.

Don't nag. Do not go on and on about something – nagging is an absolutely sure sign that you are not communicating effectively. And nagging is almost always veiled criticism about something that your partner is doing wrong, or failing to do at all. They won't listen. No matter how frustrating it is to realize that they're not taking any notice of you, you will not improve things by saying it repeatedly in ever more irritated tones.

Don't say one thing and communicate another by the way that you say it. We like to think of this as the 'Darling' example. See for example the following, said through teeth gritted so hard that you might break your jaw: 'Darling, why didn't you take your rugby boots *off* before you walked through the house?' This obviously means: 'Look, you stupid idiot, I've just cleaned the carpets and now you've trampled mud into every last square inch of them.' You didn't really mean 'Darling' did you? Don't do it. It will only annoy them.

TALKING TO PEOPLE – WHAT TO TRY

Firstly, do make sure that you know how you really feel. If you are trying to explain something to your partner it will be much easier if you are clear about what it is. If the problem is that you are confused and actually you can't quite pin down what the matter is, then be explicit about this, and maybe your partner can help you work it out.

If you are trying to talk about something important to you, it might be helpful to practise it on your own before-hand. Talk to yourself in the mirror and see how you would feel if someone said that to you. Are you talking in a way that makes it possible for the other person to listen to you, or are you saying things that will make them feel defensive and cross?

Talk in a way that avoids blaming, criticizing and gener-alizing. If you are washing up and are frustrated because no one is helping, it won't be productive to say: 'You are so lazy, you never help with anything.' Would you get up and help in those circumstances, or would you blow up and storm out of the room? Let them know how you feel instead – they can't argue with that. Try saying something like: 'I'm really tired and I want to get this finished quickly. Please could you come and give me a hand?'

TIMING

We know that anger, and other strong emotions, makes it very difficult for people to listen and communicate clearly. The angrier you are, the more you want to prove that you are right and the other person is wrong, the more you want to hurt and blame them – and the less able you are to really listen to the other person and give them a fair chance. Once relationships start to go wrong it can become very difficult to talk about anything without falling immediately into patterns that just perpetuate difficulties.

So if you decide that you would like to try communicating in a different way, do not try to do it when one or both of you is already angry, or you simply won't be able to. Try to practise talking in this way when you are both calm, and the topic is relatively unemotional. If you find that it's helpful, and that you can listen and talk a bit better, then you can start to talk about more difficult areas and with more heated emotion.

And remember, a big part of a good relationship is the willingness to accept your partner's opinions and feelings when these are different from your own, realizing that this doesn't mean that they don't love you, and practising understanding and tolerance.

6. Being nice to each other

At the beginning of relationships people are naturally on their best behavior. You want to please the other person and make them happy. You are keen to win their approval and make them like you. So you say nice things to them, and do nice things for them. But as time goes on, you start to take the good things about your partner for granted, and get increasingly irritated by the bad. They snore. They hang their wet tights in the shower. And you take it more and more for granted that they like you. So you stop saying and doing things to please them, and they stop doing them to please you. This means that the amount of reward that you get from the relationship gets smaller and smaller, and the amount of punishment – blame and criticism – gets bigger. So it is very important to try to redress this.

In the section above we showed how to avoid some of the punishing things about relationships – particularly the blame and criticism embedded in poor communication. The other side of the coin is to start to be nice. In fact, research on good relationships shows that they have a balance of about 5:1 of pleasant to unpleasant things! That is, for every unpleasant thing that one partner might do in a relationship, they do five nice ones. What would your ratio be?

So the next step is to reintroduce nice things into your relationship. Firstly, think of little things you can do. Perhaps you always used to make proper coffee in the morning while the other person was in the shower, but now can't be bothered. Perhaps you know there's a film they'd love to go to see, and although it's not entirely your cup of tea you could buy tickets. Make a list of all the things that you used to do but don't any more, or that you think your partner would like, and see if you can reintroduce some of these.

If both of you are doing this together, then you could sit down and make lists of what you could each do. These should be positive lists – 'I'd love it if you put the towels in the washing machine after football' – rather than 'I wish you wouldn't always leave the filthy towels in the bathroom'. It may be referring to the same end point but the process of getting there will make a massive difference. Remember the balance – five to one!

Stress and relationships revisited

At the beginning of this chapter we described the vicious cycle by which stress and relationships can make each other worse, regardless of which starts first. For the rest of the chapter we have spoken about relationships themselves, and how you can understand and tackle problems that arise. But there is also the other side of the cycle too – dealing with stress that arises in other areas of your life should have a positive impact on how your relationship and friendships are going, which should in turn reduce your stress and improve your mood. And just being aware of the cycle may have a positive impact. So remember: when you get home after a long and vile day at work and three hours stuck in traffic, sit for a moment in the car, take a deep breath, and think of the vicious cycle. Remember that whatever is behind the door, it is your home and there are things in it which you love and don't want to damage. Go in with a good heart, and leave the stress in the car!

CHAPTER SUMMARY

- There is a vicious cycle between stress and the quality of relationships that means that when there are problems in one of them, the other will get worse too.
- Sometimes it is not obvious which relationships in your life are actually the most stressful, and using the relationship stress worksheet to analyse this may help.
- Changing the frequency of contact with people may be a good starting-point to reduce stress or increase support.
- There are six aspects of relationships which we believe are important:
  - Firstly, relationships are systems.
  - Secondly, relationships in the present are influenced by relationships in the past.
  - Thirdly, problems in relationships are often affected by hidden expectations that each partner has about how the other should behave.
  - Fourthly, problems in relationships are affected by just the same kinds of irrational appraisals that affect other areas of our lives, and by the same kinds of cognitive errors.
  - Fifthly, communicating well does not seem to come naturally to many of us, and we need to learn how to do it better.
  - Sixthly, we need to increase constructive behavior – to relearn how to be nice.

12

Stress at work

Work-related stress is like a time bomb waiting to go off and if not addressed will lead to stress-related problems. According to a leading psychologist, Professor Cary Cooper, stress in the workplace is on the increase and studies have shown that over the past ten years every job has become more stressful. Some of the most stressful occupations are those in the public sector that include police, social work, teaching and heath service jobs. Among the least stressful occupations are those in the arts, entertainment and charity work. It might not be realistic or possible to jump ship and change your career or current working situation but changing how you manage your stress reaction at work might help. In this chapter you will be introduced to the factors that contribute to stress in the workplace and will learn how to recognize when stress at work is becoming a problem for you. We will discuss how cognitive therapy approaches can help and will suggest strategies to help you cope more effectively. These strategies include improving your communication, assertiveness and managing your time at work.

What makes work stressful?

There seems to have been an increase in work stress over the last decade or so, and there are a number of factors that might explain the reasons why. There is much more of an expectation that employees will work very long hours, and be available almost twenty-four hours a day. Developments in technology have fed into this culture since the workplace is no longer confined to the office; we carry our portable office with us – laptops, Wi-Fi, mobile phones – and can set up anywhere, whether it be the train, aeroplane, hotel room or of course home. To arrive at work late or to leave early is frowned upon by colleagues and employers. Some people believe that working extra hours will increase their job prospects and chance of promotion, so working more than other colleagues can become competitive. According to a survey conducted by trade unions, the average person works seven hours a week overtime, and most do not get paid for it. Jobs for most people are no longer for life and are generally less secure with a short-term contract culture and the threat of organizational 'downsizing'. However, the facts suggest that working long hours is not good for your health. In the short term you might get more work done, but in the long term if you work more than forty hours a week you will get sick!

Working long hours affects the work–life balance; feeling overtired and having a reduced amount of time to dedicate to relationships and leisure activities increases levels of stress. Every job has different pressures and comes with responsibilities; in the right amount, pressure at work can increase motivation and bring a healthy degree of excitement in response to new but reasonable demands. Professor Cooper suggests that the most stressful of jobs carry some common characteristics. These characteristics include situations in which there is a significant amount of change within the organization; when employees are treated as 'political foot-balls', such as in the health care and teaching professions; when there is downsizing in organizations, with threats of redundancy and amalgamation of two positions into one; and when new technology is introduced.

Two further key factors contribute greatly to work-related stress. Firstly, there is strong evidence that when people feel that they have no control or autonomy in their job they become much more stressed. This is particularly so in jobs where the individual carries significant responsibility, but does not have the power or control to balance this. And secondly, when people feel unsupported by their manager or other senior colleagues stress increases greatly.

Both the employee and employer have a responsibility to manage stress in the workplace and there are guidelines available for employers on how to best reduce and manage stress at work. It is important to realize that stress at work is not just your problem, and that sometimes there may be limited amounts that you can do because the work environment is not great. Organizations are difficult. There is increasing recognition that work stress is a significant public health issue, and legislation to protect workers is increasing, but it can't solve everything. Be aware that if you are experiencing work stress it does not mean that this is just because you can't manage. So this chapter is about helping to reduce and cope with stress in situations that it may be difficult to change. Powerlessness and lack of support at work need to be tackled at an organizational level. Although there may be a limited amount that you can do about these issues, the sections on communication and on assertiveness may help to improve conditions within some difficult situations.

Effects of stress at work

Absenteeism or presentism?

Work-related sickness caused by stress is often a hidden problem in the workplace; employees are frequently afraid to take time off work when ill in fear of adverse consequences and will often engage in a behavior called 'presentism'. Presentism involves being physically present at work, showing your face, yet thoroughly demotivated and, in reality, unproductive. As absenteeism decreases, presentism increases, with an impact both on the mental health of the employee and the organization's performance.

Work stress and health

In a study that examined stress and health at work there were key links between high self-reported levels of stress and adverse working conditions. Those who reported high levels of stress also reported having a range of health-related problems including anxiety, depression and physical ailments.

Who gets stressed at work?

Melanie, a thirty-nine-year-old married social worker in community mental health, felt undervalued by her boss, who was critical and micro-managed her work in such a way that she felt controlled. She had taken several short periods of time off sick. She felt so rundown and stressed with numerous changes at work and found that she was susceptible to picking up one virus after another. Her boss reprimanded her for taking time off sick and made it clear that her sickness record had to improve if she were to be considered for a senior position in the future. She felt fearful of losing her job, especially given talk about redundancy, and dragged herself into work through hell or high water. She quietly resented working in these conditions. Though she was careful to be seen to do her job, whenever possible she would cut corners and would waste time chatting to colleagues in the corridor. At other times she sat in her office worrying about the future, ruminating about the unfairness of her current situation and wishing that something awful would happen to her manager. Melanie had reacted quite badly to the way her manager handled the situation and was unsupported. If the situation were not addressed, she was clearly heading for further health problems.

Lewis, a twenty-three-year-old accounts administrator, worked for the county council and had been on a temporary contract for just over a year. He had approached his boss on a number of occasions and asked if the position could be made permanent and was told that she would look into it. As a temporary employee he could be dismissed without notice, was paid on an hourly rate and had no benefits such as sick pay or a pension, neither was he allowed time for training and professional development. He was doing the work of two people and working flat out and efficiently in hope of a good reference, but when he said that he was struggling he was criticized for having poor organizational skills. He resented some of his colleagues who were permanent employees: they would take extended lunch breaks, surf the Internet and often finish work early on a Friday. Every morning he hated going to work and wanted to give up his job, but was worried that he might not get another straight away and needed the money. His home life suffered because he was grumpy and bad-tempered with his flatmates and would complain incessantly about his situation. He also stopped caring for himself and would comfort eat junk food and comfort shop, spending his hard-earned cash on DVDs and games.

We immediately think of the stereotype of the stressed-out manager, but contrary to popular belief stress-related illness is lower in top-ranking professionals and managers and highest in 'chalk face' workers and junior managers. It is also easy to assume that men and women in their twenties are less likely to experience health problems related to stress at work because they have only known the current working culture and have not had to adapt to changing patterns of working practice, but studies suggest that young adults are no more resilient when it comes to stress than their older counterparts.

From a cognitive therapy perspective, work-related stress is in part explained by how the person appraises or perceives the work situation. However, the interaction between the person and the environment needs to be considered.

Gender and work-related stress

In contrast to women, men tend to see work as more of a source of stress than other areas of life. Often that stress can be severe. Men generally are reluctant to seek help for a stress-related problem because they are concerned about being seen as 'weak'. Some of the highest levels of stress in men are seen in the banking, financial and legal professions. A study suggested that one in three men turn to alcohol to try to switch off from work. Also as a consequence of work-related stress, men also tend to have aggressive outbursts and report a loss of interest.

Signs of work-related stress

To see whether work-related stress is a problem for you, go through the list below and see how many of these items resonate with your own:

- Are you feeling dissatisfied with your job?
- Are you being asked to take on more and more work?
- Do you feel that what you do is not always valued by others?
- Do you feel that you have no control over important aspects of your work?
- Do you need to work long hours to keep up?
- Do you get irritable and angry with colleagues?
- Are you regularly working more than forty hours a week?
- Do you feel that you are being treated unjustly?

- Has work disrupted your home life?
- Has working too hard stopped you from doing leisure activities?
- Do you feel unsupported by your colleagues and your organization?
- Have you had conflicts with colleagues that are unresolved?
- Would you leave your job if you had the opportunity?
- Do you start to feel unhappy on Sunday afternoons thinking about the week ahead?

If you think that work-related stress is a problem for you it might be helpful to keep a diary of your stressful automatic thoughts (SATs) and behavior to pinpoint the problem areas for you (for more on SATs, see pp. 135–9). An example of Lewis's diary is displayed below:

TABLE 12.2 LEWIS'S SATS DIARY

Date and time	Situation	Emotion (0–100)	SATs	Behavior
Monday 3 March, 3 p.m.	Called in to the big boss's office because I was behind with my work and told it was unacceptable	Shock 80% Disbelief 100% Disgust 50% Frustration 90%	Hypocritical idiot! I can't take his opinion seriously. I've done my best but my best is not viewed as good enough. It's an impossible situation. Even if I try	Cried. Started to look for other jobs. Stopped chatting to the boss casually.

Date and time	Situation	Emotion (0–100)	SATs	Behavior
	and had to improve. I was overloaded with work and working flat out.	Despair 90%	harder it won't make a difference because there is still too much work to do. It doesn't matter what I do, I'm probably going to be fired. There goes my reference. I've wasted an entire year for nothing.	Talked to a friend.
Wednesday 5 March, 1.30 p.m.	Told off and having to make up the time for being five minutes late back. Then my boss swans in thirty minutes late with my colleague, having taken an hour and a half. They eat lunch in front of me.	Frustration 60% Anger 40% Resentment 60%	Are you going to make up that time like I have to? She never does any work when she's here anyway. It's unfair: Ann, Sarah and I do all the work and don't get any thanks for it. Silva is useless as a worker, as a manager. I wish someone above Silva would notice her behavior. I want to be spiteful — an eye for an eye.	Decided to stop and eat at the same time as them to wind them up because they can't complain given their behavior. Brooded. Ate junk food on the way home.

Using a SATs diary, over the next week keep a record of situations that triggered your SATs, your emotions and what you did to cope. Again, there is an additional blank worksheet in the back of this book.

TABLE 12.2 BLANK SATS DIARY				
Date and time	Situation	Emotion (0–100)	SATs	Behavior

Having identified your work-related SATs and the problematic behavior that might result, go back to Chapters 9 and 10 to remind yourself of the techniques for challenging thoughts and working with stress-related behaviors. The techniques in Chapter 14 may help too.

Problems with communication and stress at work

One of the ways that people have found they can improve their stress at work is by thinking about their communication skills. Often problems occur as a result of communication going wrong rather than because of more fundamental difficulties. How often have you found yourself in a work situation, horns locked with a colleague because you cannot find a way to reconcile your differences, or in conflict with others because you've spoken out of turn and acted in a critical or aggressive manner? Or have you found that you don't say anything but quietly seethe with resentment? Most of us do not think about our communication style, and often it goes well. When you are with someone who is attentive, a good listener, validating of your concerns as you are towards them, then communication is easy. But, how do you communicate when someone is angry or critical towards you, and you feel hurt and vulnerable? How well do you manage when you are angry and having a disagreement with someone else? These challenging situations put our communication skills to the test. If communication breaks down and difficult situations are not resolved effectively, they tend to escalate and can lead to a negative working environment and a great deal of stress. Although communication has many forms, for the purpose of this chapter we will focus on verbal communication. What are the signs of poor communication habits at work? See the list overleaf.

If you recognize some of the patterns, then it may be that making changes in your communication could make a big difference to how you relate to others, and reduce your levels of stress.

Good communication skills

Here are five core communication skills that will help reduce your levels of stress:

Listening skills

You might think good listening skills are easy, but in fact this is one of the hardest skills to learn. Before we go any

THE SIGNS OF COMMUNICATION PROBLEMS AT WORK

If you see a problem in somebody's work, do you tend to criticize them rather than explain?

Do you tend to put other people down and be critical of what they do?

Do you feel as if you are a victim because you don't dare explain what you need?

Do you say yes to things and then wish you hadn't?

When there's a problem, do you think there's no point saying anything because no one will listen?

Do you feel that you should be treated in a better way but refuse to ask directly for what you want?

Do you deny what you are feeling – perhaps angry, hurt, sad, green-eyed – yet your emotions are seeping out and obvious to those around you at work?

Does your non-verbal behavior communicate passive aggression – for example, giving others the silent treatment or cold shoulder, making noise such as closing your desk drawer loudly or slamming down the phone – without really describing what the problem is for you?

Do you take the blame for things and put yourself down rather than try to defend yourself?

Do you immediately leap in and try to solve other people's problems while not really listening to their concerns or acknowledging how they might be feeling?

Do you respond badly to criticism and react by becoming critical of others and not acknowledging their concerns?

Do you avoid disagreement or conflict at all costs?

Do you find it difficult to express your point of view just in case you're criticized?

When there's a problem at work, do you tend to overreact and become overly emotional, either in floods of tears or fuming with anger? Are your emotions overwhelming or full on, and everyone can see exactly how you are feeling?

further you might wish to try the following exercise. You need to find a friend or a colleague who is willing to do the exercise with you. You both need to think of a current concern that is on your mind (a genuine concern and not a made-up one). One of you is the listener and the other the speaker. As a listener you just need to listen without interrupting, asking questions or making comments – just look and listen while your friend or colleague talks for six minutes. Once you've done this, swap roles and repeat the exercise. Now discuss what it felt like for you to listen and be listened to. How often do you actually listen without being distracted by your thoughts or butting in with a comment before the other person has finished speaking? Practise listening and remember it's a skill.

Open questions

When someone is talking to you, you might not always understand what they mean. Before jumping to conclusions or assuming you know what the other person is thinking, check it out. It's important to be in tune with each other and have a shared understanding of the issue being discussed. Open questions allow your colleague to elaborate on what they are saying to achieve clarity and understanding. For example, your colleague might say: 'What do you feel you need in order to do your job? What sort of help would make a difference?' You might reply: 'I'm not sure I fully understand. Could you explain that again?' Your colleague can then clarify: 'What areas of your work do you think can be improved?' And so on.

Empathy and emotional validation

Empathy in simple terms is about being able to put yourself in the other person's shoes and to acknowledge their concerns: in other words, tuning in to their mindset. To show your colleague that you have got the point, repeat out loud what they have said. For example, if your colleague says, 'This job is going really badly, there's no real future for me in marketing', you might repeat back, 'There's no real future?' You might also use the open question technique to check that you've got it right. Some examples of open questions are: 'it sounds like…', 'let me see if I've got this right…', 'I just want to make sure I fully understand what you're saying.' For emotional validation or emotional empathy, this involves picking up on what someone might be feeling and naming the feeling; this will help your colleague to feel understood. For example, if a colleague says, 'I've been rushing about all day at work and haven't had a chance to take a break', you might respond by saying, 'You must feel exhausted.' Emotional validation also involves feeding back observations in a positive way, for example: 'I've noticed that you put a lot of thought into that report, you've really grasped the key issues' or: 'That meeting was really tough! I thought you handled it really well, especially when the accountant was critical about the finances.'

Summarizing

This involves pulling together the threads of the communication and providing a brief summary, then checking out that your colleague has the same understanding. For example: 'Just let me see if I have got this right. Over the last few months you have been feeling under a lot of pressure at work. Understandably that has been difficult for you given that you are trying to manage this job as well as childcare. Having given this a lot of thought, what you are suggesting is that you would like to reduce your hours by eight a week, and to think about flexible working hours. Is that correct? Is there anything I've missed?' Summarizing demonstrates that you are listening, trying to understand the situation while being emotionally validating.

Being clear about what you want to say

In order to communicate what you want clearly, you need to be clear about this yourself. If you are not quite sure what you want, or what you think about something, then you are unlikely to communicate well.

Be aware of negative thoughts that might interfere with what you want to communicate. If half your mind is full of fearful thoughts about how the other person is likely to react then it will not be easy to explain your point of view. Try to put these thoughts out of your mind and concentrate on the task. In Chapter 14 we will talk more about how to do this (see pp. 265–77).

If you are in the middle of a debate and are not quite sure of your ground, stop and think before saying anything. Don't be drawn into saying things that you will later regret. Try saying 'Give me a minute, I want to think about that' or if you disagree try just saying 'I don't accept that'.

Practise beforehand if you know it's going to be difficult. Say what you feel or think without attacking the other person's position. Just reiterate your own views, and don't get personal. Try not to ramble.

Using the skills: Positive or negative challenging

Having established five key communication skills, let's look at ways to use these skills when faced with challenging situations.

We want you to imagine for a moment that you notice that a junior colleague whom you manage always arrives fifteen minutes late, takes an extended lunch break and is the first to leave the office. Obviously this needs to be addressed, but what is the best way to challenge the situation? Below are two different responses; which do you think is more likely to produce positive change?

> *I've noticed that for the last two weeks you have been late into work, late back from lunch and go home early and frankly this is unacceptable. You are contracted to work forty hours a week and will either have to pay back the time or I will have to deduct the hours of missed work from your salary.*

> *I've noticed over the last two weeks that you have been less punctual than usual, which seems slightly out of character and I was wondering what was going on? ... It sounds like you've been having a difficult time lately and I'm sorry to hear that. In terms of the problem with your time-keeping, what changes do you think you could make?*

Both responses to the situation were challenging but in slightly different ways; the second response (*positive challenging*) drew upon the key communication skills that we discussed earlier, whereas in the first response (*negative challenging*) the manager handled the situation in a controlling way. As we know, when people feel they have little control and low autonomy at work, they are likely to get stressed. Positive and negative challenging are not only used when there is a problem in the workplace; they are often used when there is a difference of opinion. The consequences of negative challenging are that often people's feelings are hurt and you can become alienated from your colleagues. If we were to unpick the process of positive challenging, these are the steps:

Listen to your work colleague and acknowledge that you have heard them.

Ask questions if necessary to clarify the situation.

Respect their opinion even if you don't agree with them – everyone is entitled to have a view. It's unusual for someone to be completely wrong.

Before putting across your view, find something positive to say about the other person's contribution, for example: 'That's an interesting take on the situation. Though I don't fully share that view, I was wondering if we might consider . . .'; 'Your suggestion to do X is spot on but I think your other ideas need to be developed further before deciding on taking any action; I have an idea that might help take that forward . . .'

Watch out for 'buts' and 'yes, buts'. A positive statement followed by a 'but' becomes a criticism, for example: 'You've done a great job with writing the operational policy but you really need to be focusing on preparing for the meeting with the stakeholders.' Using 'but's in your verbal communication serves to reduce motivation because of the implicit criticism. Practise using more 'ands' instead.

Assertiveness, aggression and placatory submission

Assertiveness is an important communication skill and involves expressing what you need, what you would like to happen, and your feelings. In doing so you should leave a situation without having hurt other people's feelings or feeling hurt yourself. Assertiveness is absolutely not the same as aggression. Aggression may be overt, with people actively being rude, critical or threatening, but may also be passive, where people just make sure that they block your ideas and make life unpleasant without ever admitting that they are doing so. Both have the same impact: people feel frightened, attacked and bullied. And if you are being passive-aggressive, it means that your views will not be heard and often you will not get what you want. Everyone can see your anger oozing out as you pout, sulk or even cry. You are communicating: 'It's not fair; take care of me: I'm helpless.' When your colleagues give you opportunities to talk about the problem you will either say there is nothing wrong or complain of some physical symptom such as a headache. This behavior can be very frustrating for colleagues and might leave them feeling controlled and manipulated by you. Rather than taking care of you, they are likely to give you a wide berth.

Some people are fearful of speaking up because they confuse assertiveness with being aggressive and arrogant. They worry that if they were to behave in that way people would be rejecting towards them. So instead they adopt a position of being submissive and become caught in a trap of placating others. We're sure you can think of colleagues who always offer to make refreshments, or those who are overly attentive to everyone else's needs even if this means going out of their way to help others. The bottom line is they can't say 'no' to demands from others and ultimately end up feeling stressed.

Learning to become assertive in the workplace will help reduce your stress levels. As a human being you have a right to say 'no', to make your own decisions, to be able to change your mind and to express your opinions and feelings.

Steps to becoming assertive in the workplace

- Identify how you feel about the situation.
- Use 'I' statements.
- Be direct; state things clearly. Here are some assertive statements: 'Let me get this clear . . . in other words you . . . so you felt that . . . what I hear you saying . . . so you believe that . . . am I hearing you correctly?' These statements are precise, prevent manipulation and convey self-confidence and conviction.
- Give the bottom line first instead of rambling.
- If your point is not being heard use the 'broken record' technique that involves saying the same thing in different ways.

- Don't assume you know what the other person is thinking.
- Avoid sarcasm, labelling and 'why's.
- Ask for feedback.
- Practise saying 'no'.

If you are asked to do something which is more than you can manage, or not within the terms of your job, or if you just have too much on to fit something else in, then it is very important that you communicate this clearly, and don't agree to things that you just can't manage. Here's how to do it:

- Firstly, remember that no matter whom you are talking to, you have the right to be in control of your life and your decisions. If the request is unreasonable you have the *right* to say 'no'.
- Secondly, explain clearly what the problem is. Say that you would like to be able to do it, but don't have the time/the skills etc. Be as clear as you can about the reasons.
- Thirdly, think of the broken record technique. No matter how long people go on at you for, think of yourself as a broken record (assuming you are old enough to remember records!) and just keep sticking to your point. Once you have explained, you don't have to elaborate. If the other person won't stop, then try saying: 'I'm sorry, but I have explained my decision and I need to stick to it.'

- Fourthly, try rehearsing different ways of saying no: 'I'm afraid not . . . that won't be possible . . . I'm not able to help on this occasion . . . I won't be able to make that . . . that's not going to be possible.'

Day-to-day coping strategies

No matter how well or badly work is going, there are things that you can do to release stress on a day-to-day basis.

Firstly, remember to take breaks. This sounds incredibly obvious, but many people completely ignore it. Do take your lunch break – don't eat with your sandwiches in one hand and the computer mouse in the other. Do get up and make yourself a cup of tea. And when you get up, stretch, walk around, look out of the window.

Secondly, think about whether you could organize a 'stress-busting' activity with colleagues. Do you have a room big enough to do yoga in? Could you get someone in one lunchtime a week to hold classes? Can you get together and think about what else you could do jointly that would help?

Thirdly, are there reminders of nice things in your life that you can have around, preferably unobtrusively, at work? Some people use screen savers or photos of their children or home. Of course, if you use photos then you need to be aware of the impact this might have on other people coming into your office. But, if you can, carry something with you; when times get tough, it'll help you remember that you have another life and may help you to manage.

Fourthly, are there stress gadgets that you can carry with

you? Try experimenting with stressballs or other stress toys.

Fifthly, think about the space that you occupy at work. Do you have your own desk? Your own room if you're lucky? How messy is it? It does seem that people find it stressful to work in cluttered spaces. Can you declutter?

Unhelpful attitudes

Finally, think about your own attitudes to work. Because sometimes, no matter how difficult the situation is, you can bring things with you that are likely to make it worse. Look at the questions below, and see if they could be true of you:

- Are you convinced that you are always right and the other person is wrong?
- When you have actually done something wrong, do you refuse to own up or show any imperfection?
- Do you find it difficult to own up to problems and tend to blame others?
- Do you try to take over and make everything all right for others, rescuing the situation and taking full responsibility?

If any of these are true for you then it may be very helpful to think about why you feel like this, and what you can do. Try using the cognitive therapy techniques of challenging thinking to help (see pp. 139–46).

Travel stress

So far we have been talking about the problems that can occur at work that make you stressed. But there is of course another aspect to our working lives which can cause immense stress. We have to get there! Some research has found that a long commute is one of the most important factors in reducing overall life satisfaction. People who move to better jobs at the cost of increased travel time found that they got used to the positive aspects involved – more money or more status – but found the travelling increasingly stressful over time. And travel often meets one of the most important criteria associated with stress – conditions seem completely out of our control, and we feel helpless and trapped. But since the reality is that many of us do need to commute, we can try to see if there is anything that we could do to make it more bearable.

Roads

Mickey was driving from home to an evening meeting in a neighbouring town which she really did not want to go to. Midway to the next town she found herself joining a queue of traffic which stretched as far as the eye could see, and was more or less completely stationary. For the first hour of the wait Mickey was absolutely spitting with rage at the stupidity of her life, the world, fate, her colleagues for insisting she go to the meeting, stupid careless drivers, incompetent emergency services, irresponsible police for not preventing traffic getting on to the road – and so forth. But after about an hour she realized that at the front of the queue was an accident in which it was very likely that somebody had been seriously hurt, if not killed. She also realized that if she were involved in the accident she would give anything to be one of the people in the stationary queue. As soon as she thought that she started to think that although this was a complete pain, it was not the worst thing in the world. And then she thought that since she was stuck she might as well try to work out how to tune her car radio. She also decided that she would keep an emergency pack in her car with books, drinks and snacks for any time it might happen again. With all of this going through her mind she was able to wait much more patiently, and to feel much less stressed.

But it is not always so easy. Many people spend considerable amounts of time commuting to and from work, and sitting in traffic jams bumper to bumper can never be a good experience. And as you sit there making no progress you realize that yes, you are going to be late for the meeting, you're not going to have time to shower before going out on that date, you are going to miss the children's bathtime – and so it goes on. Then you need to move into the inside lane to turn off and some aggressive idiot blares his horn at you, gestures obscenely and keeps level with you, refusing to give way. And all of this makes you feel apoplectic with impotent rage, with your body fired up and your heart pounding, your muscles tense, your head bursting . . .

So what can we do to try and prevent this? Firstly, there

are a number of practical things – probably pretty obvious but still worth repeating. Can you negotiate the hours you work with your employer so that you can travel at slightly less busy times? Can you work at home at all?

But assuming that you have already thought of this, what else could be done? Firstly, be realistic about how long the journey takes, and allow for this. The temptation is always to underestimate how long the journey will take, and leave later than you really ought to. But if you know that there is always a half-hour traffic jam when you get to the edge of town, then there is no point hoping that it won't be so bad today. It will be much easier to accept if you are realistic about it.

Secondly, is there anything that you can do in the car while the traffic is moving slowly? CDs of stories or language learning can be much easier to hear in slow-moving traffic than when you are driving faster. Could this half an hour be when you get a chance to really hear what the pronunciation of that Spanish phrase is? Could this be when you catch the more subtle parts of the novel you've been listening to, not just the rough story line?

Thirdly, can you work out any physical exercise that you could do in the car when stationary? Isometric exercises which don't involve much movement can be really useful here. Try doing stomach exercises: pull your stomach muscles in and imagine you are trying to touch your spine with your belly button. Hold for ten seconds, then release. Do ten repetitions. Or put your hands palm to palm in front of you (the car really does need to be stationary at this point!) and press as hard as you can. Again, hold for ten seconds and repeat ten times. At least you are doing something with your body! You could also run through some of the tense and release cycles in the relaxation exercises in Chapter 15.

Fourthly, try putting on a CD with music which you really like and sing as loudly as you can – singing is pretty good exercise, and seems to be pretty good for stress too. So what if other people can hear you? You are never going to see them again!

Fifthly, at the end of Chapter 15 we talk about mindfulness meditation. Some people have found that at times of stress when there is not much you can do, then switching into mindfulness mode can be very calming. Become aware of tension in your body. Are your hands wrapped tightly around the steering wheel? Are your shoulders raised, stomach tight? What does this feel like? And does it help you to get to where you are going more quickly? What can you do about it? Remember that you have more control over these things than you might think.

Sixthly, and most importantly, when you are in the queue and someone else is behaving like an idiot, don't react. Take a deep breath and remember that there are a lot of stupid idiots in the world, and you are *not* one. Do not stoop to that level by entering into a competition or battle (we're thinking of young men who end up racing each other on the motorway – my car is more powerful than your car . . . .). Don't take someone else's rage personally or to heart; they don't even know you so it's not worth getting upset. And if someone needs to move in front of you, try letting them in and see how you feel. Alternatively, if someone is driving close to the back of your car, flashing their lights while in the fast lane, pull over into the slow lane and let them pass: this is the safe option. You may also generate a very small amount of goodness in the world by doing this, and hopefully the person you have helped will extend this by being considerate to the next person – and so it goes.

Trains

Unless you are incredibly rich and get driven to your private airport in your lovely limousine in time to hop lightly on to your private jet – in which case someone is probably being paid to be stressed for you – then transport is always likely to have its down sides. But there is an added problem with public transport. One reason why public transport may have declined in use is that we are all now much more used to having our personal space, and at least cars preserve this (hence we're so unwilling to get out of them). You only have to see people sit down and place bags on the seat next to them to realize how important the concept of personal space is – something that pretty much disappears in rush-hour traffic.

Ben lives in a provincial town. His wife and family are very happy there, and he doesn't want to move. But he works in London, and has to commute for about two hours each way to work. Friends expect that he will find this extremely stressful, but Ben says that no, it's fine. He has found ways not to be stressed about it, and to discover positive aspects to the experience. Let's look at how he has done this – and how it might help you.

Firstly, do you have any choice about your route? Ben experimented with different combinations of travel. There is no direct train to London from his market town, so he has to drive some distance. He chose to drive a bit further and to get a slower train because parking is easier and cheaper at the station he has chosen, and there is no traffic getting to and from it. The faster train goes from a much busier town with notorious traffic problems, and using that station practically doubles his overall journey time. So it may be possible to experiment with different combinations and times of travel to find something that avoids aspects of the journey you dislike most.

Can you network? If you get the same train at the same time, do you start to recognize other people? Can you find people whom you would like to talk to, or feel companionable around? Ben said that he has a group of travelling companions who sit and read the paper together, or chat about work. If he doesn't feel like chatting, he'll go and sit in the corner with his paper. His father, who also commuted, used to run language lessons on the train! He and some friends would reserve seats together and use the journey time to learn a new language.

Can you work? This is fairly obvious, but using technology to work on the train is a very good way to make the journey time productive. Can you have breakfast? Snooze? Read the paper? Do sudoku? Catch up with the news on the Internet?

Ben also said that at the end of the week he would catch a different train because that one had a bar. So he would end the week, as he put it: 'Having a drink with some chums and a laugh about the trials of work – how can that be stressful?'

So with all of this, he had managed to change a potentially immensely stressful part of his life, which certainly took up about four hours of his day, into something that he would use in the most constructive way. Admittedly his journey was easier than some, involving a single train journey, and not involving rush-hour tube trains or buses, but it was still a very significant part of his life.

So, what can you do? No matter how tricky your journey, are there ways in which you can adapt it to make constructive use of the time, or to minimize the most stressful aspects for you?

There are also a couple of more practical aspects to what you can do.

Firstly – and this is absolutely vital – leave enough time. This sounds very obvious, but often we pretend that it takes less time than it does to find a parking space at the station, or for the bus to arrive, and then get stressed because things don't happen as fast as we had hoped. And secondly, as with problems with driving, look at the description of mindfulness at the end of Chapter 15. Become aware of your body, and how tense it might be. Are you frowning and gritting your teeth? Are your shoulders raised and tense? Make a conscious effort to relax and release the tension, and see if this makes you feel any less stressed.

CHAPTER SUMMARY

- Work stress is a frequent problem. Common causes for stress at work include lack of control, lack of support, reorganization of the workforce, 'downsizing' and the long-hours culture.
- We raised a number of questions to help you identify whether work stress is a problem for you.
- General cognitive therapy techniques can help you to manage work stress, but there are additional techniques which may be very helpful. These are:
  - Communication skills
  - Assertiveness
  - Day-to-day coping strategies
  - Considering your attitudes
- Finally, we considered the problems of travelling to work, and gave some guidance on ways to diminish the stress of commuting.

13

Organizing yourself and your time

Let's begin with some questions:

- Do you feel in control of your life?
- Do you have enough time to spend with your family and friends?
- Are you always on time for appointments and meetings?
- Do you manage to complete your work on time?
- Are you able to prioritize tasks and goals?
- Are you able to say 'no' to people's requests?
- Do you have time for leisure and relaxation?

If you have answered 'no' to many of these, then it is likely that time management may be an issue for you.

In this chapter we will introduce you to strategies that can help improve your time management skills and reduce stress. But before we go on, it is worth thinking about what good time management is *for*. In essence, it would be best for all of us if the way in which we spend our time reflects those things that are important to us, that are in line with our values and the things we care about. There is little sense in becoming an efficient robot who can get a huge amount done, but who doesn't really care about any of it. We need to think about what is important to us – good time management will help us to achieve that.

Paul is a nurse who had children in his late thirties. When his first child was born, Paul decided that he was going to work part-time so that he could spend time with him. He was lucky enough to be able to negotiate this with the hospital in which he worked. He thought really carefully about what this would mean to him, and the fact that it might have an impact on his overall career. But as Paul said: 'When I die, do you think I'll say on my deathbed that I regret having spent so much time with my children? I don't. But I think I'd regret it if I said I hadn't spent enough.' And he stuck to this absolutely over the next years. Despite opportunities to do things that might have interested him, and despite pressure from his manager to work extra shifts on his days off, he always resisted. He knew exactly what he wanted to achieve with his time management, and was tough enough to stick to this. He became expert at saying 'no'.

Thinking about priorities

So when we are thinking about time management, it is important to try to think first about your values and your principles. What would time spent well mean for you? What are your priorities? Once you are clearer about this you can go on to think about the more day-to-day aspects of how you try to fit things in.

One way to think about priorities in your life is to draw a 'spider' diagram:

- Draw a circle with yourself in it at the centre of the 'web'.
- Then think of the key areas in your life, such as work, your family, your interests and future directions. Place these on the web around you.
- Beyond the key areas, put the things that you would like to achieve in relation to them, or ideas that you have about things that you could do.

Clive was a fifty-one-year-old self-employed photographer who felt completely overwhelmed with stress. He regularly lost work because he put off returning telephone enquiries, and took too long to give quotes to clients. He had got behind with his accounts and was deeply worried about his finances. His private life was very difficult because he had two ex-wives, both of whom made very erratic – and competing – demands on his time with regard to childcare commitments. When he felt completely overcome with stress he would cope by hiding under the duvet, sleeping instead of working, and then staying up late drinking with friends. He was on the edge of giving up and longed to escape all responsibilities by moving to Spain and taking his chance with life, but recognized that was not a long-term solution. When he came for therapy he drew the spider diagram in Figure 13.1.

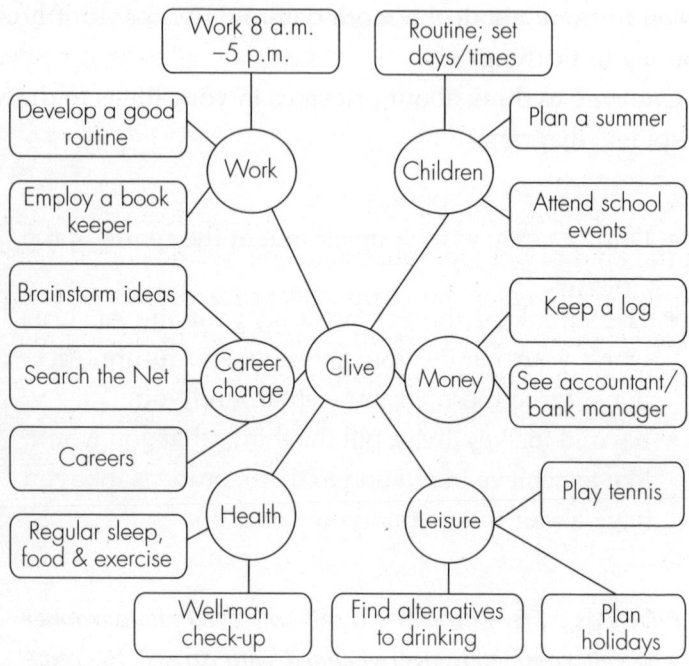

Figure 13.1 Clive's spider diagram

Using the diagram to define priorities and goals

Looking at your diagram, see which are the areas that you are most concerned about, and list them in order of importance to you. Are there any that stand out? Are there areas on the diagram which actually you don't care that much about but seem to be spending time on anyway? Are there areas which you would definitely like to spend more time on? Are there any you could drop? Because there are only a limited number of hours in the day, these priorities will determine what you choose to do, and what will go to the bottom of the list.

Once you have decided which areas are a priority for you, it would be good to create goals for what you would like to achieve. How do you want your situation to change? What would you like to be different in both the short and the long term?

Clive realized that he did not want to spend more time on the kind of photography which he had been doing and did not really enjoy, but would like to explore a different career. He also wanted to work out a way of having more consistent and stable time with his children.

The acronym 'SMART' can be useful when setting your goals. We discuss this in Chapter 8 as well, but to re-iterate: goals need to be Specific; Measurable; Achievable; Realistic and Time-based:

- *Specific*. A vague goal would be: 'I want to manage my time better at work.' This sounds sensible, but it is not really clear what it entails. A more specific goal would be: 'I want to learn to prioritize what I need to do so that I can leave at 5.30 p.m.'
- *Measurable*. This refers to how you will *know* that you have achieved your goal. In the example above, it would not be clear how you would measure whether you are managing your time better. But as soon as you say that your goal is to leave work at 5.30 p.m. it is very clear that you will know whether you are achieving it or not.
- *Achievable*. Are the actions needed to attain your goals within your capacity?
- *Realistic*. Are your goals something that fit in with the real world, or are they so perfectionist or

idealistic that you won't be able to reach them?
- *Timed*. What is your time frame for achieving your goal? Will you have achieved it by the end of the week? The end of the month? In six months' time?

Goals and subgoals

In order to achieve goals, we may need to break things down into smaller steps, or subgoals, that will help us to get there.

For instance, in order to have more consistent and stable time with his children, Clive decided that he would take the following steps: (1) try to negotiate regular fixed times with the children's mothers; (2) plan an annual holiday with the children; (3) ask the school to be included on mailing lists about parent evenings and school events; (4) set up a standing order for maintenance payments.

So, having identified a goal, consider what steps you will need to take to achieve this. Write them out in order, so that you can see your progress towards your goal!

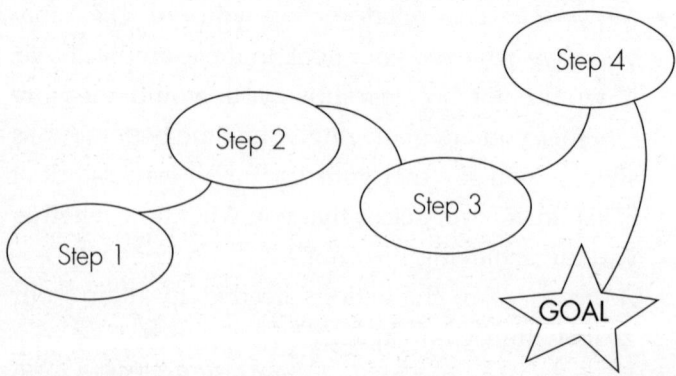

Figure 13.2 The path to your goal

How well do you manage your time?

Now that you have thought about what your priorities and goals are, you can go back to thinking about how you are actually spending your time, and whether there are changes that can be made to this. One way of finding out how you are spending your time is to keep an hour-by-hour record of your activity over the course of a week using the time log below. This is likely to be quite time-consuming, so do not let it become a stress in itself, but use it if you think it would be helpful. If there are hours when you are doing a variety of tasks, make a brief note of what these are. At the end of the day, rate how stressed you have felt overall, using the 0–10 scale (0 = not at all stressed, 10 = the most stressed you can ever imagine being). You'll find another blank time log at the end of the book.

Having done this, you can review your time log to help you identify patterns of behavior that might account for your stress response:

- Are you spending a lot of time on unimportant tasks?
- Are you putting off tasks that you really need to do?
- Have the basics of regular sleep, eating and exercise become chaotic?
- Are you spending too much, or too little time on any one activity?
- Can you relate the overall stress to what has happened in the day? For example, is the rating higher or lower on days when you go to work? Is it always higher when you see particular people? Is it higher when you are busy, or when you are not able to get going?

TABLE 13.1 TIME LOG

	Mon.	Tues.	Weds.	Thurs.	Fri.	Sat.	Sun.
8–9 a.m.							
9–10							
10–11							
11–12							
12–1 p.m.							
1–2							
2–3							
3–4							
4–5							
5–6							
6–7							

	Mon.	Tues.	Weds.	Thurs.	Fri.	Sat.	Sun.
7–8							
8–9							
9–10							
10–11							
11–12							
1–2 a.m.							
Daily stress rating 0–10							

The key to prioritizing your time

We have talked about prioritizing in the sense of being clear which *values* you want to bring to the fore of your life. Now we are moving on to consider how you prioritize your *time*. Prioritizing your time is really about making careful choices about what to do and what not to do. In order to prioritize effectively you need to be able to recognize what is important, and to see the difference between urgent and important.

Covey's time management matrix, shown below in Figure 13.3, is a useful tool to help you assess how you are spending your time and make decisions about managing your time more effectively. The matrix distinguishes between what is important and what is urgent, and what is unimportant and not urgent. Figure 13.3 shows how these two characteristics of tasks can be combined by placing them in four quadrants, with examples in each.

Essentially, an *important* task is one that is important to

	URGENT	NOT URGENT
	FIREFIGHTING	**QUALITY TIME**
IMPORTANT	(URGENT AND IMPORTANT) Examples: • Projects with a strict deadline • Last-minute preparations for scheduled activities • Medical emergencies • Crises • Pressing problems	(IMPORTANT BUT NOT URGENT) Examples: • Exercise • Building relationships • Relaxation/recreation • Planning & preparation • Prevention • Classification of values • Recognizing new opportunities
	DISTRACTION	**TIME WASTING**
NOT IMPORTANT	(URGENT BUT NOT IMPORTANT) Examples: • Some meetings • Some reports and mail • Interruptions • Immediately pressing activities	(NEITHER URGENT NOR IMPORTANT) Examples: • Junk mail • Trivia • Junk TV • Escapist activities • Some phone calls • Pleasant activities

Figure 13.3 Time management matrix

us in terms of our values and our goals. An *urgent* task is something that needs to be dealt with soon in order to cope with crises and deadlines, but not all urgent tasks are necessarily important.

On the whole, important and urgent tasks need to be completed as soon as possible – these are the ones which will get us into a crisis or into trouble if we do not deal with them. Dealing with these swiftly, rather than procrastinating or avoiding the task, should help you to feel less stressed, and it should also allow you to focus your time and attention on those tasks – important but not urgent – which are the most rewarding in the long term. When time is short, we need to make sure that we are not spending time on unimportant tasks.

TABLE 13.2 SALLY'S TIME MANAGEMENT MATRIX

	URGENT	NOT URGENT
IMPORTANT	Preparing the end-of-year report for a meeting with the chairman and board of trustees. Taking the cat to the vet following an accident.	Giving a mock interview to a colleague at work. Going to the theatre with Ben on Friday and having friends for Sunday lunch. Taking my mother for a hospital appointment with the rheumatologist.
NOT IMPORTANT	Interrupted by Jenny who was in crisis because her husband had left her for another woman. She was distressed and in need of support so we spent the rest of the day talking through her problems, even though I don't know her that well and she has better friends.	Attended a training course on how to use the new database when I already had the knowledge and consequently found the day unproductive and didn't learn anything new.

Sally is a thirty-seven-year-old manager. She reviewed her time log and completed a time management matrix, and was pleased to see that she had achieved a good balance of important tasks, both urgent and non-urgent, which gave her a great deal of satisfaction. But she also recognized that she wasted a lot of time doing unimportant tasks and could understand the reasons why she constantly felt stressed, rushing through the day and often needing to take work home.

Looking at your time log, see how the activities would fit into the time management matrix worksheet below. There is a copy of this worksheet in the back of this book.

TABLE 13.3 TIME MANAGEMENT MATRIX WORKSHEET

	URGENT	NOT URGENT
IMPORTANT		
NOT IMPORTANT		

Now, analyse how you are spending your time:

- How much of the time are you concentrating your efforts in the important and urgent/not-urgent quadrants?

- How much of the time are you concentrating your efforts in the unimportant and urgent/not-urgent quadrants?
- Were there tasks that were a waste of time, or could have been dealt with more efficiently?
- Were there tasks that you could have delegated?
- Have you given yourself time off and had fun?

You can use this system of prioritizing to plan activities, but also as a guide to how to respond to unplanned ones. For example, in Sally's case, Jenny came into her office in floods of tears and interrupted her completing a quotation for a client. She thought it would have been inappropriate for her to ask Jenny to leave her office because she was busy completing a task, and that it was right to spend a little time talking to her. However, it was beyond the call of duty for Sally to drop everything and spend most of the rest of the day trying to fix Jenny's problems. In hindsight she realized that she should have taken a few moments to listen and understand Jenny's situation, but then could have suggested that Jenny take some time out and seek the support of family and friends.

Planning activities: The value of lists

Try to make it a rule to draw up a list in the evening for the day ahead or, if you have time, first thing in the morning, with your first cup of coffee ... Many people reading this book will already be doing this, but for those of you who are not, it could prove invaluable. There are four steps to making lists as effective as possible.

Firstly, write down everything that has been buzzing around your head all night/all day/all week. Put anything down that comes into your head as a task you need to accomplish or attend to. Strange though it may sound, once the tasks are written down you should find that the pressure of carrying all that around in your head gets better, and your head feels a lot lighter.

Secondly, think about whether the task is important or urgent. What needs to be done today? What can wait? What order do you need to do things in? What's the priority?

Thirdly, once you have decided which tasks have priority you need to mark the list or reorganize it in some way to reflect this. There are many ways of doing this, and whether you use one of the ones suggested below or decide on your own doesn't matter:

- One way to mark the priority is to assign every task a letter – A, B or C. 'A' is for those tasks which are both urgent and important. Tasks in the 'B' category should only be done after you have finished with 'A'. If you have time after finishing these, then you can move on to the 'C' tasks.
- Another way is to use a highlighter pen to mark tasks which you must do today. Only when the highlighted tasks are complete should you move on to others …
- Or use sublists – write the tasks you want to prioritize on a post-it note and stick this at the top of

your list. Use a second post-it note for tasks that you'd like to accomplish but it won't be the end of the world if you don't.

- Or if you are organized in advance and have a sense of importance and urgency, you could write the list in columns to reflect what needs to be done first.

Fourthly, at the end of the day review your list. Put a tick by everything that you have managed to complete. If you have done something important that is not on the list, then write this down and tick it too – it will help you to see what you have accomplished. Have you managed to complete the 'A' tasks? Are there tasks that need to be carried over to the next day? Write a new list and prioritize again.

Keep an eye on 'C' tasks that keep getting moved from one list to the next. Is the task something that you don't really want to do, or that would make you anxious to think about? Are you fooling yourself into thinking that it is unimportant as a result? Or is it just that you want to keep the task in mind, even though it isn't a priority for you at the moment?

Our lives are messy and at times unpredictable; when faced with unplanned activities, we often need to make a quick decision about prioritizing and don't have time to analyse the situation in full. But you can keep your values and your goals in mind, and rely on your gut reaction. And sometimes taking time out and doing things for fun is a great stress reducer, so if your gut reaction tells you to do this – listen!

Structure and routine

Sometimes when our time management really gets out of hand, then we can start to become very chaotic in the way that we are living our lives. We don't have time to eat properly, and our sleep can get very disrupted. We stay up all night finishing assignments, or doing housework that we didn't have time for in the day, and end up being exhausted and irritable the following day. If this is happening to you, then the first step that you should take is to redraw the lines of structure and routine in your life to help yourself feel back in control.

Decide on what time you are going to bed, and look at the section on sleep in Chapter 15 to help with this (see pp. 301–08). Make sure that you are eating regularly and sensibly, and if at all possible build some exercise into your day, even if this is only walking up a few flights of stairs instead of taking the lift, or parking your car a little further from where you are going.

Keeping a diary

Keep a diary to plan when you are going to do things. Record the fixed activities that you have to do, such as taking children to school, walking the dog or arriving at work by 8.30 a.m. Then see where you have time to include additional things. Allocate sections of time according to the priority of what you need to do. See what free time you have.

Building in breaks and leisure

We say more about this in Chapter 12 on stress at work. But it is worth mentioning here that no one can be expected to be efficient and on top of everything for twenty-four hours a day. We need breaks in our day, even if only ten minutes to get a cup of tea and catch our breath. And we need breaks in our week for leisure, fun and relaxation. No matter how pressed you are, don't give in to the temptation to be busy all the time. You will be more efficient if you have breaks.

Delegating tasks

It also helps to remember that you don't have to be superman or superwoman and do everything yourself. There is no shame in asking other people to help, or in delegating tasks to other people. Do you have someone at work whom you can delegate to? Can you delegate to your partner or children? Is there a friend that you can ask for help? You may think that you will feel more of a sense of accomplishment if you do it all, but you will end up by being able to do less. Do not be a martyr!

Saying 'no'

One reason why people can get in trouble with their time management is that, just when they think they have everything worked out, someone comes along with another request and throws the whole system out. Sometimes you will want to do what you're asked, and it fits with your values and priorities. At other times this will not be the case, but you might find yourself unable to say 'no'. We have talked about saying 'no' in the section on assertiveness in Chapter 12, but will reiterate this here.

Firstly, remember that no matter whom you are talking to, you have the right to be in control of your life and your decisions. Your priorities and your plans are as important as anyone else's. You have the *right* to say 'no'.

Secondly, do not make excuses for why you can't do what you've been asked. You don't have to justify yourself. As soon as you start to make excuses or give reasons, people can pick you up on facts and details, and alternatives, and you will find yourself in the middle of a conflict. Just say you are sorry you can't help, but you can't.

Thirdly, think of the broken record technique. No matter how long people go on at you for, think of yourself as a broken record and just keep sticking to your point. You don't have to elaborate. Just keep saying 'no'. If the other person won't stop, then just say: 'I'm sorry, but I have made my decision.'

Fourthly, try rehearsing different ways of saying 'no': 'I'm afraid not … that won't be possible … I'm not able to help on this occasion … I won't be able to make that … that's not going to be possible.'

CHAPTER SUMMARY

- Organizing your time means starting with an idea of what values are important to you, and what your priorities for spending time are.
- You can use the 'spider diagram' to help identify priorities.
- There are a number of strategies for analysing and improving your use of time, including:
  - Keeping a time log;
  - Using a time management matrix;
  - Using lists and diaries;
  - Delegating and saying 'no'.

14

Overcoming barriers and enhancing coping

There seem to be a number of styles of thinking that can contribute greatly to how stressful we find things. We have spoken previously about the *content* of people's thoughts when they get stressed, but in this chapter we will look at more general *patterns* of thinking and feeling that can contribute greatly to difficulties in coping and which add to how stressed we can get. We will also look at techniques that could help with these.

- Problematic patterns include procrastination, perfectionism and worry.
- Techniques include TICs and TOCs, problem-solving and regulating stressful emotions.

Procrastination

Very simply, what we are referring to here is the generally tendency to put things off – to procrastinate. We do this for all sorts of reasons, but whatever the reason, what is clear is that once we start to procrastinate we become more and more stressed, since getting behind with important problems means that they pile up and, undealt with, intensify. And like many aspects of stress, there is a vicious cycle here, since we are more likely to procrastinate when we become stressed and start feeling that we cannot cope. Of course, most of us procrastinate to some degree without running into serious difficulties, but when the problem becomes very severe it can have pretty serious consequences for dealing with problems, and can affect people so that they are unable to achieve things that they are really capable of.

The key to overcoming procrastination is to understand the reasons why it happens and then to use the techniques of cognitive therapy to start to tackle these. So why do we procrastinate if it makes us feel more stressed? Some of the reasons are illustrated below.

Lilly, a twenty-eight-year-old assistant editor, had regular deadlines to meet, but often found herself making excuses not to tackle the work. She would say to herself, 'I'm not in the mood to do this now; I'll wait until later', and then distracted herself by surfing the Internet or completing unimportant tasks. She constantly felt overwhelmed and stressed and felt worried that she would lose her job.

Lilly was showing a pattern of thinking that underlies a great deal of procrastinating – that is, waiting for the moment when she *would feel like doing what needs to be done*. We will say more about this later.

Oliver, an undergraduate studying physics, had missed a term of work. He avoided going to lectures and started feeling more and more worried and stressed. Oliver came from a high-flying academic family, and had always been expected to do well. He had in fact done very well in his first year, but had started to struggle a bit in his second. But his self-esteem was very dependent upon doing well and keeping up the family tradition – he found the thought of failure (which in his case meant not getting a first!) unbearable, and would become so stressed at the thought of failing that it felt safer to do nothing at all.

Lilly, on the other hand, had always felt that she wasn't good enough, and that other people were expecting her to do badly. She always felt like an imposter in her job and was terrified that someone would spot that she didn't belong there.

So for some people procrastination is a response to their fear of failing, and to complicate matters this can occur either because people feel they are expected to do well, or because they feel they are expected to do badly. You can't win!

Linda was severely overweight and wanted to slim down. But her family kept putting pressure on her to lose weight, and she ended up feeling that they did not care about her for what she was, and that they were trying to control her, to make her fit in with how they thought she should be. So she would dig her heels in and rebel and do the opposite of what they wanted – such as eating a large cream cake in front of them. She kept putting off starting to diet, but at the same time felt terribly stressed that she wasn't losing any weight.

Linda became stressed when she felt controlled by others. Behind her procrastination about starting to try to lose weight was her resistance to being controlled, which could be summed up by the thought: if I must then I won't.

Similarly, Daisy worked as a PA in a law firm and had difficulty being assertive. When demands were made of her to do things that she didn't think really came into her work remit she would always agree, but then feel quietly resentful and stressed and would procrastinate.

Lastly, Mark's cause of procrastination was his lack of interest; he knew he had things to do such as dig the garden and file his papers, but he just didn't want to do them. He found those tasks uninspiring and boring – but he would feel stressed because he hadn't done them.

These causes of procrastination are summed up in the box below.

CAUSES OF PROCRASTINATION

1 Waiting for the right mood or right time
2 Fear of failure because of:
   - too high expectations (perfectionism)
   - too low expectations
3 Feeling controlled by others
4 Lack of assertiveness
5 Lack of interest

All these people are procrastinating for different reasons. Do you recognize yourself in any of them? Are there times when one side of you knows it would be sensible to do something, but the other puts its foot down? When you talk to yourself about why you are putting something off it may seem quite reasonable. But whatever the individual reason, the impact is the same. When you put off doing something that is important in your life, you may avoid stress in the short term, but you are very likely to add to it in the long term. So we need to try and find ways to overcome procrastination.

Overcoming procrastination

There are a number of different strategies which you can use to tackle procrastination. Firstly, the general strategies of cognitive therapy are extremely useful here. If you know that you are procrastinating, make yourself examine the thoughts going through your mind. What can you pinpoint about the reasons why you are putting things off? Can you then go on to use the techniques of questioning and challenging thoughts (see pp. 139–46) to try to tackle some of these reasons, and to come up with a way of behaving that might be less destructive? There are a number of other strategies that are useful in procrastinating:

- Firstly, understanding the links between motivation and action.
- Secondly, weighing up the advantages and disadvantages of what you are doing.

- Thirdly, breaking tasks down into manageable steps.
- Fourthly, looking at TICs and TOCs – see section below.

Action and motivation

Lilly very clearly wanted to 'wait until she felt like it'. But what her story showed was that this never happened – she never started to feel like it and missed more and more deadlines. The idea that many of us have about motivation and action is that it should go like this:

Motivation

Action

But in fact, because there are so many complex reasons why we don't feel like it – in Lilly's case the fear of failure – then what happens if we wait for motivation is that we never do anything. In fact, the system really operates like this:

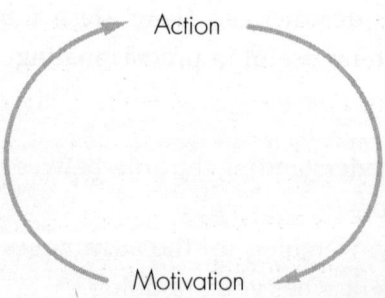

Action

Motivation

In other words, if we wait to feel motivated we won't do things. But if we can find ways to force ourselves into action – to do whatever we are putting off – then we start to feel better, and we start to feel more motivated. And this motivation then allows us to take the action further. In the section below we will discuss things that you can do to make yourself start to take action. But remember – waiting to feel like it means it won't happen!

Weighing up the advantages and disadvantages

One strategy to address procrastination involves weighing up the advantages and disadvantages of putting things off.

James was a twenty-two-year-old administrator. He had lived his student life with friends who were all as indifferent to housework as he was, but had recently returned to live with his family for a while. His bedroom got into a terrible mess, with old food plates going mouldy in corners, dirty clothes and soaking towels everywhere, and dust and grease gathering. His mother had asked him to clean and tidy his room. He felt bored and resentful about this, but on the other hand, living in an untidy and dirty environment did cause him a great deal of stress; he could never find important things such as clean clothes for work or papers. Using the worksheet in Table 14.1, he considered the advantages and disadvantages of procrastinating about tidying his bedroom.

TABLE 14.1 JAMES'S ADVANTAGES AND DISADVANTAGES WORKSHEET

Procrastination
Identify what you are procrastinating about and make a note
Tidying my bedroom

Advantages of procrastinating	Disadvantages of procrastinating
1. Get to do more interesting stuff now 2. Hassle to do immediately 3. Waste of time – it will be messy again in a week 4. It's messy but I know where everything is	1. Constantly on my mind – feel stressed 2. Struggle to walk around the room 3. Putting it off makes it worse, my bedroom will get messier 4. Would feel happy when it's done, everyone likes a clean room 5. Get Mum off my back

Take a moment to think about something you are procrastinating about and make a note of it on the worksheet below. Next consider the advantages of putting off the task and make a note in the left-hand column. In the right-hand column record the disadvantages of procrastinating about the task. Another copy of this worksheet is included at the back of the book.

TABLE 14.2 BLANK ADVANTAGES AND DISADVANTAGES WORKSHEET

Procrastination
Identify what you are procrastinating about and make a note

Advantages of procrastinating	Disadvantages of procrastinating

Looking back at his worksheet, James could clearly see that the advantages of tidying his bedroom outweighed the disadvantages, but he was still no closer to getting started with the task and was feeling just as stressed. It was the weekend and he considered the advantages and disadvantages of getting started today by using the worksheet overleaf.

TABLE 14.3 JAMES'S SECOND ADVANTAGES AND DISADVANTAGES WORKSHEET

Advantages and disadvantages of getting started today tidying my bedroom

Advantages	Disadvantages
1. Smell less	1. It will take up my free time
2. Because I've started, it will give me motivation to finish	2. The task is enormous. I always underestimate how much time it takes and it's depressing. Starting the task smacks me back down into reality
3. Less likely to break something	
4. Can move the mattress back into position	
5. Would feel less embarrassed about the state of my room	

In identifying the disadvantages of getting started today, James found a number of potential problems that he listed in the left-hand column of the worksheet below, then generated some possible solutions that were likely to reduce stress.

TABLE 14.4 JAMES'S ACTION PLAN

Problems	Solutions
1. Underestimating the time required leads to further procrastination	1. Based on past experience, be realistic about the time required. Watch out for kidding myself
2. Not knowing where to start	2. Don't worry; dive in and get on with it
3. Anticipating frustration when I know I'm going to start	3. Plan breaks, chocolate, play music whilst working
4. Knowing that I could be doing something more interesting with my time	4. Think of the benefits, the positive effect a tidy room would have.

Having completed the worksheet in Table 14.2 that helped you to identify the advantages and disadvantages of procrastinating about an important task, now consider the advantages of getting started right now. If potential problems arise, use the action plan worksheet below and think of all the solutions you can.

TABLE 14.5 BLANK ACTION PLAN WORKSHEET

Problems	Solutions

Breaking the task down

Sometimes we procrastinate because the task just seems too overwhelming, and the end goal can seem unobtainable. One strategy is to break the task down into bite-size chunks that are manageable and doable. Focusing on what you can achieve and being realistic about the time frame involved will help reduce stress. For example, James made the following list of the tasks required to tidy his room; he decided to concentrate his efforts on one at a time:

1 Collect the litter into black bags.
2 Take all the cups and plates downstairs and stack in the dishwasher.
3 Put the laundry in the basket.
4 Put the CDs and DVDs into their boxes.
5 Put the books back on the shelves.
6 Vacuum the floor.
7 Clean the desk.
8 Change the bed sheets.

The following questions will help you to work through the process of breaking a task down:

- What is the task I'm putting off doing?
- What does completing that task involve? If I were delegating the task to several people, what would be the different components?
- Are my expectations unrealistic?
- Am I telling myself to just get on with it?

Now write the steps down on your to-do list and tick each one off as you go. Just think how much better you will feel once you make a start.

Perfectionism and stress

In the previous first section of this chapter we spoke about procrastination. This goes hand in hand with what we are coming on to talk about – perfectionism. Perfectionists are driven to perform everything that they do absolutely to perfection – anything less will mean that they have failed. Often they are concerned that others will see them as a 'fraud' unless their performance is exemplary. They worry about not meeting the mark and doing things imperfectly. As a result, people who are perfectionist often become completely immobilized – they are so afraid of doing something less than perfectly that they become extraordinarily stressed, and will end up by putting off doing it at all.

Sofia, a twenty-six-year-old anthropologist employed by a major bank as a researcher, was underperforming. Her working hours were flexible and she would often work at home, but accomplished very little. She had an intense fear of failure and would procrastinate in order to feel less stressed – at least in the short term. She was unable to tolerate any criticism and believed that everything she did had to be perfect. She would make herself sick with worry over minor mistakes and would avoid things just in case she might not be at her best. She described feeling like a pressure cooker about to explode.

For many people, being a perfectionist sounds like something to feel proud of. It seems as though you would always reach the highest standards, and would never accept mediocre or second-best performance. People often also think that being a perfectionist makes you more effective. But, in fact, studies have shown that perfectionists tend to become more stressed in challenging situations than people who have more attainable standards, and are at greater risk of mental distress when things don't turn out just right. Perfectionism becomes a problem when it takes over your life and you begin to see major stress. Learning to shed the burden of perfectionism can greatly reduce the stress you experience on a daily basis.

ARE YOU A PERFECTIONIST?

Below is a list of some of the characteristics perfectionists have. If some of these items resonate with you, perfectionism might be a problem:

1 Do you often think that you should be doing better no matter what you do?

2 Do you spot tiny mistakes and imperfections in your work, to the point where you have trouble seeing anything else?

3 Are you never satisfied with your performance or with that of others?

4 Do you set yourself goals of unreasonable excellence?

5 Do you constantly push yourself harder?

6 Do you tend to focus on the results and not the process involved in getting there?

7 When your goals don't go to plan, does this lower your mood?

8 Do you believe that doing your best equals perfection, and nothing less will do?

9 Do you find that your standards just can't be met?

10 Do you feel tense a good part of the time?

11 Do you never seem to have enough time to do your best?

12 Are you fearful of making mistakes?

13 Is striving for perfection driven by a fear of failing or being exposed as a fraud?

14 Do you respond aggressively or defensively to constructive criticism?

15 Is your self-esteem low?

16 Do you have difficulty taking risks in fear of putting your reputation on the line?

17 Do you believe that there is a right way and a wrong way to do most things?

18 Do you hold high moral and ethical standards?

19 Does your perfectionism affect your relationships?

20 Do you find it difficult to trust others to do the job to your standards?

21 Do you check other people's work even when this might not be necessary?

22 Do you feel the need to be in control? Do you worry that if you relinquish control the quality may suffer?

23 Do you have difficulty making decisions and worry about making the wrong decision?

What keeps perfectionism going?

Broadly there are two key factors that maintain perfectionism. Firstly, some people have an intense fear of criticism or fear of being punished for performing less than perfectly. So they strive to achieve extreme goals that are usually unobtainable and end up with further self-criticism and an increase in stress levels when they are unable to meet the goals. Secondly, in other individuals, the drive to perfectionism is the desire to be approved of by others, or by themselves. People become dependent on pleasing others, hungry for approval and validation for doing things perfectly, or they become desperate to achieve unrealistic goals in order to be able to approve of themselves.

Ryan felt annoyed with himself when he got 99 per cent for a maths exam that was part of his master's degree because he had expected 100 per cent. He was unable to feel a sense of achievement and set the stakes higher: to be top of his year. When he actually achieved a sense of satisfaction it was short-lived, and the goalposts shifted yet again. Ryan had to keep on striving in order to feel slightly okay about himself; he could not let up on himself. Not surprisingly, he felt constantly stressed.

Perfectionism: Good or bad?

Perfectionists can make excellent employees, have exemplary organizational skills, be a good friend or neighbour. Perfectionists have the highest standards, and are prepared to do what it takes to reach them. But this is when things are going well. We have seen how perfectionism increases stress and can lead to great distress. It is clear that perfectionism has its costs. You might believe you must be perfect to feel worthwhile; or that if you make a mistake, you've failed.

Alex, a forty-year-old IT specialist, was aware that his style of thinking was all or nothing. He absolutely agreed with the old saying 'If a job's worth doing, it's worth doing properly' – although in his case, properly meant perfectly. He felt proud of this and believed that it meant that his standards were high. But he seemed to be getting into trouble with colleagues quite frequently. He was asked to consider the advantages and disadvantages of being a perfectionist, and completed the worksheet below.

TABLE 14.6 ADVANTAGES AND DISADVANTAGES OF PERFECTIONISM: ALEX'S WORKSHEET

Advantages of being a perfectionist	Disadvantages of being a perfectionist
• The job gets done well and to a high standard • Never make mistakes	• Tiring. Every job takes too long and sometimes I don't even finish the job • Annoy the lads I work with • I feel the need to control everything • I expect perfection from others and when they don't come up with the goods I feel disappointed and blame them • People tell me that I lack judgement. I focus on the 1% and not the other 99%

If this rings a bell with you, consider what the advantages and disadvantages of being a perfectionist are to you, using the worksheet below.

TABLE 14.7 ADVANTAGES AND DISADVANTAGES OF PERFECTIONISM: WORKSHEET

Advantages of being a perfectionist	Disadvantages of being a perfectionist

Taking control of your perfectionism

If you have decided that you are being too perfectionist and can see that there might be disadvantages to this, then there are a number of steps you can take.

Banning 'should', 'must' and 'ought to'

One strategy involves spotting the thinking error of 'should', 'must', 'ought to' and 'have to'. Telling yourself that you *should* do something leaves no room for error and places a great deal of pressure on you to meet this expectation.

How would you feel if someone else was talking to you in this way? Probably, you'd feel criticized and demotivated. If you were talking to someone else in this way you would probably come across as rather bossy. Adjusting your expectations involves talking to yourself in a kinder and more accepting way. Instead of 'should', try saying to yourself: 'I'll have a go', 'I'll try', or 'I might'; you will immediately feel less stressed and pressurized.

Defining your standards

Do you have to approach absolutely everything with perfection? Can some things you do be just good enough? In the grand scheme of things does it really matter that your sheets are ironed, or that your house is gleaming clean, or that you respond to every email? The pressure just builds up and something has to give, so take control and make some choices. One way into this is by experimenting with changing your behavior. Margaret was convinced that if she didn't keep the house immaculately clean, people would think she was a slattern; she predicted that people would criticize her and show their disapproval and disappointment in her. She experimented by not vacuuming for a week and leaving some dirty dishes in the sink and to her surprise no one seemed to notice. You might often fear the worst and, based on your fear, keep on maintaining your high standards. But as a consequence you never discover what will really happen. Even if the worst came true, what's the worst that can happen? You are human after all.

How to lower your standards, reduce your stress and be more productive

We have already established that having high expectations of yourself is self-handicapping and that, paradoxically, the more you strive for perfection the less you are likely to achieve it. This can push you into trying harder, to the point of exploding with stress.

Mandy was a copy-editor and had been in a junior position for years; every time she applied for promotion she didn't get the job and was furious given the high-quality work she produced. She would spend hours checking and re-checking manuscripts for spelling mistakes and grammatical errors, but spent twice as long as everyone else doing the task without twice the results.

Lowering your standards not only reduces stress but means, paradoxically, that you are likely to achieve more.

Here are some questions to help you challenge your fears about lowering your standards.

1 Does lowering your standards mean that you don't do the job as well?
2 If you were unable to do more, what would you focus your time on doing?
3 What is more valuable: doing the task perfectly yet feeling stressed and not really getting ahead, or doing fewer tasks and focusing your energy on doing these well?
4 What are the consequences of allowing yourself to take a chance?

As a perfectionist, your rules are likely to be the ideal; reducing your stress levels involves changing your rules to doing the best you can or a good enough standard.

Matt procrastinated about sending texts and emails; he would pore over every word, writing and rewriting them until he was satisfied. His SATs were: 'they will think I'm stupid', 'I'll write gobbledygook and will make a fool of myself'. His perfectionism was driven by his fear of criticism and failure. Matt defined what good enough would be with regard to email and text communication and decided that checking the content once and running a spellchecker was fine. Initially he felt uncomfortable with this change but quickly discovered that his fears were unfounded.

Dealing with worry

Although we all worry from time to time, people who have high levels of stress often worry very excessively, making the stress even worse. Worry ties us up in negative aspects of our lives, focusing our attention on what can go wrong. Because we are imagining the bad things that can happen, we tend to react emotionally as if those things already have occurred, and our mood gets worse accordingly. This makes us worry even more. Interestingly, we also start to worry about worrying. People who worry a lot may think:

- 'If I can't stop worrying I'll go mad.'
- 'There must be something wrong with me – I can't control my worrying.'

Even more interestingly, however, people who worry a lot may also have a lot of *positive* beliefs about worrying:

- 'Worrying is a way in which I can think about the problem and sort it out.'
- 'If I worry, it might stop something bad happening – it's tempting fate not to!'
- 'If I don't worry and something bad does happen, I won't be prepared.'

Psychologists call these ideas about worrying 'metacognitions' or thoughts about thoughts. Very often it is these metacognitions that play a part in keeping us worrying, and we will come back to them later.

Is worry a problem for me?

1 Do you consider yourself to be a born worrier?
2 Do you feel the need to worry when there is nothing to worry about?
3 Do you feel worried if you are not worrying about something?
4 Can small concerns escalate into major worries?
5 Once you start worrying, do you find it difficult to stop?
6 Do you feel so stressed with worrying that it stops you enjoying things?

If you answer 'yes' to any of these questions then it is likely that worry is a problem for you.

Productive or unproductive worry?

Sue was worrying that her gearbox was faulty. She noticed that at times while changing gear she would momentarily lose power; this made her cautious about overtaking other cars. She was worried about going in the fast lane of the motorway just in case her engine cut out. Because she was worried she took her car to her local garage and asked her mechanic to take a look.

Sally was on holiday with her husband, and phoned her seventeen-year-old daughter. She got no reply and initially thought nothing of this but phoned twice more and still did not get a reply. She started to feel worried. She began to think of all the bad reasons why her daughter had not contacted her, and was unable to sleep that night, desperately trying to find a solution. She imagined her daughter involved in a car accident, locked out of the house, in the middle of a wild party, taking drugs and trashing the house, in trouble with the police, and so on ... Eventually she became so worried that she started to ask her husband if he thought they should fly home. He, not being a worrier, thought this was a bad idea, and in fact the following day her daughter telephoned and it transpired that she had stayed at a friend's house and left her mobile at home.

The difference between these two examples is that Sue's worry was related to something that was happening, and led quickly to a course of action that would solve the problem that she was worrying about. But Sally's worry involved constructing a whole range of negative visions with very little grounding in reality – her daughter often stayed with friends or didn't answer her phone.

The difference between these types of worry is that productive worry quickly leads us into problem-solving. Sue did not dismiss her worry and tell herself she was being silly, but realized that she had better get her car checked out. But Sally spent her time constructing scenarios of all the things that might be going wrong, and became unable to think of more reasonable explanations. Worrying unproductively actually makes us less good at solving problems, not better.

It is important to be able to distinguish between

productive and unproductive worry. The questions below can help:

> • Are my worrying thoughts based on fact or on something that hasn't happened yet?
> • Is there an actual problem or is it just that I think there is?

Another way to distinguish is to think about the amount of time that you worry for. If your worry is productive then it should quickly lead into problem-solving. At the point where you start to think about solutions you should find that your worrying decreases. But if you are continually thinking about the problem without that leading anywhere, then it is likely that the worry itself is now the problem. At the end of this section we talk about strategies for problem-solving. But for now, we will think about the worrying itself.

What keeps worry going?

Often the kind of things we do to manage our worries actually makes them worse.

Reassurance-seeking. During the day when she was becoming more and more anxious and stressed, Sally frequently asked her husband for reassurance. The first time that he told her that everything was fine and their daughter was probably at a friend's, Sally felt much better, but not for long. She quickly started to think about all the terrifying alternatives. We know that when people worry, their worry tends to be made worse in the long run by reassurance-seeking. The problem with asking for reassurance is that you don't just do it once; you keep on going back for more. You might momentarily feel reassured and can feel the stress ease away, but then the doubt sets in: 'He's just saying that to shut me up', 'He is holding back from telling me what he really thinks because he doesn't want me to worry', 'It's all well and good him saying this, but what about ...'.

Checking. When Sally was no longer reassured, the other thing she did was to telephone her daughter's best friend several times to check if she had seen her. Sally became more worried when the friend said she hadn't seen her. She also found herself looking on the Internet for accounts of accidents in their home area. Like reassurance-seeking, the more we check, the more we tend to worry. It is as if every time we check we are giving ourselves the message that there really is something to worry about here.

Struggling with uncertainty. People who are worry-prone tend to feel very uncomfortable living with uncertainty, even in small amounts, and are tormented with the sense of not knowing what is going to happen next. Of course, uncertainty can be difficult for many of us, particularly if we are anticipating major life events like the possibility of redundancy or the result of medical tests. But when people cannot live with this uncertainty they tend to worry constantly. Somehow this feels safer than letting things take their course.

Strategies for dealing with worry

The essence of worry is that we spend a lot of time imagining what might happen rather than seeing things as they really are. Cognitive therapy approaches will help you put your worrying thoughts into some perspective so that you can look at reality and see it for what it is.

Identifying worrying thoughts

Before you can tackle your worry, it is important to keep track of when you worry and how this affects you. Donald, a management consultant, noticed that he would worry when he was faced with situations where he felt judged. His worry diary can be seen below.

TABLE 14.8 DONALD'S WORRY DIARY

Date and time	Situation and what triggered your worrying?	Brief summary of your worry	How stressed did you feel? (0–100%)
3 March, 2 p.m.	Driving to an interview.	I'll blow the interview. They will think I'm an idiot. What if I go blank and don't know what to say?	Stressed 100%

Using the worksheet below, start to track your worry and see if any patterns emerge. Think about the triggers for your worry. Are there particular kinds of situation which are more likely to start you off? Can you try to tackle these in a different way? When you look back later, did the trigger really justify that amount of worrying? (You can find blank copies of this, and many of the other worksheets, at the end of this book.)

TABLE 14.9 WORRY DIARY			
Date and time	Situation and what triggered your worrying?	Brief summary of your worry	How stressed did you feel? (0–100%)

Challenging worry

Challenging worry involves many of the techniques of cognitive therapy that we have discussed already. Worry is particularly susceptible to thinking errors, and learning to spot these in your worrying thoughts is the first step to challenging worry. Common thinking errors reflected in worry are:

- *Catastrophizing* – you take one single fact and assume the worst-case scenario: 'What if I fall off the horse and I'm paralysed and in a wheelchair for the rest of my life?'
- *All or nothing thinking* – things are either black or white, with no shades of grey: 'Either everything is all right, or it's a total disaster.'

- *Overgeneralization* – on the basis of a single fact, you assume that a negative pattern will follow in other areas: 'After that disappointment I know that every-thing will go wrong from now on – I'm doomed.'
- *Mind-reading* – you assume you know what the other person is thinking: 'He'll be thinking I can't do my job and he will fire me.'
- *Fortune-telling* – you believe you have the ability to look into the future and predict what will happen: 'I just know that something bad is going to happen.'
- *Emotional reasoning* – you assume an emotion equals a fact: 'I feel anxious, so something bad must be about to happen.'
- *Discounting the positive* – you discount any evidence that contradicts your worrying thoughts: 'I know that nothing bad has happened in the past but it could still all go wrong.'

Look at your worry diary and see if you can spot what your thinking errors are. Sometimes just being able to label the thinking error can put an end to your worry.

How likely is it that your worry will come true?

When we worry we tend to think of all the bad things that could happen. Not only do we imagine these, but if asked how likely they are we would probably say 'very'. The more worried people get, the higher they estimate the prob-ability of the bad things occurring – so that it becomes pretty definite that these terrible outcomes will occur. How often have you been convinced that your worrying thoughts are absolutely true, and then at some point looked back and realized that nothing bad happened at all? When you are caught up in worrying, it is very difficult to remind yourself of this, but we can learn to think about probability in a more realistic way.

- How often have I had a worrying thought and it's turned out not to be true?
- If a friend had this worrying thought, what would you say to them?
- What's the likelihood of this worrying thought becoming true?
- How important will this worry seem a week from now?
- What are other possibilities besides a negative outcome?

See if asking yourself these questions will help you to lower your estimates of probability. It can be helpful to keep a log of your worrying thoughts and to record the actual outcome. This will help you see the contrast between the worry and what really happens.

Thoughts about thoughts: Dealing with metacognition

At the beginning of the chapter we saw that people can have different kinds of beliefs about worry itself – both negative beliefs that worry can harm you, and positive beliefs that it can somehow protect you. Both kinds of belief can make worry worse, the first because you get so anxious that you can't stop worrying, and the second because you get anxious that something bad will happen if you do stop. The psychologist Adrian Wells highlighted the importance of tackling these *metacognitions*, or beliefs about worry, as we describe below.

Let's look first at negative beliefs about worry. If you are afraid that your worrying is out of control or that it is harmful to you, then you are likely to worry more, not less, and to feel more stressed and anxious. But like other stressful thoughts, these worries tend to be biased and exaggerated. Once you are aware that you hold these beliefs about worry, you can subject them to the same kinds of cognitive therapy processes that we have outlined above (see pp. 270–72). Is there any evidence that worry is harmful? It is certainly unpleasant, and makes you feel more stressed, but there is no evidence that it is harmful to you. You may feel that you are about to crack up, but in fact this does not happen as a result of worry. And there is no evidence that worry causes physical problems. Similarly, if you worry that your worry is out of control, think about times when something has happened that has distracted you – maybe the phone rang, or you made a cup of tea – and the worry did stop.

Now let's look at positive beliefs about worry. Try asking yourself the following questions.

- Can I think of times when I did not worry and things turned out well?
- Does worry really prevent bad things happening,

or make good things happen? Or do these things just happen, regardless of whether I worry or not?

- Does worry really help me cope, or does it interfere with my coping?
- What are the *real* effects of worrying – how is it really affecting my life?
- Am I really doing something productive when I worry or am I just making myself feel upset?

If you ask yourself these questions, it may help to weaken the idea that you need to worry. However, one of the best ways to find out what worrying does for you is to stop and see what happens. Try the following experiment:

For one day, keep worrying. Record what happens throughout the day, and how stressed you feel at the end of it. Rate this on a scale of 0 (not at all stressed) to 10 (absolute maximum stress).

The next day, don't worry. Give yourself permission to let the worries go. Again, record what happens throughout the day, and make a note of how stressed you feel.

Keep alternating 'worry' and 'no worry' days for a week or so. Then compare your records for 'worry days' and 'no worry days'. Did worrying really help? How did worrying affect your stress levels?

Try to use these findings to help to give yourself permission not to worry.

Planned worry time

If you have been worrying for a long time it may be very difficult to stop completely. But one thing that you can do is to try to confine it to specific times of the day, so that you don't have to spend the entire day worrying. Decide on a good time of day when you can spend fifteen minutes just concentrating on worrying. You can use this time to go over things that are really concerning you, and that you feel you really do need to think about. Once you have made this decision, then any time during the day when you notice that you are starting to worry, make a note of what you are worrying about. This could be just a mental note, or you could jot it down in a diary or notebook. Tell yourself that you will think about it as much as you need to later, and then get on with what you are doing. When you get to your worry time, you can bring it out again. It would also be helpful to keep a note of how many of the things you jot down seem worth worrying about when you get to your worry time. Some will. But you may find that there are quite a few that don't.

This can be summed up in the following three steps:

- As soon as you notice that you are worrying, postpone it by telling yourself you will worry later.
- Choose a time of day when you can devote fifteen minutes to worry – preferably not in the hour or two before bedtime.
- Allow yourself to worry for fifteen minutes and no longer. Set a timer if you need reminding. Only spend the time worrying if you still feel it is necessary to worry.

Task-interfering cognitions and task-orienting cognitions – moving from TICs to TOCs

When we are contemplating doing any sort of task, it is very common to have thoughts that interfere with our ability and motivation to do the task. The psychologist David Burns called these task-interfering cognitions, or TICs, and showed how they can be replaced by task-orienting cognitions, or TOCs, which help us to focus in a more productive way.

Examples of TICs are:

- I'll do it later
- I won't be able to manage/I'll fail
- I can't be bothered
- I'll never get it done
- I'll make a mess of it
- I'll be judged
- It will be really bad
- I don't know where to start
- I'll leave it to someone else
- No one will notice if I don't do it
- I'll go off sick and then I don't have to face it
- I'll get wound up/feel bad

If you think like this when contemplating doing a task, it is not surprising that you would be reluctant to do it. The idea is therefore to change these TICs to TOCs or task-orienting cognitions – thoughts that orient you towards the task and your ability to get it done. In the example on p. 251, James's TICs and TOCs might look like this:

Task-Interfering Cognitions (TICs)	Task-Orienting Cognitions (TOCs)
I can't be bothered; I'll do it later when I have more time.	The sooner I get started the sooner I'll finish.
I only have an hour and there's not a lot I can do in that time.	Spending an hour on my room is at least making a start; I could put the rubbish into bags.
Yes, but there's so much more to do.	Thinking about what you are unable to do defeats you before you start. Just concentrate on one small goal at a time.
I'll be embarrassed if my mum sees all my rubbish.	Come on — as if she doesn't know what your room is like now! She is more likely to be pleased that you are doing something about it.

TABLE 14.10 JAMES'S TICS AND TOCS

However, TICs do not just occur at the point where you are planning to do something. They can be just as important when you are in the middle of a task, and can cause massive amounts of stress. You can be hit by TICs at any time. For instance, in the middle of an interview you might find yourself thinking: 'Oh no, I'm making such a pig's ear of this question, they will think I'm a complete idiot. They are never going to give me this job.' Then you get so tied up with worrying about what they think of you that you simply can't concentrate on the next question. Or in the middle of an essay, or report writing, you might think: 'This is stupid. I'm too thick to do it properly.' These TICs mean that we get tied up in thoughts that make us more and more stressed, and take more and more attention away from the task itself, so that we do in fact end up doing it less well. So the trick is to substitute the TICs for TOCs – thoughts that orient us towards the task, and keep us focused and positive about it. This means that as soon as you notice you are having TICS, say 'Stop!' And then think of TOCS that will orient you towards the task. Examples might be:

- 'I have done this kind of thing before and it's always gone okay.'
- 'Stop going on at me stupid TICs' – strange but sometimes effective!
- 'I know I can do it – I wouldn't be here if I couldn't.'
- 'I am going to think about the question, not about how I'm doing.'
- 'Good question: what are my research plans/ business forecast/personal development objectives for the next five years?'

In other words, you are not getting tied up with all the stressful thoughts that impair your performance but are orienting yourself back towards the task itself. Although incredibly simple, TICs and TOCs can make a massive difference to how you feel about doing a task.

If you realize that TICs are a problem for you, then you could record them on the worksheet below, particularly if these are TICs that are stopping you doing something. Having recorded them, you could also try to come up with TOCs.

Very often, however, TICs occur when you are in the middle of something and you can't always take time out to write them down and examine them – this is especially true if they occur in interviews or exams. But you can still notice that you are having them and say 'Stop!'. If you know that TICs are a problem for you in stressful situations, it may also be helpful to plan and rehearse in advance what TOCs you can bring to mind. It is often easier to think of these when you are calmer than when you are in the middle of the situation.

TABLE 14.11 TICS AND TOCS	
Task-Interfering Cognitions (TICs)	Task-Orienting Cognitions (TOCs)

Problem-solving

We saw at the beginning of the section on worry that sometimes worries turn out to be problems that can be solved. And sometimes, even if you are not worrying excessively, you might put off making a decision because there doesn't seem to be an obvious way forward and you can't quite work out what to do. So one way of helping avoid getting stuck going over and over the same unhelpful thoughts, or putting off making decisions, is to have a very clear and specific way of focusing on how to solve the problem. The steps below are one way of doing this.

Define the problem. Try to be specific and to decide exactly what the problem is. If possible, break it down into smaller problems.

Think about your resources, and list all possible solutions. Have you ever solved a problem like this in the past? Do you have any personal skills or strengths that would help you to tackle it? Is there anyone who would be able to help you? Write down all the possible solutions that you can think of, even if they seem silly or unlikely to work – you are just generating ideas.

Choose a solution. Think about the pros and cons of each of the solutions you have listed. Think about the likelihood of success, and also about the time and effort they would require, and if you would need help from other people. Then decide on one solution that you can put into action. You don't have to have a solution that will solve the problem completely, as long as it moves you in the right direction. *Make a plan.* Break the solution down into small and manageable steps. Make each step very specific so that you know exactly what you are going to do. If your plan is vague or unmanageable it will be very difficult to put it into practice. For example, if your solution was 'I need to get a job', your steps might include: 'Get a newspaper tomorrow and review the adverts in my area', 'Update my CV on Tuesday morning', 'Make my first application by Friday'. Make sure you decide which step you will work on first.

Do it! Try out your solution, even if it is only the first step to solving the problem.

Review the outcome. If your solution works, that's great. Congratulate yourself and remember this experience for the future. If your solution does not solve the problem, review what happened. Does your plan need to be reworked, or do you need to try again? Remember that, even if you haven't yet solved the problem, you are at least facing up to it – and this is likely to help you solve it in the future.

Regulating stressful emotions

There may be times when, despite all your best intentions and plans to manage your stress, you find that you are just overwhelmed with emotion and don't know what to do. If this ever gets to be the case with you, then some of the strategies below might help. Most of these are things that you can do immediately, though others may need a little planning. The important thing is that you choose something that you think will work for you to distract yourself from the intensity of emotion.

Mindfulness: Mindfulness was originally described by a psychologist called Jon Kabat-Zinn who developed a mindfulness-based stress reduction program, which research has shown to be effective in managing stress as well as a range of other problems. We describe mindfulness in detail in Chapter 15, and there is information about how to find out more at the end of the book in the Resources and Bibliography sections. Essentially mindfulness helps you to do two things. It keeps your mind focused on yourself in the present moment, so that you are not constantly being drawn into fears for the future and regrets about the past.

It also helps you to detach yourself from these unhelpful thoughts, so that even if you have them, you just let them drift through your mind without engaging with them. Mindfulness teaches you that thoughts are just thoughts, not reflections of reality.

Activities: Try exercise, walking or running, cleaning or washing up, playing computer games, phoning a friend, gardening.

Emotions: Try doing something that will create a different emotion in you. Try watching a scary movie – this should create a strong enough emotion to counter the stress! Or watch a funny film, or read cartoon books. Try going into a shop and reading funny greeting cards.

Thoughts: Try to think of someone who is suffering worse than you are. Sometimes seeing pictures of the terrible things happening in other parts of the world can help to put our own problems in perspective. It may also help to create a different emotion – of pity and compassion.

There are also a number of mental tasks that you can do that require a surprising amount of concentration and can really help to break into cycles of stressful emotion. Try counting backwards in 3s or 7s from 1,001, or doing other mental arithmetic tasks.

CHAPTER SUMMARY

- There are a number of styles of thinking that make coping with stress more difficult.
- These include procrastinating, being a perfectionist and worrying.
- We discuss a number of strategies for dealing with these.
- We also discuss additional ways of enhancing coping by considering TICs and TOCs, problem-solving, and regulating stressful emotions.

15

Taking care of yourself

Most of us will feel that we have been inundated with advice about eating, exercise, not drinking too much and so on. Nevertheless, it is true that you can make stress a lot worse if you neglect these areas, and can make huge improvements in how you feel if you look after yourself well. So a lot of what follows will just be reminders of what you know already, but we hope that there may be some points in it that could be helpful.

Diet

In general, eating the odd hamburger and chips will do no harm at all and give huge pleasure. Chocolate too! But we all know that if this is all we eat then our bodies will start to suffer. There's no such thing as a bad food, but there is a need for balance. Aim for a balanced diet, containing protein such as lean meat, fish or pulses, starchy carbohydrate such as rice, pasta, bread and potatoes, fruit and vegetables, milk and dairy products, fats (as long as they are the right sort – see below), fibre, fluids and sugar in moderation: this will help to provide essential nutrients for the body. Tempting though it is to cope with stress either by reaching for junk food that makes you temporarily feel better, or by barely eating at all, resist.

Melissa, a twenty-four-year-old PA living in London, found that when she was stressed her appetite reduced and she tended to skip meals and snacks. She found that as the day progressed she lost concentration, generally felt sluggish and found herself making simple mistakes and feeling more stressed. In Melissa's case, her reduced performance might be accounted for by prolonged fasting, followed by a negative appraisal of the situation.

Ben, on the other hand, a thirty-two-year-old designer, found that if he ate something sweet or high in fat when he felt stressed, then he could calm himself down a bit – so he would snack all day on confectionary and eat junk food. Inevitably he started to gain weight and that made him feel self-conscious; he worried that other people would no longer find him attractive and snacked even more.

But why should these things be bad for us? We will describe below the ways in which either not eating, or eating the wrong kinds of food, can contribute to stress. We will deal with the problematic aspects of junk food first, which contains high proportions of fat, sugar and salt.

What's wrong with fat? There are four types of fat:

- polyunsaturated
- monounsaturated
- saturated
- trans fats

Polyunsaturated and monounsaturated fats are generally found in foods of vegetable origins (for example, olives, rapeseed, oily fish, soya, avocado, nuts and seeds). These are healthier than saturated fat found in foods mainly of animal origin (such as meat and full-fat dairy produce), as well as in hidden sources such as cakes, biscuits and choco-late. Diets high in saturated fat are associated with coro-nary heart disease and atherosclerosis (hardening or furring of the arteries), because they adversely affect the choles-terol profile. The fourth type of fat is trans fats, which are mainly found in processed food; these are created when vegetable fat, which is liquid at room temperature, is hydro-genized (by pumping hydrogen gas through the vegetable oil) in order to harden the product. The consumption of trans fats is associated with an increased risk of heart disease. In order to reduce the quantity of trans fats in the diet it is important to eat fresh produce rather than processed junk foods.

What's wrong with salt? Having too much or too little salt in our diet can lead to high blood pressure, muscle cramps, dizziness and electrolyte disturbances. Electrolytes are central to maintaining many mechanisms in the body – for example, they help to regulate heart and nerve function. Salt is added to many foods to preserve the product, but more often than not we eat too much of it. In order to reduce the quantity of salt in your diet, it is advised that you minimize the quantity you add to what you eat and again aim for fresh rather than processed or junk foods.

And what about sugar? A common misconception is that eating foods containing refined sugar – for example, confectionary, cakes and biscuits – causes a large rise in blood glucose followed by an extreme low, triggering fatigue and food cravings, periods of overeating and subsequent weight gain. The idea of a 'sugar high' followed by a 'sugar crash' is, in fact, a myth. In people who are healthy, the body has a sophisticated mechanism which ensures that blood glucose levels stay within a narrow range day and night (1 teaspoon or 5 grams of glucose is constant in your bloodstream regardless of whether you have eaten any sugar). Your body is able to do this by releasing a hormone called insulin into the blood. A gradual rise after eating, followed by a slow decline, is a normal part of the body's regulation of blood glucose. Sugar provides the body with essential energy; however if eaten in excess in response to stress then you will put on weight, and in addition you will not develop other strategies to help reduce stress.

So, to summarize, the problems are:

- Junk food eaten over a long period of time has certain health risks.

- If you are eating lots of junk food you are probably not eating as much healthy food and so are missing out on food that contains the essential nutrients that your body needs.
- It is much easier to overeat junk food than healthy food. Lab rats fed on appropriate rat food judge the amount of food that they need and maintain a healthy body weight. But when experimenters substituted chocolate bars for the healthy food the rats did not adjust their eating to their body's requirements, but consistently overate and put on unlimited amounts of weight.

Why is reducing what you eat harmful in stress?

Restricting food in response to stress can also be problematic. When coping with stressful situations we need to be alert, with our concentration and memory functioning well, and with enough physical and mental energy to do what we need to do. If we restrict our eating, then there are likely to be problems with our energy, and some research indicates that there are also effects on memory and concentration which do make it much harder to focus. The brain consumes 20 per cent of your total energy and, although it only accounts for 2 per cent of your body weight, it is a high-energy organ and needs feeding.

Some people may experience a feeling of being a bit 'high' or buzzy when very hungry. This can give them the illusion that they are functioning well, but in practice they may not be making the most sensible decisions.

And finally, people who restrict their eating very often end up having hunger binges in which they overeat, and may paradoxically end up putting weight on.

How do your eating patterns change when you are feeling stressed?

One of the best ways of controlling your eating is to make yourself write down everything that you eat. *Nothing* should pass your lips without you making a note of it and writing it down as soon as possible. It would also be helpful for you to make a note of what is going on at the time that you eat, particularly if you realize that you are eating in an unhealthy way. Take notice of what is going on when you eat in this way. Can you relate it to stressful events going on around you, or to experiencing stressful feelings? If you realize that you are writing down very little, then review at the end of the day to see if you can identify stress. Once you have identified stressors that are connected to problems in your eating, you can use the stress management plan to introduce techniques that should help you to reduce the eating difficulties.

TEN TIPS FOR COPING WITH STRESSFUL EATING

1 Adopt a regular pattern to eating: eat regularly, three meals a day and snacks.
2 Always eat breakfast; studies have shown that any breakfast is better than none. This will help with your memory and concentration.
3 In order to avoid overeating when stressed, get an idea before you start to eat of what is reasonable, and stop when you have

reached it. You don't have to clear your plate if there is too much on it, or have second helpings. Avoid the kind of buffet meals where there is no natural end to the meal.

4 If you know that you eat junk food when stressed, try to take steps to avoid it.

Prepare things that you can grab from the fridge that won't be so harmful. Make a fruit salad that can be stored in the fridge, prepare a vegetable soup that you can snack on when feeling peckish, or peel and chop up raw veggies such as celery and cucumber into strips and keep them in an attractive container. Cut lean leftover meat into bite-size chunks. Food rich in protein such as lean meat, fish, bean curd, yoghurts, milk, nuts and seeds tend to be more filling than carbohydrate-dense or fatty foods; they can potentially help to reduce your appetite by making you feel more satisfied from the food you have eaten.

5 If you find it difficult to eat when stressed, make sure that you have food that you can eat easily. If you can't face eating a meal, make sure you have healthy and nutritious snacks like milkshakes, cereal bars, dried fruit and nuts, easily available in your bag or in the fridge. Try eating them while reading or watching TV to see if that makes it easier.

6 Remember to drink enough to keep hydrated, but this does not mean having to drink two litres of water a day. Fluids do count if they are in tea or even coffee provided that this is not too strong and it's not all you drink. There is a lot of fluid in some food, particularly fruit and vegetables, or soup or milky drinks.

7 Eat at least five portions of fruit and vegetables a day. Eating a rainbow of vegetables and fruit will help you get the range of nutrients you need as well as provide you with essential fibre. In

addition, choose unrefined carbohydrates that include whole grains. These are good for roughage and should help with keeping your bowels regular.

8 Reduce your intake of saturated fat through cutting down on fatty meat and full-fat dairy products. Instead choose oily fish, lean meat, and low-fat dairy food. Choose unsaturated fat such as olive or rapeseed oil.

9 Be mindful of your salt intake and try to use other flavourings instead, such as herbs, spices, garlic and lemon juice.

10 Avoid too much tea and coffee, cola and other fizzy drinks. These are all okay in moderation, but they contain a lot of caffeine which will increase some of the physical responses associated with stress and make you feel more tense and anxious.

Vitamins and minerals

Vitamins and minerals are a crucial part of our diet, but it is almost certainly better if we get them from food, rather than buying supplements, because the body appears to absorb them better. Excesses of some minerals can be potentially as harmful as deficits, so when taking supplements you must always be careful to check with your family doctor that you are not taking excessive quantities, and on the other hand are getting enough of what you need for your body.

Stress and alcohol

It is clear that alcohol is extremely useful as a ready tool to help us handle stress. As a family doctor once said to us: 'When I get home at the end of the day I'm opening the gin bottle practically before I'm out of the car!' Alcohol has many benefits and pleasures that it would be foolish (we think!) to try to persuade people to give up. But there is an obvious difference between drinking for pleasure and drinking because we cannot handle stress in any other way. If you feel that the latter is closer to how you drink, then it may well be time to take stock.

The other obvious issue is that it is very easy to drink much too much when we are stressed, and there is no doubt that drinking enough to get a hangover the next day is *guaranteed* to make us more stressed. We don't need to drink very much for our bodies and minds to be affected the next day. We are tired, our concentration is impaired, we are irritable and anxious, we are probably in pain somewhere, we are dehydrated. All of this makes coping with the world much more difficult and makes us much more stressed.

All of this means thinking about stress and alcohol in two ways. Firstly, are there other stress management techniques that you could use instead of alcohol? Hopefully you will be able to find something in this book that might be helpful for you. Secondly, if you think you might be drinking too much, then be careful. We know that alcohol is undoubtedly harmful in large quantities, though the jury is out on whether it may have benefits in smaller amounts. Some research does show benefits, such as that alcohol seems to thin the blood, reducing the risk of thrombosis. So the key, obviously, is moderation. There is probably a great deal of wisdom in the saying 'A little of what you fancy does you good' – but be careful how you interpret 'a little'.

Tips for reducing alcohol consumption

First of all, monitor your alcohol intake for a week so that you know exactly how much you are drinking. Keep a record of everything that you drink every day for a week, and then add up the total unit value. Just as a quick reminder, a unit is:

- A small glass of wine
- A pub measure of spirits
- Half a pint of ordinary-strength beer or lager; strong beer or lager is two units

If you are drinking more than the government guidelines (up to 14 units a week for women, and up to 21 a week for men) then it is time to take steps. Government guidelines also say that women who regularly drink over 35 units a week and men who regularly drink over 50 may be at risk of damage to their health.

TEN TIPS FOR REDUCING YOUR ALCOHOL CONSUMPTION

1 Cut down your alcohol intake to no more than the recommended weekly allowance, and less if you can manage it.

2 Try to keep a record, so that you write down every drink you have.

3 Always eat before having your first drink: the valve at the bottom of your stomach will stay shut for longer and the alcohol will be absorbed more slowly. Drinking sparkling wine leads to a

build-up of gas in your stomach, which causes the valve to open; this is why you seem to get drunk more quickly with sparkling wine.

4 Plan how many drinks you'll have. If you plan to drink half a bottle of wine, buy wine in half bottles rather than whole ones. Although it might work out to be a bit more expensive, you will know when you have had half a bottle. It's much harder to open another bottle than it is to keep drinking from a bottle that's already open.

5 If you are going to a social occasion, don't let people fill your glass before it's finished. You will lose track of what you've drunk. Wait until you have finished your drink before letting your glass be refilled. For every drink you have, make a sneaky mark with a pen on your napkin or the back of your hand. When you get to the number you've allowed yourself, stop.

6 Alternate glasses of wine or beer with glasses of water or other non-alcoholic drinks.

7 Practise saying 'no'.

8 Limit the amount of alcohol in the house. Only buy drink when you have decided beforehand that you are going to have a drink so that you reduce the likelihood of reaching for the bottle out of habit. Only buy what you plan to drink.

9 Have alternative strategies in place like taking a hot bath or a walk outside.

10 If you know that you binge drink when stressed, be aware of the triggers. Write out a plan for what you should do when you are tempted, using the techniques outlined in this book, and put your plan into action.

Stress and smoking

Smoking, on the other hand, is different. Having a cigarette may make us feel temporarily calm, help our concentration, reduce our hunger pangs, make us look cool (or so we think – at least in the alternative still-smoking culture growing up on back door steps and in pub gardens) and have many other very short-term benefits. But its longer-term consequences are without redeeming features, and can only impair our health. And sadly there is absolutely no doubt that nicotine is an addictive drug; it's just not that easy to give it up. Thankfully the NHS recognizes this now, and almost all family doctor's surgeries will be able to direct you to organizations that can help, or will have help available themselves. But if you want to stop now, then there are a number of things that you can do.

TIPS FOR STOPPING SMOKING

1 Write down the advantages and disadvantages of smoking. Divide a piece of paper into two columns, and in one column write down all the good things about smoking that you can think of, and all the ways in which you benefit. In the next column write down all the bad things about it that you can think of, and all the ways in which it has a cost for you. These should be personal to you and your life – the real advantages and disadvantages to you – not just what the media or other people say.

2 Look at the columns and decide – overall, do the advantages outweigh the disadvantages, or the other way round? If the

advantages really seem to you to outweigh the disadvantages then now is probably not the right time for you to stop smoking. However, if the disadvantages outweigh the advantages, then make this the time that you will act!

3 If you haven't already included the financial cost in your analysis, remember that if you smoke twenty cigarettes a day you will be spending £167.29 a month, or a staggering £2,007.50 a year! This may not be a problem for you, but if it is, then it is worth factoring into your equation. Even if you can afford it, you could put the money you would spend on cigarettes in a piggy bank and plan to spend the money doing something else that would act as a treat or reward for you.

4 If the disadvantages of giving up smoking do outweigh the advantages, then decide when you are going to stop, and fix a date. Prepare yourself for stopping and accept that it's going to be difficult. Withdrawing from nicotine can leave you feeling irritable, headachy and stressed. Remind yourself that this is expected, and that it will get better if you can tough it out.

5 Watch out for thoughts such as 'I'll finish the 200 cigarettes I bought in the duty-free shop and then I'll stop', or 'I'll smoke until I'm sick and then I'll never want to smoke again' (who are you kidding!) or 'I'll just wait until after the meeting next week'. We would refer to these as 'permissive thoughts' – that is, they give you permission to carry on with things that are really not helpful to you!

6 If this seems too difficult for you then don't panic – there is quite a lot of help at hand now. Your family doctor will almost certainly have information about help available in your area, and can discuss nicotine replacement treatments like gum or patches that will help with the initial withdrawal stages.

7 Think about the danger points for you – when are you most

likely to want to smoke? As part of your preparation for giving up, make plans for how you are going to get through the danger points. If going to the pub after work is the problem, then go without your coat so it's just too cold to smoke outside. Ask your friends not to give you a cigarette even if you beg. Don't go to the pub at all for the next couple of weeks until you are more confident in your ability to resist.

8 Remind yourself of the benefits, and that you can do it!

For more advice on how to stop smoking, have a look at *Overcoming Your Smoking Habit* by David F. Marks.

Exercise

One of the most effective stress-reduction techniques is regular exercise. Exercise helps to relax tense muscles, can help you to sleep, will improve your health, and should reduce physical stress caused by being unfit. There are many other positive benefits to exercising; it makes you feel good because chemicals called 'endorphins' are released into your bloodstream which can positively affect your sense of well-being and give you a feeling of happiness. You may also feel virtuous given that you have made the effort to exercise when you'd rather be watching junk TV. Improving the flow of blood to your brain can have added benefits of greater mental alertness and concentration. Physically fit people are more likely to have less extreme physical responses when under stress than those who are not. The more physically fit you are, the greater your capacity to manage the long-term effects of stress without burning out or suffering ill-health.

There are many types of healthy activity and exercise that help reduce stress; it isn't only about playing a sport or working out in a gym to the point of getting sweaty and panting. All moderately intense activity counts, such as going for a brisk walk, cycling, digging the garden, DIY, or going to a dance class. These will all have health benefits. You need to aim for a minimum of thirty minutes, exercise, five times a week.

Making any change is difficult and you will need to find ways to motivate yourself. Below are some common automatic thoughts that stop you from exercising:

- I'm too tired.
- I don't want to go to work looking hot and sweaty.
- I'll start tomorrow.
- I'm too busy.
- I need to lose weight first.
- It will hurt.
- I'll make a fool of myself.
- I'll be the biggest person in the class.
- I'd rather be doing something else.
- I'm never going to get fit so why bother?
- I'll be so exhausted it will spoil the rest of the day.
- I'll look ridiculous in sports clothes.

James, a twenty-three-year-old office worker, hadn't exercised since leaving school and was very unfit. He hated his job and would feel particularly stressed when his boss would spend the day surfing the net while he was working hard. He felt so angry that his body ached with muscle tension and would cope by 'treating' himself to junk food on the way home. Over time he gained weight and started to feel very self-conscious about his appearance. This in turn made him much more prone to feeling low and out of sorts. Eventually he decided that he had to make changes, and knew that exercise would help reduce his levels of stress as well as help him lose weight. He started walking to and from work, and then joined a local kendo class. This had the added advantage of helping him to make a new group of friends.

TIPS FOR INCREASING YOUR MOTIVATION TO EXERCISE

1 Consider what you want to achieve through exercising – what are your goals?

2 Find something that you think is fun – doing something that you find tedious is going to be difficult to sustain. It's also important to vary the activity if at all possible so that you don't get bored.

3 If you haven't exercised for a while it is important to start gently, and then gradually increase how often you exercise, and how much you can do. Remember that if you have a medical condition that might be affected it is important to seek

the advice of your doctor before embarking on an exercise program.

4 Set yourself both short- and long-term goals that are realistic and achievable. Managing the small steps will give you a great sense of satisfaction and should motivate you to keep going, especially if you have noticed a reduction in your levels of stress and other benefits. Remember to keep your goals SMART (see pp. 129–31).

5 Find an exercise buddy or join a club or sports team: it's always more fun and more motivating to exercise with others.

Stress and sleep

Sleeping badly seems to be one of the worst and most distressing effects of stress. Most of us will be familiar with that awful feeling of tossing and turning, unable to get to sleep, or jolting awake in the middle of the night, mind racing with all the ghastly things that might happen the next day, mistakes we made the day before, things we have to do that we don't feel able to cope with – and so it goes.

Despite how bad it seems, there are a number of things that you can do to help with sleep.

Problems when you're lying in bed

Sleep and coping

Part of the problem is that when we have difficulty sleeping we lie awake and think: 'Oh no, I can't sleep. I won't be able to cope tomorrow.' And of course this thought winds us up and makes sleep more difficult. So the first important idea is – although this will seem hard to believe – we can cope with much less sleep than we think. Junior doctors are notorious for working long hours on call for emergencies with little sleep, and yet they manage to cope amazingly well. Many parents with a new baby are very sleep-deprived, and although they may feel tired, they still manage to do everything they need to do, and function reasonably well in the day. Research shows that sleep deprivation *does* have an effect on our performance on dull and repetitive tasks, but much less on those where we need to use our skills and strengths. So the first thing to remind yourself is that if you have a bad night, or several nights, you may feel lousy, but you will be able to cope much better than you think.

Don't watch the clock

Furthermore, as we lie awake, we look at the clock by the side of the bed. What time is it? How long have we been trying to get to sleep? We have to get up at 6.00 a.m. and it's 2.30 a.m. now – even if we go to sleep straight away then we'll only have had three and a half hours, and that's not enough … Every time we look at the clock we are reminding ourselves how bad the problem is and feeling more and more panicky. So: move the clock. If you need an alarm clock then put it somewhere in the room where you can't see it. Checking the clock and working out the hours of sleep you've missed only makes the problem worse.

It doesn't count if you think it at night

Remember when we talked about the stress response evolving during a much earlier period of our evolution? We are animals who live by day and rely heavily on vision rather than smell or even hearing. So night-times are dangerous for us, since there are nocturnal predators around who function much more efficiently than us at night and might find and kill us. So it was sensible of us to feel scared at night, and to take anything alarming very seriously. Sadly this translates into our modern lives. If we think about a problem by day it might seem difficult or upsetting, but we can try to see how we can cope, and be realistic about how bad it is. But when we think about the same problem at night it seems a million times worse. We see only the worst outcomes, the most traumatic conclusions – this is our night-time alert system working.

But unless you are in a place of physical danger, then the system is not relevant to us any more. So the rule is this: *anything you think at night doesn't count.* It is only nocturnal anxiety kicking in. Remind yourself of this over and over again, and tell yourself you will think about whatever it is in the day when you can see more clearly – but not now. Try just sitting up and saying *'Stop!'* If you find yourself assailed by worries and are afraid that you won't remember them in the morning, then get out of bed, jot them down on a piece of paper, and leave it. It might even help to take the paper out of the room, so the worries are physically removed as well.

Counting sheep?

Sometimes our minds become so caught up in worries and problems that we get more and more anxious and alert, and less and less likely to sleep. In order to break into this vicious cycle, it can be very helpful to use some quite simple distraction tasks. These will stop the chain of thoughts that is making you so wound up. Despite the title, counting sheep is *not* a good idea – you can do this automatically and don't need to think about it. We need distraction tasks that take up our mental capacity and don't leave us room to think about worries. Try:

- counting backwards from 101 in 3s
- going through every number multiplying it by itself: $1 \times 1 = 1$, $2 \times 2 = 4$, $3 \times 3 = 9$ and so on. By the time you get to 13 it becomes quite tricky!
- listing the ingredients of five favourite recipes
- reciting poems or songs.

Try getting up

As we have seen, when we sleep badly we tend to lie in bed fretting more and more. If you have tried dealing with your thoughts in the ways described above but it's not working, then don't carry on lying there. Make yourself get up and go and do something boring – the ironing, or reading a dull book. Stay up until you start to feel tired and calmer, and then go back to bed. But again, if you don't go to sleep and start fretting again, repeat the process. Eventually you will sleep. This will stop your bed being associated with tossing and turning, and help it to be more associated with sleeping.

Preparing to go to bed

Be careful about what you drink

There are some things that will definitely make sleep worse and should be avoided. Caffeine is very obvious, though as we saw earlier, it is less obvious which drinks or foods contain caffeine. But avoiding consuming any caffeine for some hours before bed is really helpful. If you like the idea of warm milky drinks, then look for decaffeinated coffee and tea. But be careful of this too – if you drink too much liquid in the evening then you are much more likely to need to get up for the bathroom.

Alcohol is also tricky. Drinking does make it easier to fall asleep. But because alcohol makes you need to pee more than usual you are much more likely to wake in the middle of the night needing the bathroom. And if you have drunk more than a small amount you will wake with the beginning of a hangover, with all the mental agitation and physical discomfort that this involves, and find it very hard to go to sleep. Alcohol also affects the quality of your sleep, and you are less likely to feel refreshed. If you are having a lot of trouble with sleep it may be worth trying to cut out alcohol for a couple of weeks to see if this helps.

Don't exercise at night

Exercise during the day can be helpful as part of an overall healthy approach to life that is likely to make you sleep better. But if we exercise energetically then our bodies get pretty aroused – our temperature rises, our heart rate increases, our pulse rate goes up – which is exactly the opposite of the calm and relaxed state our bodies need to be in for us to sleep. So don't use the latter part of the evening to exercise, but give yourself at least a couple of hours for your body to return to a calmer state.

TV and computers

Tempting though it is to relax by watching TV, or to play games or work on the computer, there is a problem! The light that comes from TV and computer monitors is extremely bright – really equivalent to bright midday sunlight. So the message that our brains get if we look at the screens a lot prior to bedtime is that it is the middle of the day. We would not expect to sleep if we went to bed then! So, annoying though it may be, if you are really having difficulty falling asleep, then it may be better to stop looking at any kind of screen for at least a couple of hours before bed to see if this helps.

Make your room a haven

It is worth looking at the room in which you sleep too. Is it full of clutter? Is it the last room that you clean? Do you have electrical equipment that hums and buzzes? Is it too hot or too cold? If you can make your room a calm and peaceful place to be, then the chances of falling asleep in it are much greater. Make sure you have soothing lighting in the room, and that it is as quiet as it can be.

Sometimes, sadly, our sleep is disrupted by the person that we sleep with. Sleep laboratories have shown, very unromantically, that most of us sleep better when we sleep alone than when we sleep with our partners. If you are sleeping badly and your partner tosses and turns or – oh enemy of sleep! – snores, then you are much more likely to find it difficult to sleep. Fiona, a thirty-one-year-old research assistant, told us that her husband falls asleep easily and then wakes in the middle of the night. She, on the other hand, finds it incredibly difficult to get off to sleep. On some nights she is just starting to fall asleep when he starts stirring and wakes her up! So if you are having a lot of trouble sleeping, and if you can accommodate this in your house, it may be better to have a period where you sleep apart in order to get your sleep pattern well established. This is not a sign of a failing marriage, but of one able to adapt!

Bedtime rituals

Many people find it helpful to have a kind of wind-down ritual before going to bed. This might involve something simple – getting into night clothes, making a hot-water bottle, dimming the lights in the bedroom and getting into bed with a good book and a warm drink. Having a bath is a slightly contentious issue, since most people find this relaxes them and helps them to sleep, but occasionally people find that their temperature is raised too much and this stops them sleeping. Like many things, experimenting with what works for you is the best way. Some people may find it helpful to do something more formal, such as relaxation exercises or meditation, as part of their night-time ritual. But what does not seem to be helpful is going from busy, stressful activities straight to bed without the chance to wind down in between.

For more information on improving your sleep, we recommend *Overcoming Insomnia and Sleep Problems* by Colin A. Espie.

Relaxation

There are many different ways of learning to relax, and people vary greatly in those they find most helpful. There are a number of commercially available relaxation CDs. One technique which is used to very good effect, and which we're going to focus on here, is known as *progressive muscular relaxation*. This is based on the idea of tensing and relaxing muscle groups around the body. Although it may seem strange to use tension to help you relax, the idea is that it works like a pendulum – the further you pull it in one direction, the further it will swing in the other when you let go. So by tensing your muscles and then releasing the tension you will experience a greater feeling of relaxation. You will also become more aware of which groups of muscles in your body are holding the tension when you're not doing the exercises. The relaxation exercises also talk about keeping your breathing deep and even, so have a look at the section below on controlled breathing first.

Controlled breathing

When we are tense and anxious we tend to breathe rapidly, and from the top of our chests. We can calm down more easily if we learn to breathe deeply and calmly, from the bottom of our stomach, not panting from the chest.

As with the relaxation exercises, make sure that you are sitting or lying in a comfortable position. When you become practised you will be able to do this anywhere, but to start with you need to make sure that you are comfortable.

1 Place one hand on your chest and one on your stomach.
2 Breathe in deeply and slowly through your nose, allowing your tummy to swell gently. Look down at your hands. If you are breathing from the bottom of your lungs, you will see that the lower hand, the one on your stomach, is moving as much or slightly more than the one at the top. If only the top hand is moving then you are breathing from the top of your lungs only. If this is the case, then try push-ing your stomach out a little as you breathe in – this will encourage breathing from your whole lungs.
3 The in-breath should be slow and gentle and quiet. Hold the breath very briefly, and then breathe out slowly and gently.

4 After breathing out, pause for a moment. Don't take the next breath in until you feel that it is 'time'.

5 Repeat the process, and try to get a rhythm going. Keep your breathing slow, deep and gentle.

Progressive muscular relaxation

Preparing to relax

First of all, choose a time and a place where you know you will not be interrupted – the exercise will take twenty to thirty minutes. Switch your phone off, and if there are other people in the house ask them not to disturb you. It will help if the room that you choose is warm and pleasantly lit, and has somewhere that you can sit or lie comfortably.

Tensing and relaxing

Below we will go through each of the important muscle groups, with suggestions about how to produce tension in those muscles. For each muscle group, the process is the same. Take a deep breath and tense the muscles as hard as you can for three to five seconds – a second is about as long as it will take you to say 'one thousand'. Concentrate on the feelings of tension and tightness in those muscles. Then exhale and let go of the muscle group completely. Notice the difference between how the muscles feel now and how they felt when you were tensing them. Sometimes the relaxed feeling will be one of warmth or heaviness in the muscles. Keep breathing slowly and with every out-breath let yourself feel this sense of relaxation, of warmth and heaviness. Wait for about twenty to thirty seconds and then go on to the next muscle group.

Keeping the feeling going

At the end of the series of muscle groups let yourself wait for a while, focusing on your breathing, and imagining yourself in a calm, relaxed state. Some people find it helpful to think of an image to bring to mind at this point. It may be of yourself on a quiet beach, or walking in beautiful countryside – anything that will bring a sense of peace and calmness to you. As you start to feel relaxed, let your mind focus on this image.

Practise

If you find that this is not working as well as you'd like, don't lose hope. Learning to relax is like any other physical skill – it needs practice. Try to find time to do the exercise once a day for a couple of weeks and you will discover that you get better and better at it.

THE MUSCLE GROUPS

Hands: Clench your fists as tightly as you can and squeeze hard. Breathe out and let go, letting your fingers and hands fall open.

Arms: Pull your elbows in to your sides and press your upper arms against your body as tightly as you can. Let go and let your arms and hands drop.

Shoulders: Roll your neck from side to side to loosen the muscles, and then raise your shoulders up to your ears. Let go and feel them drop as low as they can.

Feet: Scrunch your toes downwards as tightly as you can. Let go and let them straighten.

Legs: Straighten your legs in front of you and pull your toes up towards your head, pushing your heels out. Feel the tension all along your legs, then let go and let them drop.

Bottom: Clench your buttocks together as hard as you can, then let go.

Stomach: Suck in your stomach muscles and tighten them as hard as you can. It can help to imagine that you are trying to get your tummy button to touch your backbone. Again, let go and feel the muscles relax.

Neck: Tilt your head back as far as it will go, keeping your teeth together. Feel the tension pulling in the muscles going up to your jaw. Then relax and let your head fall forward. Now pull your chin in as far as it will go towards your chest, and imagine that you are trying to get the top of your head to reach your knees. Feel the tension in the muscles going down the back of your neck, and then let go, letting your head fall into its natural position.

Mouth and jaw: Clench your teeth, and pull the corners of your mouth as far back as you can, as in a very exaggerated false smile. Let go and feel the corners of your mouth fall back and your teeth part.

Eyes and nose: Close your eyes as tightly as you can and wrinkle your nose up. Feel the tension across your eyes and then let go and let your eyelids fall.

Forehead: Raise your eyebrows as high as you can up your forehead. Feel the tension in your brow, and then relax and let them fall.

Shortening the procedure

When you have practised these exercises, and are tuned in to the feeling of relaxation that they produce, you can use a very shortened form in situations when you are in a crisis, or have no time to do the exercises properly. Shut your eyes, if you can, and choose one muscle group that is particularly effective for you – often it will be the hands, neck or shoulders, but could be any of the others too. Tense the muscles and then release them. At the same time, if you have been using a calming image, bring this to mind and focus on it.

Because the image, and the tension in one muscle group, will be associated with the feeling of relaxation, then just summoning them will re-create the feelings from the longer exercises.

Problems with progressive muscular relaxation

If you have problems with your muscles, because of arthritis or other medical conditions that might weaken them or cause you pain if you tense them, then this may not be the right form of relaxation for you. It can be helpful just to go round the same muscle groups and try to let them fall into a relaxed state, concentrating on keeping your breathing calm and slow, and focusing on a calming scene. Or try just doing the breathing exercises without doing the muscular tension.

Meditation and mindfulness

There are many different approaches to meditation. One of the most popular and easily accessible of these is the technique of meditation taught by Buddhists. Most cities and big towns will have centres where meditation is taught, where people are welcomed in to learn. Yoga and some martial arts also combine approaches that use your body as well as your mind to help you to focus and relax, and can prove extremely helpful in stress control. The variety is so great that we will not review them all here, but there is a great deal on offer in most places in the UK. If this sounds like something that you would like to try, then have a look in your local library or health centre, or on the Internet, to see what you can find. Go and talk to the people running classes about what they are trying to achieve, and see if you can chat to someone who attends too, to find out what they are getting out of it.

Here we're going to focus on an adaptation of meditation which has been incorporated into cognitive therapy, which we call *mindfulness* and which has been shown to be very effective in stress reduction. The psychologist Jon Kabat-Zinn developed the philosophy and practice of mindfulness in his work with a variety of clinical conditions, and it has been picked up and used to very good purpose for treatments of depression and stress. There are a number of centres in the UK where you can learn mindfulness in a very intense and thorough way, and there is a much fuller account in *The Mindful Way Through Depression* by Mark Williams, John Teasdale, Zindel Segal and Jon Kabat-Zinn. Details of this book and of UK centres are given in the

Bibliography and Resources sections below. But it may be possible to gain some benefit even from a very modest understanding of the principles and practice.

Mindfulness means paying attention in a particular way:
On purpose,
In the present moment,
And non-judgementally.

What does this mean? One of the things which mindfulness tries to overcome is our tendency to think negatively and chaotically. How many of us are aware that when we are doing something we are not just thinking about the task in hand, but about all the other things that we need to get done that day, the horrible conversation we have just had, whether we are going to be able to get away at the weekend, how uncomfortable our trousers are … and so on and so on? Mindfulness sees that this style of thinking is very harmful to us. It means that we are never fully engaged in what we are doing, but are caught up in the stress and pain of things that have happened in the past and things that might happen in the future. So mindfulness says that we should always try to pay attention to what we have chosen to do at that moment. That is, we should be thinking on purpose about what we are doing. And we should try to stay in the present moment – to keep our attention on what we are doing *at this moment*, and not let our minds drift to the past or the future. And finally, our attention should be given to what we are doing and thinking without judging either what is going on, or ourselves, or other people in the situation.

Like other forms of meditation, mindfulness can start with thinking about our breathing. Mostly we are not in touch with our breathing – it's just there, forgotten. So we can start to be mindful by bringing our attention to our breath. Allow yourself ten minutes to go through the following exercise.

Bring your attention to your breath, and let yourself be aware of all the physical sensations in your body as you breathe. You do not have to try to control the breath, just to be aware. As you try to bring your attention to your breath, you will find that other thoughts come into your mind. Do not trouble yourself about this, but just see that it has happened and return your attention to your breathing. As other thoughts come to you, imagine that your mind is like the sky. Your thoughts are like clouds that drift across the sky. They will come into your mind, but you do not need to worry or judge – just watch as the clouds enter and leave your field of vision, and bring your attention back to the breath.

There are many other small things that you can do to try to stay in the present. Remember to use your body as a way to awareness. You are probably sitting as you read this. What are the sensations in your body at this moment? When you finish reading and stand up, feel the movements of standing, of walking to the next activity. Be *in* your body as you move.

Whenever you eat or drink something, take a moment and breathe. Bring awareness to seeing your food, smelling it, tasting it, chewing and swallowing. Look at the food and realize that it was connected to the earth, to the sunlight and rain.

Whenever you bring your mind to the present, allow thoughts that come into your mind to drift through. Do not judge. Do not engage with these thoughts – just watch.

One aspect of this attempt to be mindful in the present moment is that the thoughts that trouble us start to be seen as just that – thoughts that trouble us. When we are stressed or depressed, the weight of our thoughts is overwhelming. But these are just thoughts. Our attention is on the present, on our breathing, on our bodies, on the sun or the rain or the frost. We can watch the thoughts go past us, as we would watch the torrent of a river flowing past. We do not have to be in the river.

Hopefully the practice of mindfulness meditation will help you to detach yourself from your thoughts, and see them for what they are – just thoughts! It is at this point that the similarity between mindfulness and cognitive therapy becomes clear. Cognitive therapy tries to get people to examine their thoughts and to realize that these are just thoughts – they are their constructive appraisals of things, not reality, and there are other ways of seeing things. By detaching yourself from your thoughts through the practice of mindfulness it becomes much easier to really believe this. You may not always be able to stop yourself having stressful thoughts, but you do not have to believe them!

Your plan for taking care of yourself

We have covered a great deal in this chapter. In order to make the best use of this, think about which of these issues are most important for you. Do you need to cut down your alcohol? Eat more sensibly? Do you want to find out more about meditation or mindfulness?

Chapter 8 described the stress management plan and the problems and strategies you can try to use. But the other aspect of the plan is to take care of yourself physically and emotionally so that you are in the best possible shape to cope with stress. In the worksheet below, note the areas which you would like to tackle, set yourself goals, and think how you are going to make a start. Review your progress on a weekly basis. There is another copy of the worksheet in Appendix 1.

TABLE 15.1 TAKING CARE OF YOURSELF WORKSHEET

Area I would like to tackle	Specific goal I'd like to reach	Specific activity for the week

CHAPTER SUMMARY

- Stress can affect the way we eat, which in turn can make us more stressed and less able to cope. We discuss ways in which you can try to ensure a healthy eating plan.
- Stress can also affect how much we drink, and make it harder to cope. We list some ways to help reduce your consumption. We also look at ways in which you could motivate yourself to stop smoking, and to start exercising a bit more.
- Sleep is often disrupted by stress, and sleep deprivation makes people feel more vulnerable. However, you can almost always cope better than you think, even if you have much less sleep than you want. We discuss ways to help with some of the main barriers to sleep.
- We also talk about a common and effective technique of relaxation, involving controlled breathing and muscular tensing and release. We also talk about the practice of mindfulness meditation, which has proved very effective in cognitive therapy.
- Finally, we suggest that people should look at areas which they would like to make changes in, and keep track of these using the Taking Care of Yourself worksheet. This can be kept with the Stressors and Goals worksheet on p.127 for a complete stress reduction package!

16

Attending to the positive

There is one final part of stress management that we should think about. We have spoken about a range of techniques and strategies to help you manage stress and to enhance your ability to cope. As a result, we hope that you have started to feel more confident about dealing with stress, and about yourself in general. We hope that this means that your self-esteem, and your sense of self-efficacy, will be improving too, and that when this happens you will find it increasingly easy to think of solutions and to make plans. (To remind you: self-efficacy has two components to it – your ability to *think* of solutions to problems, or generally to understand how to be effective in the world, and your belief in your ability to *carry out* the things you think of.) And just as we have spoken about negative cycles, we can think about positive cycles too.

So in this chapter we will consider ways to enhance this positive cycle, and to emphasize the positive things that you are doing.

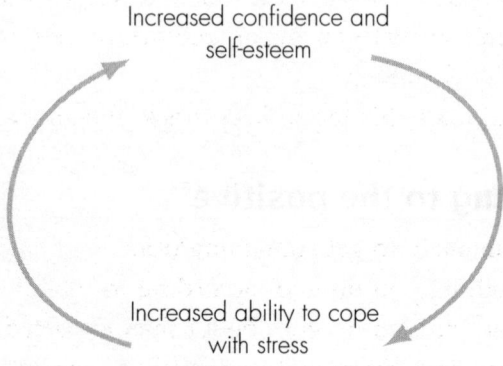

Increased confidence and
self-esteem

Increased ability to cope
with stress

Figure 16.1 The positive cycle of increased confidence and ability to cope with stress

The positive data log

Firstly, it can be the case that when you are making changes step by step you forget how far you have come. If you have been keeping records of your stress levels, look back at how bad things were at the beginning, and congratulate yourself on any changes you have made.

However, if you are making changes slowly, or haven't been using the worksheets, or sometimes just if you are very stressed, then you may find that you just don't notice good things that you do, or good things that other people say to you. Good things just disappear into the abyss of stressful feelings, and you turn your attention to the next problem rather than remembering that you have just solved the last one. If this is happening, it may be worth keeping a separate record – a positive data log – to keep track of what you've done so that you make sure you notice and don't forget the good things.

You could use this log to keep track of times when:

- You manage to get something done.
- Something you do goes according to plan.
- Something you do goes better than expected.
- You do something that you think is worthwhile.
- You think of a solution to a problem.
- Somebody compliments you.
- Somebody thanks you.
- Somebody contacts you.
- You can ask someone for help.
- You recognize good qualities in yourself.

When you are keeping this log, remember that nothing is too small or too minor to be noted. Often when people are very low in confidence they feel silly putting small things down, as if it proves how little they have accomplished. But, in fact, most of our lives are made up of small things that build up into a bigger picture. Just as vast and beautiful houses can be made of very small bricks, so each of these tiny pieces of positive information about ourselves can build up into a picture of ourselves as good and confident people. Try to fill in at least one thing every day, even if at first the things you put down seem silly. At the end of the week, look back and see how things have added up.

If you really have put nothing on the sheet, then it is possible that you are setting the bar much too high. Remember that we are talking about bricks, not buildings. (You'll find another copy of this worksheet at the back of this book.)

TABLE 16.1 POSITIVE DATA LOG WORKSHEET	
Date and time	Positive event (What I've done well, nice things other people have said etc.)

Creating a more positive image of yourself

Often when we are very stressed we run ourselves down a lot and tell ourselves that we are hopeless, or incompetent, or failures. We forget good things about ourselves. In fact it's quite hard to focus on good things about ourselves at the best of times, since we are mostly encouraged to be modest and not to boast. This means that recognizing our positive points can be doubly hard. So how can we build up a good image of ourselves? One way is to use the positive data log above and to recognize the good qualities that have brought the positive things about. Try to add one thing about yourself that you recognize as positive every day. But if this seems too hard, then try the following exercise.

Look at the list of adjectives below and give yourself a rating for each. A rating of 0 means that you have none of that quality, 1 means that you have a little, and 2 means that you have quite a bit. Now go through the list and pick out all the qualities that you have rated with a 2 or 1 and write them down. If you are feeling brave, ask someone who likes you to go through and give you ratings too.

Of course, there are many other good qualities that are not on this list, and if some of yours are not listed here, then it doesn't mean they're not important! Write them down too. Now that you have them in mind, see how often they crop up on your positive data log. If you only have a few ratings of 1 or 2, then that is a start – you can use these to start to build up a better and more positive image of yourself.

kind	assertive	caring	honest
efficient	considerate	entertaining	responsible
flexible	determined	funny	genuine
helpful	forceful	creative	incisive
smart	giving	thoughtful	compassionate
practical	forgiving	loving	conscientious
organized	clever	loyal	warm
quiet	intelligent	good cook	unselfish
gentle	well-read	artistic	good listener
forthright	mechanical	generous	imaginative
attractive	sympathetic	hard-working	good housekeeper
tidy	cuddly	punctual	good manager
relaxing	good handyman	tough	good gardener

When you have made your list, and spent a week or so filling out your positive data log, look at it and rehearse the good things in your head. This way the great job you are making of life will really sink in.

Your resourceful self

All of us have different aspects to ourselves, and behave better or worse at different points of our life. But we deserve to be the best that we can, and to bring out the best in ourselves – our most resourceful self.

To do this exercise, go somewhere where you can have ten minutes undisturbed and reasonably quiet. Read through the instructions, and close your eyes when you start to imagine things.

Think of a problem that you are trying to deal with, but perhaps not having much success with. Notice how you feel about yourself when you are thinking about the problem. Perhaps you feel tense, anxious and stressed. Are your shoulders hunched, your stomach clenched, your face tense and lined? Do you feel pretty low and incompetent?

Now try to change the scene. Imagine that you are yourself at your absolute best. You are your most confident, your most resourceful, your best self. You like yourself, and you have respect for yourself too. Picture yourself in your imagination. Think of all the details of what it feels like to be that self. How are you holding yourself? Are you standing, or walking, or sitting? What clothes are you wearing? How is your hair? What are you aware of around you? How does it feel inside yourself? Let yourself keep this image in your mind as strongly as you can for several minutes, and just enjoy being in this self in your imagination.

Bring your mind back to the problem that you were thinking of in the beginning; but now it is your best and most resourceful self who is thinking of the solution. This resourceful self is not fazed, and is not stressed and put off by the problem. See what this self can do.

If you have found this helpful, then practise being your best self in your imagination, and become familiar with all the details of how it feels. You can bring this self into your real life more and more as it feels increasingly familiar.

Reward yourself

Finding a way to give yourself positive rewards for what you are doing is also important. Learning new ways to tackle stress is hard work, and you deserve to reward yourself for any achievements that you make. When you are treated well you feel better, and this is true even if the person treating you well is yourself! You give yourself the message that you are worth bothering about, and that's very important.

Of course, your ability to reward yourself may be limited by lack of money or time, or by other practical problems, but there may be some things that you can do. What about going for a walk when the sun is shining? Or having a long bath? Or spending half an hour reading a book? Watch out for thoughts like: 'I don't deserve a reward for this – I should be doing it anyway.' Think about what you might enjoy – then do it!

CHAPTER SUMMARY

- As your ability to handle stress improves, we hope there will be a knock-on effect for your self-esteem and confidence.
- We discuss some ways to improve these positive aspects by:
  - Using the positive data log.
  - Creating a positive image of yourself.
  - Getting in touch with your resourceful self.
  - Rewarding yourself.

17

Your stress plan revisited

Having completed the overcoming stress program, we now need to consider how you can continue to practise and develop your cognitive therapy skills further. The following chapter will help you to review the stress plan that you put together in Chapter 8 and to identify what stress problems are remaining and how you might continue to work on these.

Review your stress plan

To recap, the stress management plan outlined in Chapter 8 involves five stages:

1. *Identifying stressors*: Which areas of your life are causing you the most difficulty, and could be changed?
2. *Pinpointing goals*: What is your ultimate goal for this area, and what subgoals do you need to specify on the way?
3. *Choosing techniques*: This involves looking through the book to see which of the techniques we have talked about might be useful to help you reach your

goals. If you have got this far then we hope that you will have been able to find techniques to help.

4 *Using the stress management plan worksheet to monitor and review progress*: Using the worksheet in Chapter 8 (see p. 127), you can keep track week by week of how you are doing.

5 *Including strategies to take care of yourself*: Now that you have had a chance to look at Chapter 15, you could add goals relating to taking care of yourself to your weekly plan.

When you are using the stress management plan, remember the four stages:

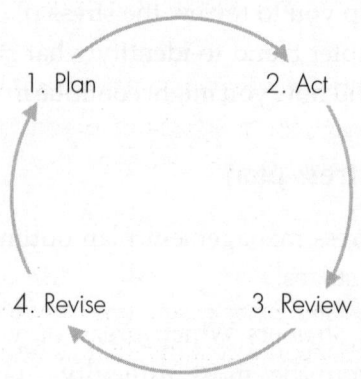

1. Plan

2. Act

3. Review

4. Revise

It is good practice to take a step back and think about all the progress you have made in addition to identifying what you have found difficult about making changes. When reviewing the plan you could consider the following questions:

1 What have I learned about my stressors and how these affect me?
2 How far have I come towards achieving my goals and subgoals?
3 Can you think of specific examples when you have achieved your goals (write these examples in your positive data log)?
4 What stress-reducing techniques have you found helpful?
5 What stress-reducing techniques have you found unhelpful?
6 What steps have you taken to take care of yourself?
7 What areas do you need to continue working on?

Now that you have reviewed your stress plan, you need to think about how you can continue practising your cognitive therapy techniques to deal with stress.

Plan

Once you are feeling less stressed, it is easy to give up practising your newly acquired skills. Just as a musician needs to practise playing their instrument regularly, you need to make time to practise cognitive therapy. Set aside some time at the beginning of the week to think about your goals, choose your techniques, and plan exactly how you are going to put these into practice.

Act: Then do it! Now you know what you are going to do, and when, there is no further excuse!

Review: At the end of the week, look at your progress. Have the techniques that you chose helped or hindered? Can you see progress towards any of your goals, or in how you are feeling? Continue to practise those techniques that seem to be helping. But remember that some things take a while before they start to work. For instance, some people find that they need to practise the relaxation exercises for longer than a week before they really start to feel the benefit. And challenging your stressful thoughts is hard work, and takes practice. So do not discard things before you have really given them a good try. Like learning to ride a bike, most things take practice!

Revise: Look at your goals and see if you want to adjust them. Maybe you have achieved the week's goal and can now set a different one for the next week. Maybe you want to try a different strategy. Revise your goals and techniques, and then go back to the first step and plan how you are going to carry this out.

The road to hell is paved with good intentions: Keeping up the motivation

Even if you have done everything we suggest, and are your most positive, resourceful, self-efficacious self, it is likely that at some point you will have setbacks and want to give up. Or you may be struggling with getting going. In either case, watch out for a kind of thought known as 'permissive cognitions'.

Here are some examples of permissive cognitions:

- 'I'll start tomorrow. I'm too tired now.'
- 'There's no point – I know I've got no willpower to do it.'
- 'There's no point: it won't work.'
- 'I've had a terrible day. I need to have a glass of wine now.'
- 'I've tried this kind of thing before and it's never worked.'
- 'I'd rather be stressed!'

Watch out for these thoughts, and recognize them for what they are – subtle and skilled ways of making excuses and letting yourself off the hook, which stop you from making changes. Don't let these thoughts influence what you do. Challenge them as you would any other thought, or just make up your mind to disregard them.

Coping with setbacks

Nobody who sets out to make changes ever manages to do so without setbacks occurring on the way. You have probably been doing things the old way for a consider-able amount of time and many of your responses will be like a knee-jerk reaction. It takes a lot of effort to bring in new ways of behaving. Over time and with practice the new way will become more familiar and easier. The important thing to remember about setbacks is to learn from them – what happened to throw you off course? How can you do it differently next time? Don't be critical of yourself and think you've failed. Accept the setback, and then go back to your new plan.

We hope that you have enjoyed reading this book, and that you have got something out of it that will help you in your way through life. And as a final word, here is our ultimate stress management tip:

Don't write stress management books!

CHAPTER SUMMARY

In this chapter we have:

- Reminded you of the five stages of the stress management plan.
- Highlighted again the importance of the Plan – Act – Review – Revise cycle.
- Identified the 'permissive cognitions' that might undermine your motivation.
- Reminded you that setbacks can throw you off course for a while, but can also be accepted so that you can go back to your plan.

Appendix 1

Blank worksheets

In this section you'll find a series of blank worksheets for the exercises described throughout the book.

TABLE 8.2 STRESS MANAGEMENT PLAN

Stressor 1	This week's goal	Techniques 1. Identify and challenge stressful automatic thoughts (SATs) 2.	Review progress
Overall goal			
Stressor 2	This week's goal	Techniques 1. Identify and challenge SATs 2.	Review progress
Overall goal			
Stressor 3	This week's goal	Techniques 1. Identify and challenge SATs 2.	Review progress
Overall goal			

TABLE 9.1 A DIARY OF YOUR STRESSFUL AUTOMATIC THOUGHTS

Date and time	Situation (where you are, what you're doing)	Mood (e.g. sad, anxious, stressed)	Stressful automatic thoughts (exactly what is going through your mind when you feel bad)

TABLE 12.2 SATS DIARY

Date and time	Situation	Emotion (0–100)	SATs	Behavior

TABLE 13.1 TIME LOG

	Mon.	Tues.	Weds.	Thurs.	Fri.	Sat.	Sun.
8–9 a.m.							
9–10							
10–11							
11–12							
12–1 p.m.							
1–2							
2–3							
3–4							
4–5							
5–6							
6–7							

	Mon.	Tues.	Weds.	Thurs.	Fri.	Sat.	Sun.
7–8							
8–9							
9–10							
10–11							
11–12							
1–2 a.m.							
Daily stress rating 0–10							

TABLE 13.3 TIME MANAGEMENT MATRIX WORKSHEET

	URGENT	NOT URGENT
IMPORTANT		
NOT IMPORTANT		

TABLE 14.2 ADVANTAGES AND DISADVANTAGES WORKSHEET

Procrastination
Identify what you are procrastinating about and make a note

Advantages of procrastinating	Disadvantages of procrastinating

TABLE 14.9 WORRY DIARY SHEET

Date and time	Situation and what triggered your worrying?	Brief summary of your worry	How stressed did you feel? (0–100%)

TABLE 15.1 TAKING CARE OF YOURSELF WORKSHEET

Area I would like to tackle	Specific goal I'd like to reach	Specific activity for the week

TABLE 16.1 POSITIVE DATA LOG WORKSHEET

Date and time	Positive event
	(What I've done well, nice things other people have said etc.)

Bibliography

The Overcoming series:

Overcoming Anxiety, Helen Kennerley (Robinson, 2009)

Overcoming Bulimia Nervosa and Binge-Eating, Professor Peter Cooper (Robinson, 2009)

Overcoming Depression, Paul Gilbert (Robinson, 2009)

Overcoming Health Anxiety, David Veale and Rob Willson (Robinson, 2009)

Overcoming Insomnia and Sleep Problems, Colin A. Espie (Robinson, 2006)

Overcoming Low Self-Esteem, Melanie Fennell (Robinson, 2009)

Overcoming Problem Drinking, Marcantonio Spada (Robinson, 2006)

Overcoming Social Anxiety and Shyness, Gillian Butler (Robinson, 2009)

Overcoming Weight Problems, Jeremy Gauntlett-Gilbert and Clare Grace (Robinson, 2005)

Overcoming Worry, Mark Freeston and Kevin Meares (Robinson, 2008)

Other CBT Books:

GENERAL

Cognitive Behavioural Therapy for Dummies, Rob Willson and Rhena Branch (John Wiley & Sons, 2005)

Feeling Good: The New Mood Therapy, David D. Burns (Avon Books, 2000)

Mind Over Mood: Change How You Feel By Changing the Way You Think, Dennis Greenberger and Christine A. Padesky (Guilford Press, 1995)

ANXIETY

Overcoming Anxiety: A Five Areas Approach, Dr Chris Williams (Hodder Arnold, 2003)

DEPRESSION

Overcoming Depression and Low Mood: A Five Areas Approach, Dr Chris Williams (Hodder Arnold, 2006)

MINDFULNESS

The Mindful Way Through Depression: Freeing Yourself from Chronic Unhappiness, Mark Williams, John Teasdale, Zindel Segal and Jon Kabat-Zinn (Guilford Press, 2007)

Mindfulness-based Cognitive Therapy (CBT Distinctive Features), Rebecca Crane (Routledge, 2008)

RELATIONSHIPS

Love Is Never Enough: How Couples Can Overcome Misunderstandings, Resolve Conflicts, and Solve Relationship Problems Through Cognitive Therapy, Aaron Beck (Harper Paperbacks, 1989)

Resolving Relationship Difficulties with CBT: A Self-help Guide for Couples, Rod Holland, Sadhana Damani, Larissa Clay and Claudia Herbert (Blue Stallion Publications, 2008)

Other books about stress

How to Deal with Stress, Stephen Palmer and Cary Cooper (Kogan Page, 2007)

Managing Stress, Terry Looker and Olga Gregson (Teach Yourself Books, 2007)

Useful resources

Finding a therapist

British Association of Behavioural and Cognitive Psychotherapies (BABCP)

The BABCP is a national charity for Cognitive Behaviour Therapy (CBT). Its members consist of psychologists, psychiatrists, counsellors and nurse therapists. The BABCP holds a list of accredited CBT therapists.

Tel.: 01254 875 277
email: babcp@babcp.com
www.babcp.com

British Psychological Society (BPS)

The BPS holds a register of Chartered Psychologists that includes Clinical Psychologists and Counselling Psychologists.

Tel.: 0116 254 9568
email: enquiry@bps.org.uk
www.bps.org.uk

United Kingdom Council of Psychotherapy (UKCP)
The UKCP holds a national register of psychotherapists and counsellors.
Tel.: 020 7436 3002
email: ukcp@psychotherapy.org.uk
www.psychotherapy.org.uk

Other stress resources

Centre of Stress Management and Centre for Coaching
The Centre of Stress management offers stress counselling, coaching and CBT programs.
Tel.: 020 8318 4448
www.managingstress.com

International Stress Management Association (ISMA)
The ISMA is a charity that promotes the prevention and reduction of stress.
Tel.: 01179 697284
www.isma.org.uk

Living Life to the Full
The 'Living Life to the Full' is a life skills course that uses CBT approaches.
www.livinglifetothefull.com

Mood Gym

Mood Gym is an interactive CBT web-based program aimed at the prevention of depression. The program includes a downloadable audio recording of a relaxation procedure.
www.moodgym.anu.edu.au

Anxiety

Anxiety UK (formally the National Phobic's Society)

Anxiety UK provides information on anxiety disorders, they provide email and telephone support.
Tel.: 08444 775 774
General information: infor@anxietyuk.org.uk
email support: support@anxietyuk.org.uk
www.anxietyuk.org.uk

No Panic

No Panic offers support to people who suffer with anxiety disorders.
Tel.: 01952 590005
www.nopanic.org.uk

Eating Disorders

Beating Eating Disorders (BEAT)

Beating Eating disorders is the working name of the Eating Disorder Association that is a leading charity for people with eating disorders.
Tel.: 01603 619090
www.b-eat.co.uk

Mental health

The National Institute for Mental Health (MIND)
MIND is a mental health charity whose aim is to help create a better life for sufferers of mental illness.
Tel.: 020 8519 2122
email: contact@mind.org.uk
www.mind.org.uk

The Royal College of Psychiatrists (RCPsych.)
The Royal College of Psychiatrists have useful information leaflets about coping with stress, anxiety disorders and depression.
www.rcpsych.ac.uk

Mindfulness

The Centre for Mindfulness Research and Practice, University of Bangor
The centre provides teaching for the general public, and training for professionals.
email: mindfulness@bangor.ac.uk

Buddhist Centres in most major cities

Nutrition

British Nutrition Foundation
The British Nutrition Foundation provides scientifically sound information on nutrition.
Tel.: 020 7404 6504
email: postbox@nutrition.org.uk
www.nutrition.org.uk

Problem drinking

Alcoholics Anonymous (AA)
Alcoholics Anonymous is a fellowship that helps people recover from alcoholism.
National helpline: 0845 769 7555
Contacting AA: 01904 644026
www.alcoholics-anonymous.org.uk

Alcohol Concern (AC)
Alcohol concern is a voluntary organization that provides information on alcohol misuse.
Tel.: 020 7928 7377
email: contact@alcoholconcern.org.uk
www.alcoholconcern.org.uk

Relationships

Relate
Relate offers advice, sex therapy, relationship counselling and mediation.
Tel.: 0300 100 1234
www.relate.org.uk

Index

The Compassionate Mind
A New Approach to Life's Challenges

PAUL GILBERT

'As one of Britain's most insightful psychologists,
Gilbert illuminates the power of compassion in our lives.'
Oliver James, author of *Affluenza*

Compassion and particularly compassion towards oneself can have a significant impact on our wellbeing and mental health. Developing our sense of compassion can affect many areas of our lives, in particular our relationships with other people.

In this book, Professor Paul Gilbert explores how our minds have developed to survive in dangerous and threatening environments by becoming sensitive and quick to react to perceived threats. This can sometimes lead to problems in how we respond to life's challenges, and scientific evidence has demonstrated that compassion towards oneself and others can lead to an increased sense of happiness and wellbeing – particularly valuable when we are feeling stressed.

Based on evolutionary research and scientific studies of how the brain processes emotional information, this compassionate approach offers an appealing alternative to the traditional western view of compassion, which sometimes sees it as a sign of weakness and can encourage self-criticism and a hard-nosed drive to achieve.

Professor Paul Gilbert is the author of *Overcoming Depression*, which has sold more than 110,000 copies, and is Professor of Clinical Psychology at the University of Derby and Director of the Mental Health Research Unit, Kingsway Hospital, Derby.

978-1-84901-078-6
£9.99

Visit www.constablerobinson.com for more information

More psychology titles from Constable & Robinson
Please visit www.overcoming.co.uk for more information

No.	Title	RRP	Offer price	Total
	An Introduction to Coping with Anxiety	£2.99	£2.00	
	An Introduction to Coping with Depression	£2.99	£2.00	
	An Introduction to Coping with Health Anxiety	£2.99	£2.00	
	An Introduction to Coping with Obsessive Compulsive Disorder	£2.99	£2.00	
	An Introduction to Coping with Panic	£2.99	£2.00	
	An Introduction to Coping with Phobias	£2.99	£2.00	
	Overcoming Anger and Irritability	£10.99	£8.99	
	Overcoming Anorexia Nervosa	£10.99	£8.99	
	Overcoming Anxiety	£10.99	£8.99	
	Overcoming Anxiety Self-Help Course (3 parts)	£21.00	£18.00	
	Overcoming Body Image Problems	£10.99	£8.99	
	Overcoming Bulimia Nervosa and Binge-Eating – new edition	£10.99	£8.99	
	Overcoming Bulimia Nervosa and Binge-Eating Self-Help Course (3 parts)	£21.00	£18.00	
	Overcoming Childhood Trauma	£10.99	£8.99	
	Overcoming Chronic Fatigue	£10.99	£8.99	
	Overcoming Chronic Pain	£10.99	£8.99	
	Overcoming Compulsive Gambling	£10.99	£8.99	
	Overcoming Depersonalizaton and Feelings of Unreality	£10.99	£8.99	
	Overcoming Depression – new edition	£12.99	£8.99	
	Overcoming Depression: Talks With Your Therapist (audio)	£10.99	£8.99	
	Overcoming Grief	£10.99	£8.99	
	Overcoming Health Anxiety	£10.99	£8.99	
	Overcoming Insomnia and Sleep Problems	£10.99	£8.99	
	Overcoming Low Self-Esteem	£10.99	£8.99	
	Overcoming Low Self-Esteem Self-Help Course (3 parts)	£21.00	£18.00	
	Overcoming Mood Swings	£10.99	£8.99	
	Overcoming Obsessive Compulsive Disorder	£10.99	£8.99	
	Overcoming Panic and Agoraphobia	£10.99	£8.99	
	Overcoming Panic and Agoraphobia Self-Help Course (3 parts)	£21.00	£18.00	
	Overcoming Paranoid and Suspicious Thoughts	£10.99	£8.99	

No.	Title	RRP	Offer price	Total
	Overcoming Problem Drinking	£10.99	£8.99	
	Overcoming Relationship Problems	£10.99	£8.99	
	Overcoming Sexual Problems	£10.99	£8.99	
	Overcoming Social Anxiety and Shyness	£10.99	£8.99	
	Overcoming Social Anxiety and Shyness Self-Help Course (3 parts)	£21.00	£18.00	
	Overcoming Stress	£10.99	£8.99	
	Overcoming Traumatic Stress	£10.99	£8.99	
	Overcoming Weight Problems	£10.99	£8.99	
	Overcoming Worry	£10.99	£8.99	
	Overcoming Your Child's Fears and Worries	£10.99	£8.99	
	Overcoming Your Child's Shyness and Social Anxiety	£10.99	£8.99	
	Overcoming Your Smoking Habit	£10.99	£8.99	
	The Compassionate Mind	£20.00	£15.00	
	The Happiness Trap	£9.99	£7.99	
	The Glass Half-Full	£8.99	£7.99	
	I Had a Black Dog	£6.99	£5.24	
	Living with a Black Dog	£7.99	£5.99	
	Manage Your Mood: How to use Behavioral Activation Techniques to Overcome Depression	£12.99	£9.99	
	P&P		FREE	FREE
	TOTAL			

Name (block letters): _____

Address: _____

_____ Postcode: _____

Email: _____ Tel No: _____

How to Pay:

1. By telephone: call the TBS order line on 01206 255 800 and quote BROSAN. Phone lines are open between Monday–Friday, 8.30am–5.30pm.

2. By post: send a cheque for the full amount payable to TBS Ltd, and send form to: Freepost RLUL-SJGC-SGKJ. Cash Sales/Direct Mail Dept, The Book Service, Colchester Road, Frating, Colchester, CO7 7DW

Is/are the book(s) intended for personal use ☐ or professional use ☐?
Please note this information will not be passed on to third parties.

Constable & Robinson Ltd (directly or via its agents) may mail or phone you about promotions or product
Tick box if you do not want these from us ☐ or our subsidiaries ☐